ALLS · HARRY GILMER · VAUGHN MANCHA · CLEM GRYSKA · HA

GTON JR. · TOMMY BROOKER · BILLY NE

AUL CRANE · STEVE SLOAN · JIMMY FUL

NNAH · JOHN CROYLE · WILBUR JACKSON · JOHN MIT WA

· BOB BAUMHOWER · GUS WHITE · OZZIE NEWSOME · BARRY KRA

HENSON · E. J. JUNIOR III · MAJOR OGILVIE · JEREMIAH CASTII

· MIKE SHULA · BOBBY HUMPHREY · DAVID SMITH · ROGER SHU

EAL · ANDREW ZOW · SHAUD WILLIAMS · WESLEY BRITT · HOW

Y GILMER · VAUGHN MANCHA · CLEM GRYSKA · HARRY LEE · TON

TOMMY BROOKER · BILLY NEIGHBORS · JACK RUTLEDGE · DAR

STEVE SLOAN · JIMMY FULLER · RAY PERKINS · JERRY DUNCAN ·

CROYLE · WILBUR JACKSON · JOHN MITCHELL · WAYNE WHEEL

MHOWER · GUS WHITE · OZZIE NEWSOME · BARRY KRAUSS · MA

· E. J. JUNIOR III · MAJOR OGILVIE · JEREMIAH CASTILLE · TON

SHULA · BOBBY HUMPHREY · DAVID SMITH · ROGER SHULTZ · C

REW ZOW · SHAUD WILLIAMS · WESLEY BRITT · HOWARD CHAP

R · VAUGHN MANCHA · CLEM GRYSKA · HARRY LEE · TOMMY LEV

ROOKER · BILLY NEIGHBORS · JACK RUTLEDGE · DARWIN HOLT

AN · JIMMY FULLER · RAY PERKINS · JERRY DUNCAN · KEN STABL

WHAT IT MEANS TO BE CRIMSON TIDE

GENE STALLINGS
AND ALABAMA'S GREATEST PLAYERS

KIRK McNAIR

TRIUMPH
BOOKS
CHICAGO

Library of Congress Cataloging-in-Publication Data

What it means to be Crimson Tide / [compiled by] Kirk McNair
    p. cm.
  ISBN-13: 978-1-57243-752-4
  ISBN-10: 1-57243-752-9
    1. Alabama Cimson Tide (Football team)—History—Anecdotes.
  2. University of Alabama—Football—History—Anecdotes.
  I. McNair, Kirk, 1945–

  GV958.A4W53   2005
  796.332'63'0975184—dc22

                                                2005043924

This book is available in quantity at special discounts for your group or organization. For further information, contact:

Triumph Books
542 South Dearborn Street
Suite 750
Chicago, Illinois 60605
(312) 939-3330
Fax (312) 663-3557

Printed in U.S.A.
ISBN-13: 978-1-57243-752-4
ISBN-10: 1-57243-752-9
Design by Nick Panos; page production by Patricia Frey; editorial production by Prologue Publishing Services, LLC.
All photos courtesy of the University of Alabama's Paul W. Bryant Museum or Barry Fikes except where indicated otherwise.

CONTENTS

FOREWORD

What It Means to Be Crimson Tide

A football fan's first thought of Alabama is excellence. Of course, coach Bryant set the bar very high. But there is a long history of excellence at Alabama. When you think of the Crimson Tide, you think of players who play up to their potential and who win games in the fourth quarter.

Obviously, Alabama can be very proud of its great football tradition. But as much as the past is acknowledged, there are high expectations for the present and the future at Alabama. And what's wrong with that? We want our children to be high achievers. We want our students to make good grades. What's wrong with expecting our football players to play at a very high level? I know when I was at Alabama, first as an assistant coach and then later as head coach, the expectations were high. And I would not have wanted it any other way. If you can't handle that pressure, you have no business coaching at Alabama.

There have been a lot of championship teams and big wins in Alabama football history. When people ask me about big wins, my first thought is always the Vanderbilt game of 1990. That usually brings a puzzled look from people who know Alabama football. But we had lost three tough games to start that season, then finally got our first win over Vanderbilt.

I wasn't joking then, but after a few years when we had some success, I could joke that my advice to any Alabama football coach would be not to start his career with three straight losses. Even when we were losing those games, I was encouraged. We lost the opener to Southern Miss when we had about 450 yards of offense and they had less than 200, even with Brett Favre at quarterback. But we had some turnovers and more than enough mistakes.

We lost by three points. Then we lost to Florida by four points when we had a punt blocked for a touchdown. And in the third game, we had something like 25 first downs to 15 by Georgia and had a 10-point lead with 10 minutes to play and lost by a point. So I thought we were going to be a good team eventually.

But Alabama people don't really think about eventually. While Texas A&M people are still talking about the national championship the Aggies won in 1939, at Alabama they expect to win the national championship every few years. Texas A&M has a lot of tradition, but really hasn't won a lot. We had not had many winning programs at A&M until coach Bryant got there in 1954.

And when he came to Alabama in 1958, they weren't winning. In the three years before he came, Alabama had won only four games.

My first exposure to coach Bryant came in my freshman year at Texas A&M. I had gone there under coach Ray George and had played on the freshman team in 1953. I had really wanted to go to Baylor, but Ruth Ann, who was my high school sweetheart and who would be my wife, wanted me to go to Texas A&M. It was a military school with no coeds, and she thought that would be better for me.

vi

Growing up in Texas, and not having television coverage like we do now, about all we knew was the old Southwest Conference, so I didn't know anything about coach Bryant when he came from Kentucky. We had a yell practice in the grove, and he was introduced to the crowd. And, boy, was I impressed. He went up to the microphone and took off his jacket and made a speech. I don't remember exactly what he said, but I remember being impressed. I might not have known about him before then, but it didn't take me long to learn who he was.

My first exposure to Alabama football came when I got a ticket to go to the Cotton Bowl in Dallas, where Rice was going to play Alabama at the end of the 1953 season. I guess it was one of the most interesting Cotton Bowl games of all time with Tommy Lewis coming off the Alabama bench to tackle Dickie Moegle.

After my playing career, I stayed on as a student coach at Texas A&M. Sam Bailey was the freshman coach, and four or five of us were his assistants. Coach Bryant gave me an unusual job, scouting Texas A&M. I'd go in the press box and scout Texas A&M just like one of our opponents would. If I saw a tendency or a substitution or a formation that meant something, I'd

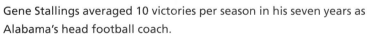

Gene Stallings averaged 10 victories per season in his seven years as
Alabama's head football coach.

make a note of it. And then I'd report to coach Bryant with the same information our opponents were getting on us.

I think doing that job may have been one of the reasons he hired me when
he went to Alabama.

When we learned he was going to go to Alabama, that was the first time
I realized that he had played at Alabama. He told me he would hire me, but

that if news got out about it before he was ready, he wouldn't hire me. And, brother, nobody found out.

Alabama was in a mess when we got there. I didn't really get there with the first wave. I helped get the Aggies ready for the Gator Bowl game against Tennessee, then came back and finished school before I went to Tuscaloosa.

Coach Bryant wasn't going to do anything the way it had been done the year before. He changed snap counts, alignments, maybe even the uniforms. He was going to change everything. And the players mostly were receptive, even though we worked them pretty hard and quite a few of them left.

It was my job to follow Jerry Claiborne around. He was the secondary coach. If I had had a title—which I didn't—I guess it would have been "assistant secondary coach." There wasn't a great deal made about titles at Alabama, though, except one—coach Bryant's.

You could feel the change coming at Alabama. We recruited some pretty good players in those early years, guys like Billy Neighbors, Lee Roy Jordan, Richard Williamson, and a lot more. Coach Bryant was an excellent coach, but it always helps when you have excellent players.

And we had a good coaching staff. I was in awe. There I was working with those guys who had coached us and now I was on that side of the ball with men like Jerry Claiborne and Phil Cutchin and Pat James. I was tickled to death to have a job, even one paying $4,500 a year.

It was hard work, demanding work. Everyone was always a little tense. It was not easy working for coach Bryant. Everyone wanted his approval. You didn't always get it.

The coaches all had games to prepare the scouting report. And that first year, coach Bryant gave a new suit from Black, Friedman & Winston to the coach who turned in the scouting report if we won the game. I had Vanderbilt and Georgia Tech. We tied Vanderbilt 0–0, but beat Georgia Tech 17–8.

Benny Marshall was sports editor of the *Birmingham News*, and he and coach Bryant had worked out a deal for Benny to write a book for coach Bryant. Coach Bryant told me he wanted me to help Benny, and he'd pay me $50. I met with Benny, but he said he wasn't going to be able to do the book. All I could see was my $50 flying away. I went to see coach Bryant and told him Benny couldn't write it, but I could. He asked me what I knew about writing, and I said I didn't know anything, but I had written down everything he'd had said for the past five years. He agreed to let me do the book and said we'd split the royalties.

Gene Stallings never expected to be Alabama's head football coach after he was passed over for the job in 1983 following Paul Bryant's retirement, but Stallings was hired seven years later.

I got a yellow pad and wrote at the top, "Book." And I knew a book had chapters, so I wrote down "Chapters." And I figured about 12 chapters was good, so under "Chapters" I wrote down "1 through 12." Then I wrote "Beginning," "Middle," and "Ending."

I called my wife, Ruth Ann, to show her what I had done. I was on my way.

I wrote it out in longhand, and Ruth Ann typed it. I even helped design the jacket. The name of the book was *Building a Championship Football Team*, and it was very well received. I don't think coach Bryant saw any of it until it was finished.

One of the nice things that happened for the assistant coaches was that a group of men from Jasper—Mr. Gardner, Ellis Taylor, and Red Pope—had a little outing for us. We went to Panama City and went fishing on a party boat. It's turned into more of a golf trip than a fishing trip, but that trip for the coaches is still going on. Bud Moore, who played for us, and the Drummonds and others have kept it up, and I don't know if there is anything like it anywhere else in the country.

I left Alabama after the 1964 season. We had just won our second national championship. I was 29 years old and had the opportunity to be head football

x

Following Texas A&M's 20–16 win over Alabama in the 1968 Cotton Bowl, Paul Bryant gave Gene Stallings a surprise "Bear hug" congratulations at midfield. *Photo courtesy of Bettmann/Corbis.*

coach at Texas A&M. I probably didn't have the best judgment at that age. Looking back, I think we may have had better players than I thought. And I worked them pretty hard.

We had our best year in 1967 when we won the Southwest Conference and went to the Cotton Bowl. And we played Alabama.

In those days, there was a lot of interaction at the bowl game between the players and coaches of the two teams. The reason I wanted to play Alabama was because I wanted my players to be exposed to coach Bryant, to get to hear him, maybe get to meet him.

We were fortunate enough to win the game 20–16. Curley Hallman, who had come with us from Northport, had a big game.

When the game ended, I went to midfield to meet coach Bryant and shake hands. He stooped down and picked me up. I was in complete shock. He was saying congratulations. Alabama had the better team, and I'm sure he was disappointed in the way his team played, but he was happy for me.

I think the majority of those who played for coach Bryant and worked for him all felt that he had a way of making us feel special. And I think he believed we were special. I loved him and appreciated that, cherished every one of his compliments.

In 1972 I went to the Dallas Cowboys to work under coach Tom Landry. I was with the Cowboys when coach Bryant announced his retirement to take place at the end of the 1982 season. I was brought in for an interview. The Cowboys were in contention for the playoffs. Alabama asked me, if I was offered the job, would I be willing to announce it on the next Monday regardless of what coach Landry wanted? I told them I couldn't do that, that I owed it to coach Landry to do what was best for the Cowboys. I don't know if I would have gotten the job or not, but they hired Ray Perkins.

A few weeks later, I was sitting at my desk in the Cowboys' offices when Linda Knowles called me to tell me coach Bryant had died. Over the years, I've realized how many people know where they were when they heard the news, like when President Kennedy died. I was stunned. I couldn't believe it. I thought he would live forever. I was sort of in a fog for a while after I got the news, and obviously the people of Alabama felt the same way. Things just sort of came to a standstill. I went to the funeral, as did the great majority of those who had been associated with him.

I couldn't say that I think about coach Bryant every day, but there are many, many times I do. One of the things you have to do as a coach is coach

Gene Stallings was confident his 1992 Crimson Tide football team would win the Sugar Bowl game against Miami for the national championship.

your own personality. I couldn't coach like coach Bryant or coach Landry. But I'd remember things coach Bryant said and the way he handled things.

He had a tremendous influence on me. If I had to pick out the two or three people who had the greatest influence in my life, he would without a doubt be one of them. He was the greatest college coach ever, in a class by himself. To be able to play for him and to be able to work for him was a thrill. I idolized him and looked forward to every day with him. I wish I could have been a better player and a better coach for him.

When I got passed over for the job in 1983, I didn't think I would ever have an opportunity to coach at Alabama. I had a great feeling for Alabama in those years after I left. Alabama played on Saturdays and we played on Sundays, so I was able to keep up to some extent. And I thought coach Bryant had made it the best coaching job in the country.

When I got the opportunity to be Alabama's coach in 1990, I can't tell you how excited I was. And I loved every minute at Alabama.

I am very grateful to Hootie Ingram, who was athletics director at Alabama, and to Dr. Roger Sayers, who was president. If there was a search committee in 1990, I'd say it was a committee of one: Hootie. And I don't even know if he interviewed anyone else.

I never had an agent. Hootie offered me the job and I accepted it. The furthest thing from my mind was how much it paid. I just wanted the job.

I never speculated on what might have been if I had been Alabama's coach starting in 1983. I never looked back. Do I think we would have won? Yes. And I think I would have stayed more than seven years.

After our rocky start, the game that put us on the upward swing was Tennessee. They were undefeated and ranked third in the nation. We weren't ranked, but we went to Knoxville and won the game. That's when I think the players bought into what we were trying to do. I'll never forget Stacy Harrison blocking their field goal attempt and then Philip Doyle kicking a long one to win the game 9–6.

We had good players and won 70 games in our seven years. And the highlight season was 1992 when we went 13–0 and won the national championship. I didn't allow myself to start thinking about the national championship until we were 8–0 or 9–0. We were 11–0 and still hadn't won the conference championship, and even though we were ranked second in the nation, there was no guarantee at that time we would have played Miami, which was No. 1. But we won the SEC Championship game against Florida, and that set up the Sugar Bowl game of No. 1 Miami against No. 2 Alabama.

I thought we would win the game. We led the nation in about three different defensive categories. I thought we could shut down the run and shut down the pass, and I thought we could run the ball. That's the way it turned out.

I guess that game had maybe the greatest individual play I have ever seen, George Teague running down their receiver, Lamar Thomas, and taking the ball away from him. Even though we were leading at the time, that could have been the turning point. A team like Miami was capable of scoring a lot of points in a hurry.

But just because I thought we would win doesn't mean I was ever comfortable. I think it was down to about two minutes to play with us leading 34–13 before I was sure we were going to win the game. And it was so gratifying to win every national championship that was awarded that year.

I'm one of those people who remembers the losses more than the wins. I only coached one losing bowl game, and I still fret about the way I prepared Alabama for the Fiesta Bowl game we lost to Louisville.

We went more than 30 games without losing and then lost to LSU, and I think that if I had put David Palmer in at quarterback a little earlier we might not have lost that game.

I'm living in Texas now, but I still go to Alabama with some frequency. And I keep up with the team as best I can. I think Alabama is on the way back. I think they've got the right man on the job in Mike Shula. It takes a while to be a head coach, but I think he's going to do a good job.

I always thought the facilities were nice when I was there, but Mal Moore has done an excellent job of moving Alabama to the top in facilities for football.

One of the best things about being at Alabama is the players want to be there. It's not a place where you have to use pressure in recruiting. Very good players have always wanted to play football for the Crimson Tide, as you will see in the following pages.

—Gene Stallings

ACKNOWLEDGMENTS

I don't know if I would rather be lucky than good, but I do know I have been lucky. Lucky to have been given early encouragement to be a writer. Lucky to have been in the right place at the right time to become a sportswriter. Lucky to be selected to work in Alabama's sports publicity office, as it was called in the sixties and seventies. And lucky to be around those who were very, very good—coach Paul Bryant, the best football coach ever, and Charley Thornton, who took a backseat to no one in the field of sports information.

Coach and Charley are gone now, as are so many others who played an important part in this work. Some of them I knew not at all, or only casually, but they were instrumental in Alabama football being known worldwide. Others have been close friends, a by-product of more than 35 years covering the Crimson Tide.

There is no tradition in college football like that of 'Bama's. Over the years I have climbed into taxicabs in New York, San Francisco, Miami, Chicago, and many points in between. Frequently, the driver will ask, "Where you from?" and upon hearing "Alabama," the response has almost always been, "Ah, the Crimson Tide."

The greatness and tradition of Alabama football is in large part owed to men of vision, former presidents of the university—notably George Denny, Frank Rose, David Mathews, and Roger Sayers.

Coach Bryant talked about surrounding himself with good people, how important it was that everyone in the athletics department have the same goal. And there have been dozens of assistant football coaches who have been instrumental in Crimson Tide success. Hank Crisp, who served in a variety of capacities, was an early legend. Ken Donahue and Bill Oliver and Homer Smith were later ones.

There were important administrators—Jeff Coleman, Carney Laslie, and Sam Bailey.

Gene Stallings restored the glory of Alabama football. And he was kind enough to be a major participant in this work that, fittingly, bears his name.

Certainly Mal Moore, athletics director at Alabama, has a special place. He was a player, an assistant coach, an offensive coordinator, and as athletics director envisioned and directed the most ambitious capital improvements campaign in Alabama history.

Senior Associate Athletics Director Kevin Almond provided critical information.

This project could not have been accomplished without the cooperation of Larry White and his staff of professionals in the office of media relations. The staff of the incomparable Paul W. Bryant Museum, directed by Ken Gaddy and including associates Brad Green, Taylor Watson, and Clem Gryska, are invaluable in any project involving Crimson Tide athletics.

Former Alabama players Harry Lee and Tommy Brooker serve unique roles in Crimson Tide football history. Harry is the permanent secretary-treasurer of the "A" Club, and Tommy is permanent executive director of the "A" Club Foundation.

Barry Fikes, photo editor of 'BAMA Magazine, has chronicled Alabama football with photographs for over three decades, and he provided many of the photographs for this work.

Research and interview assistance was essential, and I got that from 'BAMA Magazine assistant editor Mitch Dobbs and writer Erik Stinnett, who writes the Where Are They Now? feature each month.

A number of players interviewed for this book had stories of one of my very best friends, former Crimson Tide trainer Sang Lyda, whose memory of players and incidents was so helpful.

Most of all I acknowledge the players who were so generous with their time and their memories to help in this production.

This is the first book I have written about Alabama football. I have written parts of books and edited books and written hundreds and hundreds of stories of the men who have coached and played the game for 'Bama. And over the years I have been approached to produce books on Alabama football, and particularly on coach Bryant. I had always declined. But Tom Bast, editorial director at Triumph Books, gave me a deal I couldn't refuse. Not a financial deal. A philosophical one. This was the book I wanted to do, focusing on the players and what it meant—and means—for them to be Crimson Tide.

I learned many, many years ago that it is all for nothing without those who follow the Crimson Tide, and I think about our fans in everything I write.

In 1970 Vera Dowdle became the secretary in the sports publicity office at Alabama. When I founded *'BAMA Magazine* in 1979, she remained at the university for a couple of years. We still had contact as I did much of my work in the athletics offices. And then in 1981 she joined our staff at *'BAMA*, and she continues to keep me on track in my work.

My wife and children participated in the process, reading the stories and offering suggestions. And my sister, Linda Cohen, a librarian, was proofreader and much more.

I married the former Lynne Pearson in 1963. In 1967 Lynne and I sat together in the upper deck at Legion Field in Birmingham and watched Kenny Stabler run in the mud through the Auburn defense for a dramatic Crimson Tide victory. Lynne and I are still married and we still go to Alabama football games, but that is the last time we have been able to sit together. My time in the press box has made her a football widow for nearly 40 years. It is the nature of my life in sports that nights and weekends have been work times, robbing hours and days from Lynne and my children, Julia and Stuart. They were understanding then, and they have been encouraging in this project. They, too, know what it means to be Crimson Tide.

INTRODUCTION

"Mama called." Succinctly, Paul William Bryant thus said what it means to be Crimson Tide.

The most extraordinary figure in the extraordinary experience that is Alabama football demonstrated his love for The University of Alabama. When in late 1957 Bryant revealed his decision to leave his job as head football coach at Texas A&M to go to Alabama, his explanation was simple and clear. His alma mater needed him, and he could not refuse. That is what it means to be Crimson Tide.

There haven't been many hard times in the 110-plus years of Alabama football, and certainly not since the Crimson Tide became a national power in the 1920s. Today Alabama is one of a very small group of truly special places in the world of college football. And Alabama football has always been able to overcome those difficult times. At the end of the 1957 season, 'Bama was on the bottom. Dr. Frank Rose, the president-elect of the university, knew he had to do something. And what he did was tap Bear Bryant, who had played on an Alabama Rose Bowl team, to return to Tuscaloosa.

The chairman of the committee to get Bryant, University Trustee Ernest Williams, said, "We have secured, to my mind, the finest football coach in the nation." The pronouncement has never been challenged.

Alabama football is much more than the Bryant era, though 1958 to 1982 was a magnificent, unparalleled quarter of a century in the sports world. And exactly one month after his Alabama football work was finished, on January 26, 1983, Paul Bryant died.

But there were other periods of greatness. Former Crimson Tide coaches Wallace Wade and Frank Thomas are, with Bryant, in the National Football Foundation Hall of Fame. Gene Stallings should be joining them soon. There were players throughout Alabama history who have gained national honors and helped the Crimson Tide to national championships.

This work is heavy with the men who played in the sixties and seventies. Alabama was named National Team of the Decade and Bryant was Coach of the Decade in both those periods.

To be Crimson Tide is even bigger than the larger-than-life Paul Bryant. But his standard influences the feelings of those who came before and who came after, as well as those who were with him at Alabama. It is partly for that reason, and partly because for the final 13 years of his 'Bama career it was my privilege to spend some part of almost every day of the football season with coach Bryant, that he dominates this chronicle of *What It Means to Be Crimson Tide*.

He demonstrated it as a player. When Alabama went to Knoxville to play Tennessee in 1935, Bryant—"the other end" to the incomparable Don Hutson—was not expected to play. He had suffered a broken leg. Coach Thomas gave his trusted aide, Hank Crisp, the opportunity to charge the team before the game. "I don't know about the rest of you," Crisp said, "but I know one thing. Old No. 26 will be after them." Bryant was No. 26. Bryant downplayed his solid playing career, but he was truly proud of that moment (and of catching two critical passes that led to touchdowns in 'Bama's 25–0 victory). That is what it means to be Crimson Tide.

Former Southeastern Conference Commissioner Boyd McWhorter said, "When you are with him, you feel like you are walking with history." The history is well documented in the victories, championships, All-Americans, and coaches he produced. His former players expand his dimension.

From day one, I was awed by his imposing greatness. As I came to know him better, my admiration was strengthened. He stressed throughout his career that he was teaching lessons for life, not for football games. While that has become something of a cliché to justify athletics, interviews with those who played for him soundly support the notion. It didn't just ring true. It was true.

Everyone who played for or worked for coach Bryant has a favorite story. So do thousands of fans. Mine is this: I recognized early in my career in the sports information office that coach Bryant had an uncanny knack for

Paul Bryant was not the only great coach in Alabama football history, but his mark on Crimson Tide football and college football has never been equaled.

measuring his words, as if he could imagine what he was about to say transformed to print in the next day's newspaper. I never knew the background of how he happened to call Auburn a "cow college," an insult Auburn credited as the motivation for Auburn's 1972 upset of Alabama. One of my jobs was to meet with coach Bryant after practice each day to get a short report—a "trainer" in the business—to send to the wire services and selected newspapers. Unlike today's post-practice gathering of reporters, in those days few practices were covered by a writer. I was the pool reporter.

Following a 1973 spring scrimmage, coach Bryant—after lighting up an unfiltered Chesterfield and taking a long drag—said, "We couldn't have beaten a cow college today." He thought for a moment, took another drag, then instructed me, "Change that to 'barber college'."

Alabama football under Bryant succeeded because of self-discipline and self-sacrifice by players and coaches. There was organization. There was fairness. Under Bryant, and before and after him, it has been demonstrated that the right way is the best way—the Alabama way.

Crimson Tide success has not come by shortcuts. Alabama football has been goal-driven. "National championship" is a recurring theme among those who define what it means to be Crimson Tide.

There was joy—the joy of big wins and championships and heroic individual achievements in a team game. And there was heartbreak, in the loss of games, but more so in the loss of those who are part of this great tradition. The lost games linger in the mind, lost comrades in the heart.

In four decades of covering Alabama football, I have come to know players from the twenties to the present day. I consider it among my greatest experiences that these men selected me for honorary "A" Club membership in 1974. At the time, I said it meant so much because I saw each day what the real lettermen did to earn the honor. It still has that meaning. Today I enjoy the camaraderie of former players and coaches and staff—what coach Bryant called "Alabama's football family"—at games, "A" Club functions, Red Elephant Club meetings, and team reunions.

I proudly wear a national championship ring coach Bryant decided I had earned as his sports information director.

And I know what it means to be Crimson Tide.

For instance, I was not surprised when Mike Shula–led Alabama came from behind in the final seconds to beat Georgia and Auburn in 1985. I had seen Terry Davis pull off a miraculous comeback against Tennessee in Knoxville in 1972 and Steadman Shealy lead Alabama on a long touchdown march to defeat Auburn in 1979.

I was not surprised that Alabama's 1992 team, which had struggled for much of the year, romped over Miami for the national championship in the Sugar Bowl. I had seen Alabama teams beat heavy favorites like Nebraska in the Orange Bowl at the end of the 1965 season and Heisman Trophy quarterbacks like Pat Sullivan in 'Bama's 31–7 win over Auburn in a battle of unbeatens in 1971.

And I am never surprised by Alabama football players who play above their perceived abilities—little men like nose tackle Terry Rowell, who was perhaps 175 pounds. Coach Bryant pointed out that "Alabama hasn't won because of its All-Americans, but because of the men who weren't All-Americans but didn't know it."

Alabama football ranks at the very top in tradition. Crimson Tide teams have won a dozen national championships and 21 Southeastern Conference championships going into the 2005 season. 'Bama has a winning record against every SEC team and against almost every team it has played. Alabama has far and away the most victories and best winning percentage of any SEC team and ranks among the top five in the nation in those categories. Only a handful of teams, and those having played very few games against Alabama, can claim a winning record against the Tide.

No team in the nation has been to as many bowl games (52) or had as many bowl victories (29). For many years the big four were the Rose, Sugar, Orange, and Cotton Bowls. Only a sprinkling of teams had played in all four, fewer still had victories in all four. And only Alabama had won all four more than once. In 1945 Alabama's undefeated team went to the Rose Bowl and crushed Southern Cal. After that game, the then–Pac-8 made a deal with the Big Ten to provide the opposition for the Rose Bowl, perhaps tired of 'Bama squads coming out every few years to dismantle the pride of the West Coast.

No team has had as many 10-win seasons as Alabama, a total of 27.

And while Alabama is noted for national championships, it is also noteworthy that Bama has had a number of close calls, some 31 top-10 finishes.

Alabama has carried the banner of Southern football. In 1922 all the football powers were in the East. An unheralded Crimson Tide went to Philadelphia and upset mighty Pennsylvania, 9–7, a result that sent shockwaves around the college football world. In 1926 Alabama became the first Southern team invited to the Rose Bowl, and the Crimson Tide again surprised the experts by defeating the reportedly invincible Washington Huskies 20–19.

As much as I thought I knew about what it means to be Crimson Tide, this opportunity revealed I had much to learn, particularly the depth of feeling for Alabama by those who played. The common bond and feeling notwithstanding, each man has a unique story.

There is an unusual problem in selecting former players to define what it means to be Crimson Tide. A book of this type at many schools would have the problem of not enough worthy candidates. The problem at Alabama is there are too many, and it is disappointing that so many deserving subjects

Paul "Bear" Bryant is considered the greatest college football coach of all time, and those who played for him consider him to have been more than just their coach.

are not included. Every day as I worked, I would see a name and think, "He needs to be in here."

Where to start? Alabama boasts nearly one hundred All-America players, although many are deceased. And there are Hall of Fame members here. But there are others who were not All-Americans, but who have been a part of Crimson Tide tradition.

Jerry Duncan wasn't an All-American, but when coach Bryant began honoring past players with spring training awards, one of the first was the "Jerry Duncan I Like to Practice Award." And Duncan played a part in college football history because of his success as a "tackle-eligible," a tackle who caught passes owing to the formation that made him an eligible receiver. That brought about howls from other coaches and eventually a rules change that outlawed the tactic. Duncan was a favorite for another reason. As college football linemen began growing in the sixties, up to the 300-pound-plus behemoths of today, Duncan represented the "itty-bitty" linemen coach Bryant liked to brag about. Eventually, they would give way at Alabama, too, but it was a great source of pride that Duncan was more effective at his job than were men at other schools who were 50 to 100 pounds bigger.

Bart Starr was no All-American at Alabama, but who can doubt his influence on the game of football? As Vince Lombardi's field general at Green Bay, Starr was quarterback of the first two NFL-AFL World Championship Games, then informally known as Super Bowls I and II. And more than that, he has been the ultimate role model among athletes.

Kareem McNeal never had a chance to be an All-American. In July 1995, before his senior season, he was injured in a one-car automobile accident near his hometown of Tuskegee. No one else in the car suffered serious injuries. Kareem was paralyzed. His football career was over, but he persevered, earning two degrees from the university, and he continues to have hope. That is what it means to be Crimson Tide.

Walk-ons have always been an important part of Alabama football. It is a difficult road. A most unlikely walk-on was Peter Kim, who walked on from Hawaii to play for coach Bryant. Peter returned to Hawaii after graduation and is now one of the nation's most successful businessmen, and he says he owes that success to what he learned on the football field at Alabama.

Mal Moore could have cursed the luck. He wanted to be Alabama's quarterback and as a junior was back-up to Pat Trammell on the 1961 team. As a senior he had to play behind a sophomore, Joe Namath. Moore then paid his dues as an assistant coach and eventually became the architect of the Crimson Tide's famed wishbone offense that 'Bama rode to a 124–19–1 record in 12 years. Those teams earned three national championships. Mal Moore wanted to be Alabama's head football coach, but when Paul Bryant stepped down, Moore was passed over. He returned to Alabama with Gene Stallings in 1990 and was instrumental in another Tide national championship, but a few years later was forced to leave the field because of the progressive illness of his wife, Charlotte. His first quest to be Alabama's athletics director was unsuccessful. When he finally got his chance, he proved to be one of the most effective athletics directors in the nation. And he has seven national championship rings from Alabama. That is what it means to be Crimson Tide.

Certainly, there are stories from the All-Americans—Joe Namath, Kenny Stabler, Lee Roy Jordan, Johnny Musso, Ozzie Newsome, and the greatest linemen to play the game, John Hannah and Dwight Stephenson. These are household names not only in Alabama homes, but wherever football is known.

And oh what a list it would be, those Crimson Tide greats who have gone. Old-timers, for sure, including Herky Mosley, who had talked and planned about his place in this book. He died at age 89, two weeks before he was to drive from Dothan to Tuscaloosa to be at the university on Signing Day 2005 and to share his fabulous memory for these pages.

We don't have Dixie Howell and Don Hutson, the legendary passing combination of Alabama's early Rose Bowl years. Johnny Mack Brown was perhaps more famous as a cowboy movie star, but was an excellent Alabama player. Fred Sington was so outstanding in the twenties that the most popular singer of the day, Rudy Vallee, recorded a tribute to him, "Football Freddie." And Frank Howard became one of the nation's best-known coaches at Clemson after the Bard from Barlow Bend had finished playing at 'Bama. We don't have Admiral Don Whitmire, an Alabama All-American who transferred to the United States Naval Academy after the 1942 season and was awarded the Knute Rockne Trophy as the nation's best lineman.

And young ones, too, like Derrick Thomas, the Butkus Award winner at Alabama and a recent NFL Hall of Fame finalist who was killed in a car crash in the prime of his career. Derrick was one of the finest linebackers in

Paul Bryant had star players, but said the championship teams were the result of the many players who were not All-Americans, but played as if they were.

Alabama history, and one of the finest men. His father was a pilot, killed in Vietnam. While Derrick's life was mostly football, he put great value on God and country—and on literacy, a generous donor to reading initiatives in his hometown of Miami and elsewhere. And good friends, Mike Ford and Cecil Dowdy, who left us too early.

What a chapter we miss not having Pat Trammell, the unquestioned leader of Alabama's 1961 undefeated national championship team. Trammell applied the same intensity to his studies as he did to football and realized his dream of becoming a doctor. Then came the nightmare, Pat Trammell taken from his family—and the Alabama family—by cancer.

And a personal highlight would have been to talk to Robert Cope of Union Springs, a great, great ancestor who played on Alabama's first football team in 1892.

It would not have been fair to ask Sylvester Croom what it means to be Crimson Tide. Sylvester was an All-American at Alabama and an assistant coach for the Crimson Tide before going off to the NFL. And he was a finalist for head coach at Alabama, but instead ended up at 'Bama rival Mississippi State. Following his first game against Alabama, a 30–14 Crimson Tide win in 2004, Croom was asked if he was glad to have the game and the hoopla of him being a former Alabama player (and candidate for the 'Bama head coaching job when Mike Shula got it) behind him. "As long as I'm at Mississippi State and we play Alabama, it will never be behind me," he said. "I can deal with that. Plus, in a lot of ways, I'm not going to let it be behind me because I want to be where Alabama is. I want Mississippi State to play like Alabama. I want us to expect to win as Alabama expects to win. I want the kids who come to Mississippi State to expect to wear championship rings just like they do at Alabama." He went on to say that the colleges with the greatest college football tradition are Notre Dame and Alabama.

Following the 1970 football season, a disappointing one in which the Crimson Tide had gone 6–5–1, the annual football banquet was a somber affair. But it provided a moment never to be forgotten. Dr. David Mathews, who was about half the age of Bryant, was president of the university. And Dr. Mathews was called upon for a few remarks at the banquet. He had scratched out a few notes on a napkin before rising. And he defined what it means to be Crimson Tide. He said:

> No one can help but be aware of the rich tradition that is associated with this team and with this university. There are people too old now to go to the games who still remember wearing a crimson-and-white jersey, men for whom The University of Alabama has great meaning. There are also some who are too young to be left alone in the stadium who would like one day to wear a crimson-and-white jersey and to be a part of The University of Alabama. That is tradition, and it is

something which is very, very important and very much a part of The University of Alabama.

Tradition is a burden in many ways. To have a tradition like ours means that you can't quit; to have a tradition like ours means that you can't lose your 'cool'; to have a tradition like ours means that you always have to show 'class,' even when you are not quite up to it; to have a tradition like ours means that you have to do some things that you don't want to do and even some you think you can't do, simply because the tradition demands it of you. On the other hand, tradition is the thing that sustains us. Tradition is that which allows us to prevail in ways that we could not otherwise.

I'm convinced that greatness in any field has to come out of some kind of tradition. And our job is to make certain that the tradition that is The University of Alabama means as much and stands for as much for those who are yet to come as it has for us and those who have gone before us.

That is what it means to be Crimson Tide.

The
THIRTIES

HOWARD CHAPPELL

LEFT HALFBACK

1931–1933

WHEN YOU GET TO BE ABOUT 95 YEARS OLD, there's an awful lot to remember and you worry about getting something wrong. But I certainly have wonderful memories of being a football player at Alabama. I was born July 9, 1910, and I've been told I'm the oldest "A" Club member still living.

I went to Alabama from Sylacauga. I took four years and one summer semester to earn my degree. I graduated on August 24, 1934. The next day I took a bus to Tuscumbia, where they had an opening for the football coach at Deshler High School. I interviewed for the job for 30 minutes. The next day, two days after I had graduated, I was the coach.

I enjoyed offense, and my Deshler teams reflected that. We scored a lot of points. But we were never as good as we should have been on defense. One of my teammates at Alabama was Paul Bryant. I think he was the best defensive coach who ever lived. He thought defense. His thinking was that if the other team didn't score, they couldn't beat you. And after he finished, a couple of years after I did, he helped me with my defense.

My wife was a student of football. Once she said, "Howard, your team doesn't play defense as well as it should." I said, "I'm not Bear Bryant. I'm not a defensive coach. I'm offensive." She said, "You sure are."

I went to Tuscaloosa during the 1929 season and told coach Wade that I wanted to come to Alabama to play football. He said, "You're mighty small." And I said, "Yes, but I'm mighty fast." And he said he liked that because we

2

were going to be playing against teams with fast guys. And he gave me a scholarship beginning in the fall of 1930.

Freshmen couldn't play in those days. So I practiced all year, but couldn't play in games. And when the team went to the Rose Bowl at the end of the 1930 season, coach Wade told me that he was sorry, but that since I wasn't eligible to play, I wasn't eligible to make the trip. And I had practiced all year against those great players. I particularly remember kickoff practice after we had finished practice. I'd return three or four of them and be worn out.

Even though I never got to play in a game for coach Wade, I learned a lot from him. He was a wonderful coach. He was as good as Bryant, and as tough—tough as nails. He meant for you to do what he said to do.

We knew that coach Wade was leaving for Duke after the season. And in 1931 coach Frank Thomas came in from Georgia, where he had been the backfield coach, I believe. He had played quarterback at Notre Dame. He brought in a coach who had put the Notre Dame shift in at Georgia and brought it to Alabama.

I was a left halfback, but that wasn't the best offense for me. I couldn't kick and I certainly couldn't pass as well as Dixie Howell. He took the first team job, but I got to play in most of the games. We had some great players in guys like Dixie Howell, Bear Bryant, Don Hutson, Tom Hupke, B'Ho Kirkland, Bill Lee. Bryant couldn't catch too well, but he was the best on defense. Hutson was a slow starter, but he certainly finished fast. He was tops.

3

We went to the Rose Bowl my freshman year when I couldn't go, and the year after I graduated those guys went back to the Rose Bowl.

Coach Thomas was an excellent coach, but we lost to Tennessee his first two years, and that was not good. We lost to them 25–0 in Knoxville in 1931. In 1932 we had that game in the rain in Birmingham—horrible playing conditions. Both teams were kicking on first and second downs. No one passed on third down. Both teams were playing for a break, hoping for a mistake. It was a bad day to try to play football.

Johnny Cain punted for us and had a great day, something like 19 punts for a 48-yard average. Beattie Feathers kicked for Tennessee. He punted 21 times and I caught 17 of them. We lost 7–3.

In 1933 we went back to Knoxville and won 12–6. With time for just one play, we knew Tennessee would throw a long pass. I was at safety and playing behind their deep receiver. The ball went over his head and I intercepted it. I was near the sideline and just stepped out of bounds. There were a bunch

4

Howard Chappell was on coach Frank Thomas' first Alabama Crimson Tide team.

of high school kids along the sideline there and they weren't happy about us winning. They started kicking me and kicked me all the way to the end zone.

Football players were well known on campus, and it was very important that a player act with dignity. Every now and then we'd have a player who'd get the big head. Usually a player who hadn't done much. We'd get him straightened out. We wanted the athletes to be athletes, but it was also important that they be good students.

The university president, Dr. Denny, was very active around the team. He'd come to practice with that brown coat over his shoulders and that stinking pipe and kind of get in the way. If you didn't smoke you could smell that pipe from 15 yards away. He'd walk right through our practice work and we'd have to stop. But he knew every boy on the team and where he was from and what he was studying. He was a grand old man, a great person. We all thought when they built the tower for Denny Chimes that he was most deserving.

After I left Alabama, I went to Tuscumbia and stayed there as a coach and teacher and eventually elementary school principal for some 35 years.

I had four years out for navy service in the early 1940s. I was in the Gene Tunney program. The navy wasn't happy with the physical condition of the men coming out of boot camp. So they put the boxer, Gene Tunney, in charge of a program to get them stronger. He selected 50 coaches to direct the program. We went to Norfolk, Virginia, and trained for four weeks, then went to Great Lakes, Illinois, to train the recruits. We took them into companies of 150 each for about six months. And when they finished they were bigger and stronger and could complete a very difficult obstacle course. We received reports that the captains were pleased with the results.

I met some fine people there, including the great Cleveland Indians pitcher Bob Feller, who was a fine fellow, and Mickey Cochrane, who was manager of the Detroit Tigers. And we had a lot of boxers because Tunney believed in boxing to get men in shape.

I was always interested in guiding students to the university, and particularly football players. I'd tell them that if you played football at Alabama, you would be playing for a school known for its football. The university put out engineers and doctors and lawyers, but when you think about Alabama, the first thing that comes to mind is football.

I loved playing football for Alabama. I loved the coaches I had, coach Wade and coach Thomas, and also the great assistant coaches like coach Drew and coach Crisp. They certainly influenced how I coached.

I still follow recruiting pretty close, and it looks like we're picking up some good players. We've had some rough times, but I believe we're on the way back. I believe Mike Shula is going to be a good coach. His daddy certainly was. But you have to have the horses. You can't win the Kentucky Derby on a mule.

Howard Chappell is Alabama's oldest living former football player. He played on coach Frank Thomas' first three teams, Crimson Tide squads that went 24–4–1.

BEN McLEOD JR.

END

1935–1936

I'VE BEEN TOLD THAT MY SON AND I ARE THE ONLY FATHER-SON combination who played on national championship teams at Alabama. I played on the 1934 team that went undefeated and beat Stanford in the Rose Bowl, and my son, Ben W. McLeod III, was on the 1965 national championship team for coach Bryant. Of course, since I was born April 22, 1913, I have also been told that I am the oldest former Alabama football player, but I know that is not the case.

I didn't really go to The University of Alabama to play football, but it's one of the best things that ever happened to me. I know I owe everything to the university. At least eight members of my family have attended Alabama, including my brother who got his doctorate there, and youngsters from our family continue to attend.

I am particularly indebted to coach Hank Crisp. I was born in Leakesville, Mississippi, but we moved to Geraldine, Alabama, after my father became ill. My mother was a school teacher and got a job teaching in Geraldine, where she provided for our family. I played basketball, and when I made all-state in the 11th grade, coach Hank contacted me. And after my senior year, he offered me a scholarship. In those days, you could take five years, and I took all five and enjoyed every minute of my time at Alabama.

The summer before I went to the university I was fortunate enough to get a job in a hotel working as a waiter for parties. I made $30 a month. And then

Ben McLeod Jr. was a three-sport star for Alabama and played behind Don Hutson and Paul Bryant in the Rose Bowl.

when I got to Tuscaloosa, coach Hank got me a job waiting tables. And I got the greatest job of all, waiting tables for the "A" Club men. I was in heaven.

That first year I played on the freshman basketball team. I was always looking for a little job and got one that spring, raking the baseball diamond for coach Paul Burnham. Later in the spring he let me take some batting practice, and by the end of the spring I was playing baseball.

The next fall coach Burnham told me to report to the football team, and he also told me I could have a job sweeping the auditorium on Sundays for 25¢ an hour. I spent $47 my first year at Alabama.

I had played football in high school, but it had been against teams that were not very strong. I was redshirted that year, but the next year, 1934, I was on the team. I was listed as a halfback, but was really better at end and backed up Don Hutson and Bear Bryant. I wasn't very big, 6'0" and about 160 pounds, but I could catch the ball. You had to play both ways, and I was a lot better on offense than defense. I was just a spare take-along. If you weren't a starter, you usually didn't play much.

We went 9–0 that year and beat everyone pretty handily, and so I'd get some time at the end of games, but not enough to earn a letter. And we were selected to play in the Rose Bowl against the great Stanford team.

The Rose Bowl was quite a deal. We left Tuscaloosa on Friday morning and arrived in Pasadena on a Monday morning. We stopped in San Antonio, Texas, for a full practice and stopped again in Tucson, Arizona, for a walk-through. Bill Young, a tackle, suffered an appendicitis attack and was operated on in Del Rio, Texas, and, of course, he missed the game.

I played only seven or eight minutes in the fourth quarter, but I remember every play of that 29–13 win.

I did play enough to letter in 1935 when we were 7–2–1, and was a starter in 1936 when we went 8–0–1; a 0–0 tie with Tennessee keeping us from being perfect.

On the way back to Tuscaloosa after the Rose Bowl, the basketball players stopped in New Orleans and played two games against Tulane, then went up to Baton Rouge and played two games against LSU before we could go home. We beat Tulane, but lost to LSU.

I thought I was going to start the Tennessee game in Knoxville in 1935. Bryant had a broken leg. But they took him out of the cast and started him. He didn't play long, maybe a quarter, but he played well. He caught at least two passes, which he lateraled to Riley Smith. I think one went for a touchdown and the other one set up a touchdown, and we beat Tennessee pretty handily, 25–0. It was really hot that day and after the first quarter, I went in for Bryant and went the rest of the game. That was the only game I ever played where I about gave out.

That Bryant was about as tough as they come.

I won two letters in football, three in basketball, and three in baseball. We won one SEC Championship in football and one in basketball and three in baseball. My baseball coach was Happy Campbell, who had been one of my roommates and teammates on the Rose Bowl football team.

I liked the notoriety that went with being a football player, but I liked playing baseball more than any other sport. Our outfield was Don Hutson in left field, Young Boozer in right field, and me in center. Jim Whatley was our first baseman, but I got moved to first when he made too many errors.

We were getting ready to go to the 1934 SEC Basketball Tournament in Atlanta. We didn't have a big squad, only about eight who traveled, because money was tight. One of our good players, Zeke Kimbrough, took a hit that caved in his cheekbone. Coach Hank said he wasn't going to be able to play and that I would start in his place. I told coach Hank that he had brought me to Alabama and I wouldn't let him down. I had the highest percentage of field goals, 8-of-15, and we beat Mississippi State, Tennessee, and Florida and won the championship.

I didn't get to play in the last SEC Tournament because I came down with pneumonia. They thought I was going to die. My mother came down and stayed with coach Thomas while watching over me. And I came out of it. That spring I was tapped into ODK, an academic honor society.

Coach Thomas was one in a million. I think he was a great football coach because he had an uncanny knack of anticipating what the opposition was going to do. He never hollered or bullied his teams into producing their best, but had a quiet and firm control on his players. When he wanted something done, it was done.

9

After I graduated, I went to Brewton to coach football at T. R. Miller High School. In the summer, I played semipro baseball in Alabama and in North Carolina. My last two Miller teams went undefeated, and the 1942 team only allowed seven points. Coach Thomas came to Brewton to speak at our football banquet and stayed with me and my wife, Katie, whom I married in 1940. (She's a little younger than I am.) He said he thought I should move up to college coaching and that he would help me. The next day the Japanese bombed Pearl Harbor.

They were sending people everywhere to get ready to go into the service. Among former Alabama players, two of us were sent to Annapolis—Paul Bryant went in the first class, and I went in the second. We were there 10 weeks. Then I was commissioned a Lieutenant (JG) and stationed in Pensacola. I played for the Naval Air Station team that played Alabama in Mobile in 1942. Alabama won 27–0, and one of the stars for Bama was one of my former high school players, Hosea Rogers, who ended up playing and graduating from North Carolina.

I stayed in the navy for a while after the war. Then a year or so after I got out, they called me up because of the Korean War. I ended up staying in the navy for 28 years, including reserves service, and retired with the rank of commander.

And when I left active duty, I stayed on at Pensacola as special services officer and athletics director at Naval Air Basic Training Command.

In 1972 they found a growth on my ankle. I had cancer. The doctors at Eglin Air Force Base operated on me and got it all. I wanted to do something for them, so I called coach Bryant and asked if he could help me with four tickets for these doctors and their wives. He said he'd take care of it. Well, they got up there and coach Bryant had them in a box with Governor Wallace. Those doctors hadn't even known I'd played football before that.

The Lord has been awfully good to me, and being able to attend The University of Alabama has meant everything to me.

Ben McLeod Jr. earned eight letters (two in football and three each in basketball and baseball) and played on five SEC Championship teams (one each in football and basketball, and three in baseball) for the Crimson Tide.

The
FORTIES

JOE DOMNANOVICH
CENTER AND LINEBACKER
1940–1942

WHEN THE *South Bend Tribune* FOUND OUT I WAS GOING to Alabama, they ran a little cartoon of me with the Golden Dome in the background and me heading out with a suitcase that had "Traitor" written on it. Paul Bryant was an assistant coach at Alabama when I got there in 1939, and he remembered that suitcase a little differently. My wife, Elizabeth, and I went to the Sugar Bowl and ran into Mary Harmon and Bear out waiting for a cab. Bear started laughing and said, "I can still see Joe when he got to Alabama with all his possessions in a cardboard box that said 'J. C. Penney' on it."

Since I was from South Bend, Indiana, almost everyone thinks I went to Alabama because of coach Frank Thomas, who had played at Notre Dame. But I had never heard of him until Alabama started recruiting me in 1938. I will say he was a really good person.

I thought I'd go to Notre Dame. I was named the most outstanding player at my high school my senior year. I had some hip problems and went over to Notre Dame because they had a trainer who was pretty well known. I went there and got treatment every week. But when the time came, I never heard a word from Notre Dame. So I went to work for a year.

Purdue and Indiana had talked to me, but I wasn't interested. In fact, I wasn't really interested in going to college. A guy from Gary, Indiana, came

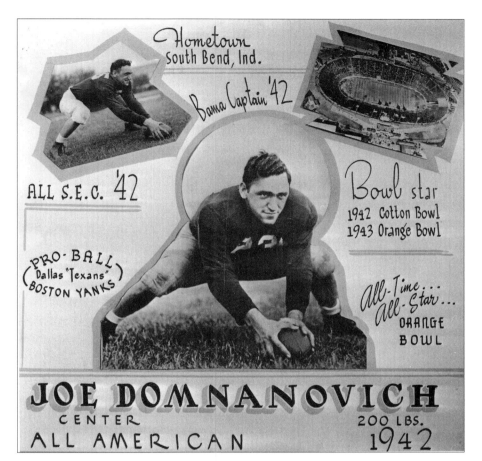

Joe Domnanovich was an All-American center in 1942 and selected to the All-Time Orange Bowl Team.

to see me about playing for Alabama. Mort Kimball had been a year behind me at South Bend, and they were recruiting him, too.

Alabama was the team that always went to the bowl games. That was the big thing for me. Notre Dame didn't go to bowls back then. Alabama used to go to the Rose Bowl all the time, so I thought I would just go down there. So Mort and I went to Alabama.

Recruiting was much different then. First of all, I needed a math course, so I went to East Mississippi Junior College to get that. Then when I showed up at Alabama, it was more like tryouts instead of a scholarship. They'd have 10 or 15 guys trying out at each position. Each day a few were on the bus going back home.

I didn't sign a scholarship until just before the first game that year.

Back then you couldn't go back in the game in that quarter if you came out, so I played center on offense and linebacker on defense. Most starting players played most of the game.

I went to Alabama to play in bowl games, and we played in two of them.

We played in the Cotton Bowl against Texas A&M, which was considered the number one team in the nation by a lot of people. That was a big event for us. Statistically, we didn't beat them, but we ran all over them. We had fumble recoveries and punt returns and interceptions and had a 29–7 lead in the fourth quarter. Texas A&M scored a couple of late touchdowns to make it look respectable. Later I would play pro ball with a tackle on that A&M team, Martin Ruby.

After the 1942 season, we played in the Orange Bowl on January 1, 1943, against Boston College. They had five guys who would play pro ball, and they were favored to romp us. They were up 13–0 in the first five minutes, but by halftime we had the lead and won 37–21. We had trouble early because we had never played against a T formation team until that game.

That was a memorable game for me because they had a snap go over the punter's head, and I got back there and tackled him in the end zone for a safety.

We traveled by train, and a lot of guys had never been on a train trip that long. It was fun. There were places where they knew we were coming, and they'd stop the train and have a little rally for us at the station.

In 1993 the Orange Bowl invited us back for a 50-year reunion, players from Alabama and Boston College. They showed a film of the game we played. We ran the Notre Dame box formation, which was a shift formation. When we were watching the film, the Boston College guys would holler that we were in motion every time we had the shift. But they were just being funny. In the shift, you all got reset before the ball was snapped.

We had about 40 players on the two teams back for the Orange Bowl reunion. There are still 12 or 13 of us who played for Alabama and we stay in touch, but it's getting harder to get together. I've lost a leg and had open heart surgery and have beaten cancer.

When I played, we didn't play Auburn. Tennessee was the big game. And to my mind, it still is. Mississippi State had good teams back then, and they were the only team to beat us twice in my three years.

They didn't make much out of being an All-American. I don't have any idea how I was selected. I just read about it in the newspaper. Afterward they sent me a sweater.

After the Orange Bowl, I had to go into the service for three years. I spent one year in Germany. I came back to finish my degree, and that's when they started talking to me about pro football. I played six years. The team moved from Boston to New York and a couple of other places, but it was the same team owned by Ted Collins. It was nice because I was playing with and against some of the same people I had played with in college.

Elizabeth and I married after my final season, after coach Thomas said it was all right. We knew we wanted to stay in the South after I finished playing pro ball. An Alabama man wrote me a recommendation. It said. "This is Joe Domnanovich. He is a good man. Hire him." I took it out to U.S. Steel. They hired me as a supervisor and I stayed there 30 years. We went to all the Alabama games until a few years ago. We still buy tickets.

Long after my playing career at Alabama it was amazing how many people knew that Joe Domnanovich had played football for Alabama.

Our son and his wife went to Alabama, and now our grandson is in law school at Alabama.

15

Joe Domnanovich was an All-American in 1942 and was captain of the Crimson Tide. He was selected to Alabama's All-Time Team for the first 50 years in 1943 and was named to the all-time Orange Bowl team. He played for the New York Bulldogs and Boston Yanks of the NFL.

DON SALLS

FULLBACK AND LINEBACKER
1940–1942

I'LL HAVE TO ADMIT WHEN I CAME TO ALABAMA in the late 1930s from White Plains, New York—about 30 miles from New York City—I thought I had made the biggest mistake a man could make. My first year was probably the toughest of my life. The heat was tough. Spring training lasted a long time. The paper mill made it hard to breathe. It seemed like there were about a hundred freshmen.

Then you saw all the monsters they had. You felt like it was going to be almost impossible to make the team because they had top-notch athletes from all over the country. You were playing against some very fine athletes in practice. I thought, "What have I gotten myself into?" I knew it was going to be tough, and it was.

Every time I saw a New York play or heard a train whistle, I wanted to leave. But I couldn't. If I didn't learn anything else, I guess I learned patience. It took me four years to make the team.

My high school coach had been a college roommate with Red Drew, who was an assistant coach at Alabama, and that was my first connection to Alabama. I was aware of Alabama from the Rose Bowls, but I was really more interested in the Eastern schools—Columbia, Fordham, Manhattan, and those types. And I was interested in Illinois because they used small backs, and I was small.

Don Salls was given mop-up duty on defense against Kentucky and turned in an interception that led to playing time.

Coach Hank Crisp and coach Happy Campbell came to New York to see me. My coach had me put my gym shorts on to meet them. He said, "I want them to see your legs." I had a lot of scholarship offers, but none like the one Alabama offered. It was room, board, books, tuition, and $10 a month. That was mighty nice, and I had it for five years.

Coach Thomas was tough, too. I think he only said one thing to me the whole time I was here. One day in spring training I ran the ball and he said, "Salls, that may be the way they run the ball in New York, but you're in Tuscaloosa now." I didn't take that as criticism. I realized he knew my name and where I was from, and I took pride in that.

I didn't do much in my first two years, but in my third year—which was my sophomore season for eligibility—I got my chance. We were beating Kentucky in Lexington, and one of the coaches said to coach Thomas, "Let's put that Salls kid in and see what he can do on defense." I was just a floater. Kentucky was passing, trying to catch up. And I intercepted a pass and went 76 yards for a touchdown, which is still listed as one of the longest in Alabama history. And that was my entrée into Crimson Tide football.

It was hard to letter then. For the most part, the starters played the entire 60 minutes. We probably only had about 15 lettermen a year. I was a fullback on offense and linebacker on defense and played in almost every game, but didn't play enough to letter. I liked defense about as much as offense. What you made on offense, you wanted to save on defense.

I was pretty light, about 170 pounds. I was the lightest fullback Alabama had had, and then Norwood Hodges came along about five years later and beat me out for that honor. He weighed about 165.

In 1941 I was the third fullback. Two big guys, John Hanson and Paul Spencer, both about 210 or 220, were in front of me. But Hanson went into the service and became a pilot—in fact, he buzzed the practice field one day—and Spencer got hurt. And so the third team fullback got the first team job.

We had fine athletes and good teams. We played in the Cotton Bowl at the end of the 1941 season and the Orange Bowl at the end of the 1942 season. That Cotton Bowl game was one of the strangest ever. We had only one first down, but we had seven interceptions and five fumble recoveries. Jimmy Nelson pretty much won that game by himself with big plays, including a long punt return for a touchdown. We had some excellent players like Don Whitmire and Holt Rast.

We didn't know it until a long time after, but that 1941 team was awarded a national championship. I moved back to Tuscaloosa in 2001, and I'd see Clem Gryska at church. And Clem has all those national championship rings. I wanted one and was going to buy one. But in 2003 at a reunion of some of my players from Jacksonville State, they presented me with a 1941 national championship ring. They didn't give rings in those days, so I have the only one. One of my Jacksonville players, Duck Hodges, was a representative for Balfour, which makes those rings.

Our 1942 team went to the Orange Bowl to play Boston College. They got two long scores in the first quarter by Mike Holovak, but we came back and won the game 37–21.

In 1992 the Orange Bowl had a 50-year reunion for those two teams. We stayed at Don Shula's Country Club and Resort. We had 22 players and they had 21. We played golf and went to the game and even went to the banquet where we heard Bobby Bowden from Florida State and Tom Osborne from Nebraska speak.

I got my bachelor's degree from Alabama and then, after World War II, came back and got my master's. I went to New York University to get my doctorate. Jacksonville State was looking for a football coach, and coach Thomas recommended me. I also had to be a professor, although I taught a lighter load in the fall. And I had two assistants, who were also professors. That was our staff.

I stayed there 38 years—the only place I ever worked—and retired in 1982. I was head football coach from 1946 to 1964, then continued just as a professor. We had some good players, like Little All-American Jodie Connell, who had just one arm. We won 97 games, which is the most of any Jacksonville State coach, and that got me into the Alabama Sports Hall of Fame, for which I am grateful.

I was a pioneer in isometric exercises in the 1960s. And in 1995 I published a book, *Live and Love to Be 100.*

In 2003 Don Salls, along with Harry Gilmer, was presented the Paul W. Bryant Alumni-Athlete Award, which is given to recognize Alabama athletes who have made exceptional contributions since graduating.

HARRY GILMER

HALFBACK

1944–1947

THE BEST WAY TO THROW A PASS IS NOT A JUMP PASS, and in my years of coaching I never taught the jump pass. It doesn't lend itself to today's ball. But it worked for me. I always felt that coach Thomas didn't like for me to do it. Sometimes we'd have younger people around practice, and if they saw me throw a jump pass they would try to do it. Coach Thomas would tell them to stop, to do it the correct way. Ed Salem, the passer who followed me, jumped and threw one time, and coach Thomas ran up to him, got in his face, and told him to stay on the ground and throw like he was supposed to.

I started throwing the jump pass when I played on the sand lots. At Wood-lawn High School I kept doing it because I could start out on an end run and then turn it into a pass. If the receiver wasn't open, I kept running.

If you just think through the actions of a passer, you know if you drop back and set up in the pocket, you certainly aren't going to jump. You're going to be on the balls of your feet so you can bounce and stay ready to throw.

But if you throw on the run, you're usually running towards the sideline, and you're going to throw at a right angle to that. So you need to get your body and your hips turned downfield. You either have to stop running to do it or you jump. If you jump, you can turn your hips around. I just naturally did that.

Harry Gilmer came to Alabama during World War II and was a four-year starter and All-American halfback who led the Tide to its last Rose Bowl victory.

Although I was the team's passer, I wasn't a quarterback. I was the left half-back in the single wing, or Notre Dame box, formation. The closest thing to it today is the shotgun formation. Ideally, the left halfback was able to run, throw, or kick.

The jumping came about because I could throw the ball on the run. I didn't have to stop to turn my body. And maybe I was a little more accurate than most people. A lot of people back then would try to jump and throw. It's not the best way to pass, but it's the best way if you are throwing on the run.

I went to Alabama during unusual times, as World War II was winding down. Alabama didn't have a football team in 1943 because all the men were in the service. They recruited us to play in 1944, and we had four years of doing all the playing. I was a junior before we had people coming back out of the service to compete with us for those jobs.

I had played for a very strong Woodlawn team. We had a great coach in Malcolm Laney and never lost a game in my four years there. I wasn't good enough to be a starter until I was a senior. I had opportunities to go to several colleges, but Alabama was the closest and the one I knew the most about, so it was an easy decision to make. I really didn't know much about Alabama before I got there, but I have a great love for the school now. I have followed Alabama closely and been proud that the football program has continued to be successful over the years.

When I got to Alabama it was the reverse situation of high school. There was no waiting. I was a starter as a freshman.

We were very successful during my four years at Alabama. We went to the Sugar Bowl my freshman year and the Rose Bowl my sophomore year. That was Alabama's last appearance in the Rose Bowl. We beat Southern Cal 34–14, and it wasn't that close. After that, the Rose Bowl shut out Alabama and the other Southern schools.

Our third year, 1946, we lost our coach, Frank Thomas. His health broke down in the middle of the season, and we lost four games toward the end of the year. Red Drew took over in 1947, and we went back to the Sugar Bowl.

I probably gained some attention when we went to play Duke in the Sugar Bowl at the end of the 1944 season. That game meant a lot to me because we only threw eight passes, but we completed all eight of them. The last play of the game was a pass I threw to Ralph Jones. He was out long and the pass was a little short, so he was able to adjust and make the catch. But that also allowed the last Duke defender to get him. The guy who was covering him dove and slapped Ralph's foot and tripped him up. He was the only guy who could have caught him. Duke was a team of veterans, navy trainees, and was heavily favored and we lost by the slim margin of 29–26.

The great old-time sportswriter out of New York, Grantland Rice, was at that game, and he called my performance "better than Baugh," referring to the great Sammy Baugh of Washington Redskins fame. He shouldn't have written that, and I probably shouldn't repeat it, but it was an honor, particularly when you consider we passed only eight times.

Alabama prepared me for a life in football. After I played at Alabama, I went into pro ball and played nine years with the Redskins and Detroit. Then I went to Pittsburgh as an assistant with the Steelers for four years. I went with Norm Van Brocklin to a new franchise, the Minnesota Vikings, and coached defensive line for four years. I got the head job at Detroit, but didn't win enough games and was there only two years. I was quarterbacks coach with Jim Hart, the quarterback at St. Louis, for three years, then went to Atlanta and rejoined Van Brocklin. After five years in Atlanta, I went back to St. Louis for seven years, then scouted for St. Louis for 11 years. If you add it up, after Alabama, I played for nine years, coached for 27 years, and scouted for 11 more. I was a scout for the Cardinals when Gene Stallings was head coach.

Add that up and it's 47 years in pro football.

I always enjoyed returning to Tuscaloosa to scout Alabama players. I have great respect for and loyalty to Alabama, and I am appreciative of the great record in football there.

I'm still in St. Louis because I have children, grandchildren, and now great-grandchildren here. You can tell where I coached by where we left our children—one in Detroit, one in Atlanta, and two in St. Louis.

Harry Gilmer was All-America and SEC Player of the Year in 1945, and MVP of the 1946 Rose Bowl. He accounted for an Alabama record 52 touchdowns, ranks second all-time in interceptions, and first all-time in punt returns. In 1946 he led Alabama in rushing, passing, interceptions, punt returns, and kickoff returns. He was inducted into the College Football Hall of Fame in 1993.

VAUGHN MANCHA
CENTER
1944–1947

I FELL IN LOVE WITH THE UNIVERSITY OF ALABAMA at an early age, when I was playing football at Ramsay High School in Birmingham. There were so many things I appreciated about the opportunity I had. I was a poor kid, but I was lucky enough to have the skills to play for Alabama, which meant I was going to get three meals a day and not have to sleep with my big brother anymore. And I was lucky enough to have a coach, Frank Thomas, who stressed education.

And everything about it I appreciate even more today. My career in athletics and education has been mostly at Florida State, but my heart has always been at Alabama.

When I was growing up, The University of Alabama was a favorite destination for a lot of Ramsay High School graduates. I used to go to Legion Field and watch Alabama play. I had such great admiration for guys like Dixie Howell and Don Hutson. And because I was a center, I really loved to watch Carey Cox. I tried to emulate him.

I've tried to apply the lessons I learned from coach Thomas throughout my life as a player, coach, administrator, and professor. Coach Thomas wanted every player to earn his degree. If you needed aid after your playing days, he would make sure you got it. I actually finished the work for my undergraduate degree just before my final game at Alabama. Coach Red Drew was our coach that last year after coach Thomas became so ill.

Vaughn Mancha was an All-American center and Hall of Fame player who became athletics director at Florida State.

I signed a professional football contract with the Boston Yanks, who are now the Indianapolis Colts. I was a number one draft choice and signed for $7,500 plus a $2,500 signing bonus. In those days that made you a rich man.

I tore up my knee and ended my playing career, but I was able to take advantage of the deal for academic aid at Alabama and went back to get my master's degree in 1950. I actually got a little beyond the master's degree, which would prove important.

That's how I got my first job in athletics. Livingston University needed a coach, but you also had to be a professor and be beyond the master's level.

I enjoyed my time at Livingston. I particularly remember a game when we were going to play Florida State in Selma. I thought Cliff Harper, who was the best high school official in Alabama, was going to call the game, but there was a mix-up and no one ever contacted him. So we were ready to play and didn't have an officiating crew. We pulled some people out of the stands to officiate. We beat Florida State, and I told them later that three of the officials had been my teammates at Alabama. And actually, one of them had been.

26

That may have led to me getting a coaching job at Florida State under Tom Nugent. I was defensive coordinator and also served as a professor for six years. I went to Columbia in 1957 and was defensive coordinator and a professor while working on my doctorate.

I went back to Florida State in 1959 as athletics director. I left athletics in 1971, but stayed on as a professor until I retired in 1990. One of the highlights of my career as athletics director was when we opened the season in Birmingham against Alabama. Alabama had won national championships in 1964 and 1965, and gone undefeated in 1966, giving up just 44 points all year. It was quite a night in Birmingham. The scoreboard went out, and when the game ended, it was a 37–37 tie.

One of my classmates at Alabama was Claude Kirk. Later, when I was athletics director at FSU, Claude Kirk was elected governor of Florida. We got a lot of things done here in those days.

My career in athletics has enabled me to know some great people. I loved going to the coaches conventions and being able to visit with coach Bryant and people like that. Tom Landry was on the Texas team that beat us in the Sugar Bowl in my last game at Alabama, and I enjoyed knowing him when he was coach of the Dallas Cowboys. And I coached some guys who did pretty well, like Lee Corso of ESPN, who was a great running back; and Burt Reynolds, who wasn't as good a player; and at Columbia I coached Brian Dennehey. He said he couldn't understand a redneck like me, but he understood a kick in the butt.

But my fondest memories are of my playing days at Alabama. I actually signed with Alabama in 1941, but because of World War II, I didn't get there until 1944. When I was six years old, we were playing bow and arrow, and I got an eye put out, but I still had to do something. I joined the Merchant Navy and was in the Pacific for a couple of years. And somehow I got out in time to get to the university for the 1944 season.

Those were wonderful times with wonderful people. We went to two Sugar Bowls and one Rose Bowl. The first one was one of the great games ever against a powerful Duke team in the Sugar Bowl, and we came within a shoestring tackle of winning that game.

After the 1945 season, we went to the Rose Bowl. We got up 27–0 on Southern Cal and won easily, 34–14, to finish undefeated. That was the last time Alabama went to the Rose Bowl. After that game, the Rose Bowl signed a contract with the Big Ten to be the visiting team.

One of the great things about playing then as opposed to now is the time factor. Today you get on a jet, go to the game, get back on a jet, and go home. I think it must have taken us about half a month to go to California and back for that Rose Bowl game. They took professors with to tutor us. The train would stop every few hundred miles for us to practice and to meet fans.

When we got to California, we got to go to Johnny Mack Brown's ranch. He had been a great player at Alabama and was a famous movie star. We met Errol Flynn on the set. He was making *Robin Hood*. He was about 6'5" and really built and wearing those tights. We thought he would have made a good addition to the team.

And over the years I kept up with my teammates. But now I look at a picture of that last Rose Bowl team and see so many who are no longer with us. My time as a player at Alabama was very special. I have a lot of great memories of the thrills we had.

I've been awfully fortunate to have honors come my way. When I was inducted into the National Football Foundation Hall of Fame, one of my students was Deion Sanders. He was impressed. He said, "I didn't know you were bad." I told him I had been 228 pounds with Deion speed.

You never know how Alabama football is going to help you. When I was at Columbia, I got pulled over for speeding. The policeman was from Alabama and recognized my name from my playing days and let me off with a warning.

I make trips to Alabama as often as I can. Unfortunately, some of them are for funerals of old friends. But my son graduated from the Alabama medical school and is a doctor in Montgomery. I wish I could have spent more time in Alabama following the Crimson Tide, but I was always tied up at another school. Now we're active in the Alabama Alumni Association in Tallahassee.

I've had a great life. I think working in athletics helped keep me young. And I owe it all to The University of Alabama.

Vaughn Mancha started every game for four years at Alabama and was a consensus All-American in 1945. He is a member of the Alabama Sports Hall of Fame and was selected to the Alabama Team of the Century. He was inducted into the National Football Foundation Hall of Fame in 1990.

CLEM GRYSKA
END
1947–1948

IN 1947, AFTER COACH RED DREW TOOK OVER for coach Frank Thomas, we switched our offense from the Notre Dame box to the wing-T, a tight formation. I had been a quarterback, which was really a blocking back in the box, but moved to right end in the T formation. We were having a practice session one day, and a pass was thrown to me. I dropped it. Coach Drew shouted, "Two hands, Gryska, two hands!" That broke the team, up. If I had two hands, I might not have been at Alabama.

I was working in a grocery store when I was 11 or 12 years old and lost my right hand in a meat grinder. The doctor did a great job to save the thumb, or I wouldn't have been able to do anything. I wrote and called him until he passed away. If he hadn't done that, I would have been helpless.

But it meant I wasn't fit for the service. I was 4-F. And when I was 17 years old I was 6'2" and 187 pounds and had good grades. In fact, I had already signed with Northwestern. Coach Thomas had a good friend who was the Coca-Cola distributor in Wheeling, West Virginia, just across the river from my hometown of Steubenville, Ohio. Coach Thomas came up and coached an all-star game they put on in Wheeling, which I played in. I really wasn't that good, but coach Thomas and his staff came by my house after the game. They promised my parents, who were Polish immigrants, that they would take care of me. And that was important to them because I was the youngest of their six boys.

Clem Gryska served Alabama as a player, assistant coach, and administrator, and after retirement from the athletics department moved to the Bryant Museum.

30

I went to Alabama, and a few months later I was in Pasadena, playing in the Rose Bowl. It was beyond anything I could have imagined. We had played in front of crowds of twenty or thirty thousand, maybe forty thousand. At the Rose Bowl, there were 92,000.

We had gone through warm-ups and then went back to the dressing room. And coach Thomas jumped on Harry Gilmer, of all people, our best player. Then we went back out and 92,000 people stood up, like a giant wave. I can still remember it. It excited us and even scared us a little to be in front of that many people.

And of course it was great to win the game and finish the season undefeated. I don't know if people realize it or not, but that team scored 430 points in 10 games. In 1973 Alabama scored 477 points in 12 games, the only team to outscore the 1945 team.

We rode the train to the Rose Bowl. We left on a Sunday. We changed trains in New Orleans. And anytime a troop train needed the track we pulled off to a sidetrack. We got to Pasadena on Thursday afternoon. We had some adventures along the way. Once we stopped in El Paso for the locomotive to get water, and coach Thomas took us over to a nearby schoolyard to work out. The thing I remember most about that is we got back onto the train and didn't have showers for 40 or 50 sweaty guys.

I also learned something about hot tamales on that trip. Steve Fortunato, who was also from Ohio, and I bought some tamales from some Mexican kids on one of our stops. They were six for a quarter. We got them back on the train and they were wrapped in cornhusks. We couldn't chew them, so we never ate them. That was ammunition for guys like Vaughn Mancha to point out what dumb Yankees we were, not knowing to take the tamales out of the cornhusks.

I was fortunate to play for coach Thomas for two years before he became too ill to coach. Years later when I was working for coach Bryant, who had played for coach Thomas, I could see where coach Bryant had learned a lot of lessons from coach Thomas. That was particularly true in organization and attention to detail. Under both, you ran a play correctly. And that meant doing it over and over and over until every detail was perfect. Any mistake and the whistle meant "Do it again."

31

In the early years, coach Bryant probably had only five or six running plays and a couple of pass plays and a quick kick. But they were done to perfection. There was never a missed block, never a man jumping offside.

Another thing they had in common was giving players direction, then letting them motivate themselves.

Over the years I saw a lot of tough guys in football, but I think the toughest may have been Charley Compton, a tackle who had been in the service and who would be a missionary. We were playing Georgia in Athens, and Charley came to the sideline and asked Fred Posey, our manager, for a pair of pliers. I guess Fred thought Charley had a loose cleat and gave him the pliers. And Charley put them in his mouth and pulled out a tooth that had been knocked loose and threw it on the ground while spitting out blood. Even coach Thomas got wide-eyed over that, but he didn't say anything.

I don't think I had any intention of getting into coaching. But after I graduated, coach Drew told me that Buck Hughes, who had been a great athlete at Alabama in the 1930s, needed an assistant coach at Huntsville. Later I went to Emma Sansom and coached with one of my teammates, Kayo Miller, and then went back to Huntsville as head coach until 1960. Benny Nelson, Mike Hopper, and Boots Elliot were some of my players at Alabama. I was president of the Alabama High School Coaches Association, and coach Bryant called me to interview. I thought he was interviewing me to coach, but he wanted me to get into the high schools and recruit.

Dude Hennessey and I came together, and we both coached one day before hitting the road as recruiters for two and one-half years. Coach Bryant wanted it done the right way. A lot of recruiters would go in, see the football coach, and then talk to the prospect. Coach Bryant told us to go in and first see the principal, then the coach, then the teacher, and finally the prospect. We always did it the right way.

I finally moved to on-the-field when Jerry Claiborne left. I was recruiting coordinator, freshman coach—later junior varsity—and helped with the kicking game.

After coach Bryant retired, I stayed on as an administrator for awhile. And I was lucky. I didn't have to completely retire or get away from athletics.

I have been fortunate enough to continue working at the Paul W. Bryant Museum. Anytime a former player walks in, it sparks a memory for me. We have reunions of a lot of teams, including a 60-year reunion of that 1945 team that I played on as a freshman. I think it has been good for me to keep active doing something I really enjoy.

Clem Gryska played on Alabama's last Rose Bowl team at the end of the 1945 season, played in the renewal of the Alabama-Auburn series in 1948, a 55–0 Crimson Tide victory, and was an assistant coach under Paul Bryant, 1960–1976.

The FIFTIES

HARRY LEE

GUARD AND LINEBACKER

1951–1954

I WAS GIVEN A CHOICE: BIG FISH IN A LITTLE POND OR little fish in a big pond. Originally from Alabama, my family was living in San Francisco during World War II. I was in the fifth or sixth grade when the 1945 Alabama team came to California and defeated Southern Cal 34–14 in the Rose Bowl. That was my introduction to Alabama football and a great source of pride.

After the war we moved back to Alabama, to Birmingham, and I became even more of a fan. I got to see a lot of Alabama games in those days. And I started to learn about the history and tradition of Alabama football, the bowl games and championships. And it seemed to me that it would mean something special to wear that crimson jersey. I took it as a great compliment to Alabama when I read that General Neyland at Tennessee had told his team, "You never know what a football player is made of until he plays against Alabama."

And even though I knew I was going to go to Alabama, I took advantage of the recruiting trips. I was recruited by most of the SEC teams, plus Army and Navy.

The state track meet was in Auburn, and while we were there, one of the Auburn coaches pulled a couple of us off to the side and said that Auburn wanted both of us. And he said to me that he knew Alabama wanted me. He said, "Y'all can come to Auburn and be big fish in a little pond, or y'all can go to Alabama and be little fish in a big pond."

Harry Lee was an offensive lineman and linebacker for teams coached by Harold "Red" Drew that played in the Orange and Cotton Bowls.

My teammate, who wasn't being recruited by Alabama, said, "I want to be a big fish in a little pond!"

I said, "Well, I want to be a little fish in a big pond and grow up to be a big fish."

The Auburn coach said, "I guess that means you're going to Alabama." And I told him I was.

I graduated from high school in January and went straight to the university. Classes started in February, and about a week after we started classes, we started spring training. Here I was a freshman walking out there in spring practice with guys I had been watching play at Legion Field a few months earlier. I thought, "I'm going to be killed."

I don't know what I did to catch the eye of a coach, but he gave me a compliment, and it was a confidence builder for me. The more pride I had in that crimson jersey, the harder I worked; and the harder I worked, the more confident I got.

I was practicing at offensive guard, and coach Hank Crisp moved me to linebacker. He told me that, with my quickness and speed, linebacker should be a natural position for me. Anything I accomplished in football I owe to coach Crisp. He took an interest in me and was an excellent coach.

I played in two extraordinary bowl games. The first was following the 1952 season when we defeated Syracuse 61–6 in the Orange Bowl.

In 1953 we didn't have as good a record as we did in 1952. We were 10–2 in 1952 and ended up 6–3–3 in 1953. But we won the SEC Championship in 1953 and went to the Cotton Bowl to play Rice.

Everyone knows that that Cotton Bowl is the game Tommy Lewis came off the bench to tackle Dickie Moegle. I was the last person Tommy spoke to before he did it. In fact, he dropped his helmet and it hit my foot. Later he apologized to Rice and Moegle and everyone else and said he was just too full of Alabama. And we understood because we all were.

They tinkered with the substitution rules all through the fifties and early sixties, and it was a crazy rule—a stupid rule—that caused the Cotton Bowl incident. You could come out of the game and go back in only one time per half. So every team started its first team, then took them out at the end of the first quarter. Then, if the second team got in trouble, the first team would go back in. There were only six seconds left in the first quarter when we punted Rice back to their 5-yard line. Coach Drew decided it was silly to leave the first team in for one play when they were way down there, so he put in the second team, which meant Tommy was on the sidelines.

Our scouting report said they didn't run outside the tackles inside their 20, so we had an eight-man line to stop the inside run. But they went outside, and so Moegle was coming down the sideline. And if he had been on the other side of the field—the Rice side—the incident never would have happened.

We all felt for Tommy and did all we could to protect him from photographers coming to our bench area trying to get a picture of him. They didn't get any pictures.

After I graduated from Alabama, I went into the Army for two years and was stationed at Fort Jackson, South Carolina, where I played service ball. We had coaches and players from all over the South. It was almost a pro team. The first day at practice we were running a drill, and I was on the offensive line. The guys on either side of me, who I didn't know, said that I must have played at Alabama. I asked how they knew. They were from Maryland, and we had played them a few years earlier.

At Alabama, the offensive linemen came off the ball charging and sounding like wild animals, grunting and growling. Those Maryland guys recognized it. I didn't even realize I did it, or perhaps I just thought everyone did it. I found out later that when we were preparing for the Orange Bowl game against Syracuse, a Miami sportswriter had written that you could stand outside the fence at our practice and think there was a zoo on the other side. But if you stood outside the fence at the Syracuse practice site, you wouldn't even know there was anyone inside.

After the Army, I went to Canada and played for Hamilton and we won the Grey Cup. But I injured my shoulder, ending my career.

I had a great idea for a career after football. I had read that in the future all cars would be washed where they got their gas. I was going to open a gas station and car wash.

I came back to Alabama in 1957 and was introduced to a gentleman in the management end of the insurance business. I began working for Mutual of New York, and I've worked there ever since. I think playing at Alabama has gotten me an audience with people who wanted to hear stories from a former player. And I know I've been able to put men in touch with companies who wanted to hire former Alabama players. People tell me they know if a guy can meet the demands of Alabama football that he will be successful in business.

37

Harry Lee lettered four years and played on Orange Bowl and Cotton Bowl teams for Alabama. He is the longtime permanent executive director and secretary-treasurer of the "A" Club, the association of Crimson Tide letterwinners.

TOMMY LEWIS

FULLBACK

1951–1953

Author's Note: Of the millions of people who love Alabama football, it is likely only one is embarrassed by an event of January 1, 1954. That was the day in the Cotton Bowl that Alabama's Tommy Lewis left the bench, without helmet, to make a tackle on Rice's Dickie Moegle. Moegle was awarded a touchdown. The incident was national news, leading to Lewis appearing on The Ed Sullivan Show *to apologize. Lewis told a sympathetic nation, "I'm just too full of Alabama." Lewis apologized to Moegle and the Rice team following the game.* The Dallas Morning News *ran a front-page editorial expressing admiration for Lewis as a "genuine competitor" and urging the event be regarded as a "forgivable error."*

I'VE NEVER WANTED TO TALK ABOUT THE COTTON BOWL incident. I knew the moment it was over that I would be hearing about it all my life. If there is one thing in my life I could take back, it would be that. I just didn't want that guy getting into our end zone. I'm still embarrassed by it. It's not my nature to do something like that. But I didn't want to lose my last game at Alabama, where I had dreamed all my life of playing. I'd do anything to keep from losing. And I did. But if I could take it back, I would.

My teammates consoled me. My friends consoled me. They knew how I felt. And Alabama fans have been wonderful to me. I have never had an Alabama fan say that I had embarrassed him. But I embarrassed myself.

I had wanted to play football for The University of Alabama since I was a little kid growing up in Greenville, Alabama. My father had been a great football player at Butler County High School, before there was a Greenville High School. I had seen pictures of him in his leather helmet and heard the stories around town of what a player he was. Everyone knew him. He was considered a tough hombre.

We listened to Alabama football games on radio when I was growing up. When I was a junior and senior in high school, I had a chance to be a junior counselor at Camp Mountain Lake near Tracy City, Tennessee. I didn't get paid anything, but I didn't have to pay to go, and it was a pleasant experience. The big drawing card for the camp was Harry Gilmer, who would bring kids up from Birmingham.

I admired every step Harry Gilmer took. After the regular camp activities each day, we'd have a football session. After it was over, I'd ask him to throw me a "Harry Gilmer pass." I'd run down the field and run either an out or a post, whatever he told me to do. And he would run out to his right and throw me that jump pass. That was almost more than I could stand, I was so happy. And you can bet I never dropped a Harry Gilmer pass.

There is no way to say how much I wanted to play for Alabama. I worked hard on my own to become a good football player. I don't know how in the world college football coaches found out about me playing in the little South Alabama town of Greenville, but I still have letters and telegrams from colleges that were recruiting me from around the country. One of them is from coach Bryant at Kentucky. But I never gave a thought to any of them except Alabama. The day Alabama offered me a football scholarship, it made my world. It was the Crimson Tide for me!

Joe Kilgrow was the freshman coach for coach Drew, and he recruited me for Alabama. And I was glad he did.

One of the men I played with at Alabama was Bobby Marlow. I tell people he is one of the main reasons I went to Alabama. Our Greenville team played his Troy team, and he just about killed all of us. I decided I wanted to play on his side.

Bobby Marlow and I were about the same size, about 195 pounds, but he was twice as powerful. He was the halfback, and I was the fullback because they wanted me blocking for him. We also had Clell Hobson at quarterback and Bobby Luna at halfback. Looking back on it now, I thought that Happy

Tommy Lewis is best known for his tackle from the bench in the Cotton Bowl, but he was an excellent fullback on powerful Alabama squads. *Photo courtesy of Bettmann/Corbis*

Campbell, who was the backfield coach, might have had an easy job, but I'm sure that's not true. He was a great coach, and he was always very good to me.

Freshmen couldn't play for the varsity in 1950, and Alabama had a very fine varsity team. We played three freshman games, beating Georgia Tech, Georgia, and Auburn. The main thing I remember about my first year is one practice. Coach Drew had a separate practice field for the freshmen. But there was a tradition that each year the freshman team would "go across the fence," which meant we went to the varsity practice field for a scrimmage. We knew one day we'd get the call, but we didn't know when. One day coach Drew said, "We're going across the fence." And so we ran—we ran everywhere—across to the varsity field. And we were scared to death because we knew there was a lot of quality talent and didn't know what they might do to us. But we held our own pretty well.

Alabama had made the transition from the Notre Dame box, but we still shifted to the box occasionally. I can remember playing an opening game in Crampton Bowl, and I can still hear the "2, 4, 7," which shifted us into what was a single-wing formation.

I was only a fullback my first two years, but in 1953 we went to one platoon, and I also played linebacker.

We had a good team in 1952 and went to the Orange Bowl to play Syracuse. In those days, the teams went to functions together. We didn't get all buddy-buddy, but we did mingle with them and get to know them, and they were very nice guys.

It was one of those days. The first team didn't play much over two quarters, but Bobby Luna and I had two touchdowns, and Bobby Marlow had one. Our defense scored; Hootie Ingram returned a punt for a touchdown; and, of course, everyone who went in was trying to score. You couldn't ask them to not try to score. And score is what they did. Bart Starr was the backup quarterback to Clell Hobson, and he got us into the end zone.

There was not a soul on our team who wanted to run up the score on anyone. Red Drew was certainly not the kind of guy to run up the score. But we beat them 61–6.

After my playing career at Alabama, I played two years in the Canadian Football League. Bobby Marlow also played in Canada because it paid more than the NFL in those days. Bobby played for Saskatchewan and I played for Ottawa. We were in different divisions and didn't play in the regular season, so I didn't have to play against him. But we played an exhibition game once. I took some of my teammates down to the train station to meet them coming in, and Bobby nearly beat me to death on the platform.

I always thought that many doors were opened for me in the business world because of my association with our great university. I consider membership in the "A" Club to be very special. I enjoyed being a State Farm agent in Huntsville for nearly 40 years, and I suspect having played football helped me to be successful. I wouldn't take "no" for an answer.

Even though my senior year did not end on a happy note, my joy at being a player for The University of Alabama has never diminished, and I will forever be grateful for that opportunity.

Tommy Lewis was a three-year starter for Alabama and scored one touchdown in the Cotton Bowl and two touchdowns in the Orange Bowl.

CECIL "HOOTIE" INGRAM

CORNERBACK AND QUARTERBACK

1952–1954

THERE WAS NEVER ANY DOUBT IN MY MIND that I was going to play football for Alabama, and the reason for that is coach Frank Thomas, even though I never got to play for him. I grew up in Tuscaloosa, and coach Thomas' son, Hugh, was one of my closest friends growing up. Even though he was not my neighbor, I thought of coach Thomas the way you would think of a next door neighbor.

That he would be instrumental in me signing with Alabama is understandable.

But not many people know that coach Thomas is probably the reason that Willie Mays signed with the New York Giants. I was at the Thomas house one evening eating sandwiches when the doorbell rang. It was an old Notre Dame classmate of coach Thomas. The guy was a scout for the New York Giants baseball team. He said he was headed to Florida to look at some players and just stopped by to say hello.

Coach Thomas was a great baseball fan. He told this scout that we were getting ready to go see the best baseball player in the world. I can remember the guy saying he knew what a poor-mouther Tommy was, and I guess that's what convinced him to go see this player.

The Birmingham Black Barons were playing at Alberta Park, and Willie Mays played for them. I guess he had a typical game. I remember he had a triple and that he threw a guy out at home.

After the game the scout said, "I don't know if he's the best in the world, but he's among them." The scout also said that the one thing they'd have to teach Mays is how to catch a ball, that he couldn't use that basket catch. The scout didn't go to Florida, and he did sign Willie Mays. And, of course, Willie Mays continued to use that basket catch and is in the Hall of Fame.

I also remember coach Thomas came back from spring training one year and said he had seen a skinny kid trying to make the Braves. He said he had the best wrists he had ever seen, and, of course, he was talking about Hank Aaron.

Coach Thomas had become too ill to coach after the 1946 season, and I played for coach Drew. But coach Thomas stayed active and interested in Alabama football. He didn't want to just sit around and die. He had people who would drive him to practice. He'd sit in his car and watch baseball games from behind the right-field fence and park just beyond the corner of the end zone to watch football games. He died in May 1954, prior to my senior season.

After I got to Alabama, I would go on Thursday nights to his house and visit with him, spending an hour or two with him. He wanted to know what we were doing in practice, how we planned to stop Georgia Tech, or whatever. He enjoyed talking football strategy. Even when he was dying, he wanted to stay in there with football, to keep up.

The last year he coached, he was unable to move, and so they built him a little house on wheels with glass all around. He had a chair and a microphone and speaker, and that's how he coached practice.

One of my great thrills was in a game at Denny Stadium when he was parked down in the corner of the end zone with Mr. Hocutt and Mr. Pate. I was playing safety, and the opponent threw one of those throwback passes that if you intercept, there is no one in front of you. I picked it off, ran it back, and kept going on straight for his car—I could see how happy coach Thomas was.

Alabama didn't have to recruit me. I had been practicing to be an Alabama player since I was in about the fourth grade. And I spent a lot of time on the Alabama practice fields watching as a kid.

Cecil "Hootie" Ingram was a record-setting cornerback in the fifties, and returned to Alabama as athletics director to hire Gene Stallings as head coach in 1990.

I got letters from other schools, but I was never going anywhere else. One day during basketball season, coach Crisp asked me when I was going to sign. I told him I didn't know I had an offer. He told me to come by his office the next day, which I did. He then sent me to coach Lew Bostick's office to sign the scholarship. Coach Bostick told me it was out on the table, to fill it out and sign it. And I did. Years later when I was working for the Southeastern

Conference, I went back in the files and found my scholarship papers that I had filled out myself.

I was playing baseball my freshman year after spring practice, and coach Crisp came by to see what I was going to do in the summer. He told me I needed to stay in shape "because it looks like we're going to have to play you next fall." It wasn't exactly a compliment.

I may have set a record in my first game as a sophomore. It was against Southern Miss in Montgomery. I fumbled three times, but I also recovered three fumbles. I only touched the ball three times—one punt return and two interceptions. It was raining, and the ball was slick, and on each of the times I had the ball, I fumbled when I got hit. But I was able to get all three of them back.

That 1952 team was good, the one that beat Syracuse 61–6 in the Orange Bowl. One of our biggest wins was against Maryland, which had won the national championship the year before. Our pregames were usually the same. Coach Drew would say the same thing every game, and when he finished he'd say, "Coach Hank, you got anything to say?" And coach Crisp would say, "Nah." But this time was different. He gave us a Knute Rockne–type speech, telling us we couldn't compete with Maryland, but to just go out and do the best we could and not get hurt. We beat them 27–7. The thing that stands out to me was that we were leading 14–7 late in the game, and Maryland had fourth down from their 10 with five or six minutes to play. And they went for it. I intercepted the ball at about the 40. If I had just knocked it down, we would have had the ball at their 10. But I intercepted it and ran it back for a touchdown. One of the writers wrote that I must have had more confidence in myself than I did in our offense.

I went into the Army after my Alabama career, but I wanted to coach. I was at Brookwood High School when coach Bryant came back. Jerry Claiborne came out to one of our practices to look at our kids. Usually those coaches would just stay a few minutes, but Jerry stayed the whole practice. When it was over, he said, "You're running our stuff," meaning the schemes coach Bryant was putting in at Alabama. I said, "No, you're running our stuff." And I took him in and showed him the playbooks that I had from coach Thomas—who had been Bryant's coach.

I couldn't help but notice over the years the number of things that coach Bryant had taken from coach Thomas. I think coach Bryant would have been great no matter where he had been, but he obviously had taken so many things from coach Thomas, like bragging on his players even when they lost, taking the blame for things that went wrong, and poor-mouthing after a win.

I had a career in coaching and then in administration. I went from the SEC office to being athletics director at Florida State, and then was fortunate enough to return to my hometown as athletics director at Alabama in 1989. At the end of that year I had to hire a football coach, and we had to get someone stable, someone who was fundamentally sound. Coach Sam Bailey had told me before that not just anyone could coach at Alabama. He said that at a lot of places a guy could get through the season and then have a hobby, fishing or playing golf. But that at Alabama being the head football coach was an everyday deal, that he had to have a thick skin and be able to bow his neck and get through the tough times.

I had known Gene Stallings when he was an assistant at Alabama and when he was at Texas A&M, and I knew he had done a great job for coach Bryant and coach Landry. I knew he could take the heat and do the job, and that's why I chose him. I think Dr. Sayers may have been skeptical, but he wasn't after he met Gene. And I don't think we could have gotten anyone who could have done a better job. And we got along great, maybe because we were both pretty ornery, two hard-headed people working together.

47

Cecil "Hootie" Ingram was All-SEC as he set Alabama records with 10 interceptions for 163 yards in returns and two touchdowns in 1952. The 10 interceptions was best in the nation that year.

BART STARR

QUARTERBACK

1952–1955

IT IS NO SURPRISE THAT ALABAMA TAKES GREAT PRIDE in Bart Starr being one of its own. Perhaps more gratifying is that despite some tough times with the Crimson Tide, Bart is proud of his association with Alabama.

There was no indication that Starr was going to be anything less than the fine quarterback 'Bama had recruited out of Sidney Lanier High School in Montgomery, beating the likes of Kentucky coach Paul Bryant for the signature. As a freshman under coach Harold "Red" Drew, Starr earned some playing time, including throwing a touchdown pass in the Orange Bowl, a 61–6 win over Syracuse. As a sophomore, he won the starting job at quarterback as 'Bama won the Southeastern Conference championship.

As Starr has said, his final two seasons at The Capstone did not make for a great résumé. His junior year he suffered a back injury that basically sidelined him for the year. Then he learned just prior to his senior year in 1955 that new head coach J. B. "Ears" Whitworth was going with a youth movement; the seniors would be used little or not at all.

"A very unpleasant year, but that's part of life," Starr said. "It can toss us some really tough sliders, curveballs, or hard tackles, but it's our decision how we respond. It says a lot about our attitude. After 'Love,' I consider that the second most important word in our vocabulary. You'll pay a price for it later if you don't have the proper attitude.

"I think everybody was upbeat our senior year. Mental toughness and courage were on display. All of us tried to handle it as best we could. Some played more than others, but as a rule the seniors played very little. However, our attitude was good, and that was something we were all proud of."

Even in Alabama's 0–10 season and relegated to only spot duty, Starr showed his talent as he led Alabama in passing.

The unfortunate events of his final two years notwithstanding, he had no regrets about his college choice.

"While maturing I realized Alabama was very, very special and highly regarded around the nation for its athletics achievements," Starr said. "I appreciated the history and tradition of the football program. After moving to the professional level, I could appreciate it even more. When coach Bryant came in a few years later, he raised the bar tremendously. I am very proud to be an alumnus, even though we experienced some embarrassing disappointments during those two years."

Starr said he was very happy while in school at Alabama. "Lifetime friendships were developed with teammates and other students."

Starr left Alabama and went to the Green Bay Packers, where, under the leadership of coach Vince Lombardi, the Packers became a dynasty. He quarterbacked Green Bay to victories in the first two Super Bowls. He was the MVP of both the 1967 and 1968 games.

Starr said his road to professional football was helped by his love of basketball. He was a regular at Crimson Tide basketball games and even practices. Johnny Dee, head coach of 'Bama basketball at that time, was a friend of Green Bay Personnel Director Jack Vainisi, and tipped Vainisi off to Bart.

The combination of Lombardi and Starr is considered one of the best ever in the NFL. Starr enjoyed what he said was "far better than a pretty good relationship. It was outstanding. Coach Lombardi was a very special gentleman, exceptional coach, teacher, motivator, and leader."

Starr said he benefited from having grown up in a military family, for Lombardi possessed the best characteristics of a great military leader. "He was meticulous in his planning, very tough and demanding, but compared to my father, coach Lombardi was a piece of cake."

Several factors, one extraordinarily unlikely, contributed to Starr being at Alabama. The first was a decision made by his father, Ben, a career military man. Although Bart was born in Montgomery, his dad's military life moved

Bart Starr did not have the best of college careers because of injuries and coaching changes, but became a Pro Football Hall of Fame quarterback for Vince Lombardi at Green Bay.

the family around. Then his father, a master sergeant in the Air Force, returned to Montgomery, which allowed Bart to spend his final four years of school there, including three years at Sidney Lanier High School.

In Montgomery, Bart became a fan of the Crimson Tide, as was his father. They had been aware of Alabama football tradition at least from the final 'Bama Rose Bowl in 1945. "I tried to attend every game I could to see Harry Gilmer play," Starr said.

The most unlikely benefit for 'Bama involved his high school sweetheart, Cherry Morton, who was going to Auburn to study interior design. Bart thought being at Alabama was as close to her as he could get, and a huge bonus, as he could occasionally see her. That worked out also. "We married after my sophomore year," Bart said. In 2004 the couple celebrated their 50th wedding anniversary.

Starr was also a big baseball fan, and a good high school player. As a young teenager, he earned money bagging groceries to make two summer trips to

Detroit, where an aunt lived. His goal was to see the great Joe DiMaggio of the New York Yankees. Years later, Bart had an opportunity to meet DiMaggio and told him that story. "He was very gracious and had a nice, light laugh about it," Starr said.

Starr did not attempt to play baseball at Alabama. "I would not have considered it," he said. "I was not gifted enough to pass up spring practice in football." After being drafted in the 17th round by Green Bay, he had a chance to spend time with another childhood idol, Harry Gilmer, who had a business in Tuscaloosa. "I think that spring I probably bugged him to death," Starr said.

Gilmer could not prepare Bart for one early experience. One of Starr's duties with the Packers during training camp was to hold for extra points and field goals. Jim Ringo was the center and snapper. Bart recalls the first time they worked on field goals after practice. "The first snap was about three feet over my head; the second three feet to the right; and the third three feet to the left. I could not get to any of them. After the third poor snap, Ringo walked back to me and said, 'Rookie, you may not remember this, but when I was at Syracuse and you were at Alabama, you guys beat the you-know-what out of us in the Orange Bowl. Today, I get even.' "

Starr and Ringo worked together several years. Bart said, "Not one time was any snap less than excellent, even to the laces never being more than an inch or two off dead center."

Bart Starr was Most Valuable Player of the first two Super Bowls, in 1967 and 1968, and was inducted into the Pro Football Hall of Fame in 1977. He lives in Birmingham and is an avid fan of Alabama football and basketball.

FRED SINGTON JR.

TACKLE

1958–1959

I HAVE HEARD MIKE SHULA SAY THAT HE KNOWS SOMETHING about having to follow a name, and I can certainly identify with that. I think when you are the son of someone who has made a name for himself and follow into that field, in the back of your mind there is always a bit of that pressure or responsibility. Most people say, "I just tried to do the best I could." And you do have to be your own self and do what you can.

I know that I was always very proud of what my father had done. I think it set a bar for me, and I tried to reach his heights, which may have helped me get a little better in some ways. But I was also able to recognize that certain ones come along just so often. I tried to do the best I could and come as close as I could.

My father was a tackle for coach Wallace Wade, 1928–1930, playing on the undefeated and Rose Bowl champion team of 1930. Notre Dame coach Knute Rockne called him the finest lineman in the nation. He was also a Phi Beta Kappa student. He played professional baseball for the Washington Senators. He was inducted into the National Football Foundation Hall of Fame in 1955. He was known as Mr. Birmingham for his civic contributions.

And my father certainly loved The University of Alabama and Alabama football.

Fred Sington Jr. (left) had a big name to live up to when he played for Alabama in the fifties, as his father (right) had been one of 'Bama's all-time greatest players, as well as a Phi Beta Kappa student and civic leader.

I had an unusual playing career at Alabama. I went to Alabama in 1953, recruited by Red Drew and coach Crisp. I think everyone always assumed I would go to Alabama, but when I was finishing up at Ramsay High School in Birmingham, I was recruited by Florida and almost committed there on my visit. But, of course, a visit to Alabama changed that.

I was injured at Alabama and had to have a disk cut out of my spine, and that kept me off the field in 1954. I played for coach Whitworth in 1955, then went into the Army, where I played service ball in 1956. I came back as a student coach under Whitworth in 1957. Then I played on coach Bryant's first two teams, in 1958 and 1959. So my career spanned from 1953 to 1959, seven years. I don't think you could do that today.

My brother Dave, who is younger than I am, had come to the university in 1955, and he was a captain with Bobby Smith on coach Bryant's first team in 1958.

54

In 1957 Dr. Frank Rose, who was president of the university, got on a plane in Birmingham and flew to Atlanta. My father was already in Atlanta. They got on another plane there under assumed names. That's something else you couldn't do today. Dr. Rose sat in the front of the plane and Dad sat in the back. In case one or the other was spotted, they didn't want to be seen flying together to Houston. (Actually, my father was spotted. I had dated the stewardess, and she said, "Aren't you Fred Sington's father?") Dr. Rose and Dad were part of a small group that was going down to get coach Bryant to leave Texas A&M and return to Alabama, which they did.

Obviously, that was a wonderful thing for the university and for Alabama football. But I'm not sure I would have agreed with it in the spring of 1958, coach Bryant's first spring practice. In fact, it started in January with what was known as the gym program. That was so tough that we thought it was a relief that we would finally get onto the football field for spring practice. We were wrong. There was no relief.

My father had told me when coach Bryant was hired that I didn't know what tough was, but that I'd know when coach Bryant got there. There was nothing he could have told me that would have prepared me for the ordeal. You really didn't know if you were going to survive. When we had a 40-year reunion of the 1958 class in 1998, we went back to the rosters. We found a pre-spring roster with 362 names. That was before 25 days of spring practice. When we reported in the fall we had 42 left. You couldn't get away today with what they did to us, but Alabama football was in desperate shape, and the coaches did what they had to do.

Intensity had increased a thousand-fold. Under coach Drew we had very large squads, and some worked hard, but there was a lot of standing around. There was no intensity under coach Whitworth. But under coach Bryant, it was there from the time you got to the dressing room until the time you left, and then some.

I think he changed everything. I believe that we could sense that things were not only going to be different and a lot tougher, but that they were also going to be better, that he would bring the program back. Even with all the pressure, we thought that was going to happen, that we were going to be winners.

I can't remember why coach Bryant missed a practice in the preseason of 1958, but he wasn't there on a day when we scrimmaged the first recruiting class, Pat Trammell and that bunch. The freshmen beat the varsity, and we were scared to death of what was going to happen to us when coach Bryant got back and heard about it. But he could surprise you. He said, "Well, we'll just throw that one out and start over." Talk about relief! We thought we'd be running until the first game.

55

In 1958 I was a tackle on offense and a linebacker on defense. But in the Georgia game I was lined up as a fullback, sort of like in the wishbone that Alabama would run later, except I was very close to the quarterback. I'd either get the tackle or the linebacker and we'd either go off tackle or pitch it. And we upset Georgia 12–0. In 1959 I was strictly a place-kicker.

There is nothing like having played football for The University of Alabama. I loved it, and many, many other people love it. And it's a good feeling to be a part of the greatest tradition in college football.

To have played for coach Bryant helped prepare me for life. He instilled in us that when things are going bad, when things are tough, you stand tough and you come out of it. You can overcome obstacles.

And from my dad, I learned a love for the university, and that you give something back to it, which I have tried to do. I am proud of the university and proud that I was a part of Alabama football.

I enjoy returning to Tuscaloosa for games and having time to visit with guys I played with, the ones who were upperclassmen when I started and the ones I finished with. I played with a lot of people.

Fred Sington Jr. is assistant to the mayor in Gadsden. He is past president of the National Alumni Association and active in the "A" Club and Red Elephant Club.

The SIXTIES

TOMMY BROOKER

END

1959–1961

I KNOW THE FIRST MEETING WE EVER HAD WITH coach Bryant when he was getting ready for his first season at Alabama in 1958 was the one when he talked about the long-range plans, how we would win the national championship if we did what he told us. I was a freshman and all I could think about was that what he told us didn't make sense. He said, "If you don't have a good day—and all days won't be good days—then come back the next day and give 110 percent." And so we had the 110 percent rule. And I couldn't figure out how you could give more than 100 percent. In fact, I didn't know how you could know whether you had given 80 percent or 90 percent or 100 percent.

But I figured it out soon enough. I learned it on the practice field, in the drills. You'd find out that when you thought you had given all you could give, that somehow you could reach down and find a little more. And that was every day as we tried to survive.

Years later I realize that coach Bryant taught us a lot. And you don't get it all at once. But over the years you'd have a situation and you'd think, "That's what coach Bryant was talking about." And you were better off for having that experience.

The reason I went to Alabama was I made them keep their word. Joe Thomas had recruited my brother, but my brother was signing with Detroit to play pro baseball, and so he went to Auburn because it was on the quarter

Tommy Brooker (No. 81) kicked a field goal to beat Auburn 3–0 in 1960. It was one of four consecutive shutout victories 'Bama had over Auburn. Quarterback Bobby Skelton (No. 11) was holder.

system, which would be easier to work around baseball. That was when I was a sophomore in high school. Coach Thomas told me, "I'll be back to get you in two years." And two years later, he came back, and I told him I was taking him at his word and that I would sign with Alabama.

But before I signed, the Whitworth group was out. Pat James came to see me. He was coming in with coach Bryant. He asked me if I was good enough to whip Auburn. I told him that was why I was going to Alabama.

When I got to Alabama, I thought maybe I had made a mistake. The first person I met was Jim Blevins. He had been in the service and was older and had tattoos. A few minutes later, one of the freshmen came in, and he had tattoos. Back then I thought only bad actors—really mean people—had tattoos, and I wondered if I was at the right place.

My freshman year we were the scout team for the varsity. We had a few freshman games, but we didn't have any plays except whatever we had been doing on the scout team that week. So one freshman game we'd play like

Georgia Tech, and another game we'd play like Tennessee, and so on. We kind of made up plays.

We had a very smart quarterback on the freshman team. He understood what coach Bryant wanted. I don't know why, but for some reason Pat Trammell and I were very close. He'd come by my room and get me to go with him to the drug store. He had a little TR7 sports car, the first one I ever rode in. I don't think I ever saw one in Demopolis. We'd go get cigars. He smoked Antonio y Cleopatra. I didn't smoke, but I'd go with him.

In the huddle with Trammell there was just one voice. If anyone tried to say anything, Trammell would kick him out of the huddle. I don't mean trying to get him to run a play or something. A guy might be blocking his man. But he couldn't say anything. Sometimes in a game someone would try to give Pat some information, and he'd spend all the huddle time cussing him out. And when I say cussing, I mean like a sailor. So we'd go to the line and he'd call the play there. It may have looked like an audible, but it was just getting a play called. Pat Trammell was the general when we were on the field.

I kept in touch with him right up until the time of his death. I was back in Tuscaloosa by then in the real estate and insurance business. He came by the office and showed me the scar where they had operated on him.

60

Pat died in 1968. Coach Bryant came up with the idea of an "A" Club Charitable Foundation, a way to help former players who might have catastrophic illnesses or other hardships. Coach Bryant told me to take care of it, and by the end of the year we had formed the corporation. I have been president of it since it was founded. I have tried to give it up but haven't been able to. We do have a large board, including a number of people who have been very successful in business, and we have helped a lot of families.

Although I was a tight end on offense and end on defense, I also worked on kicking. In 1959 Fred Sington missed a kick against Georgia Tech—we won the game anyway—and the next week coach Bryant told me he might use me. And against Auburn I kicked a field goal to give us a 3–0 lead, and we beat them 10–0.

The next year we were playing Georgia Tech and I was coming off knee surgery. Coach Bryant told me that if we had a long field goal to win the game, he'd expect me to kick it, but if we just needed a short one he would use Richard O'Dell. Now how did coach Bryant know that game was going to come down to a field goal? It did, and it was a short one. And

O'Dell—"Digger" O'Dell we called him because a disc jockey had been buried alive in some promotion and his name had been Digger O'Dell—got to kick it. We were getting killed 15–0 at halftime, but came back and, with 16 or 17 seconds to play, had a chance to win. And he made it. The radio people, Maury Farrell and John Forney, thought it was me and announced that Brooker had won the game. It wasn't Brooker.

We didn't know about the radio mistake. We flew back to Tuscaloosa, and there were probably five thousand people waiting for us. And all these college girls were there to give Brooker some sugar. They thought I'd won the game. I tried to tell them it wasn't me, that it was O'Dell, but they had heard it on the radio and knew it was me. By the time we got to the dorm, Richard was pretty upset that he wasn't getting credit. We finally got him up and went to the quad and had a pep rally. Word spread around and everyone knew that O'Dell had won the game.

In the Auburn game, we were worried because they had a great field-goal kicker in Ed Dyas. Dyas was also their fullback, but he had broken his jaw a couple of weeks before our game. But coach told us we couldn't let Auburn across our 40 or we'd lose. We didn't let them across the 40.

I missed my first field-goal chance and thought that would probably be it for me. But Chief Smelley, who was the highway patrolman who escorted coach Bryant, came over and told me not to worry about it, that we'd get another chance. I probably would have given up on myself without that pep talk. But I got another chance and made it, and we won 3–0.

After the season, coach Bryant called me, Pat Trammell, and Leon Fuller into his office and thanked us for making good grades. He said we were the main reason the football team had a better grade-point average than the rest of the university, and particularly the fraternities. That was important to him. And he said he'd pay for us to go to graduate school, and I was able to get my master's degree in the off-season from pro ball.

After Alabama I went to Dallas. There were two teams there, the Texans and the Cowboys. I was with the Texans, owned by Lamar Hunt. I was a tight end, not a kicking specialist. But I did the kicking, and we won two or three games on field goals, and we won the AFL championship. We played what was the longest game in pro football against Houston, in Houston, on a muddy field. Len Dawson was my holder, and I can still remember him trying to get the mud out of my cleats before I kicked. We were at 2:54 in the sixth quarter when I made the kick, and we won the game.

We moved to Kansas City and got to play in the first Super Bowl, although it was called the NFL–AFL World Championship Game then. And there wasn't anything like the attention there is now, of course. We played pretty well with Green Bay for a half, but it got away from us in the second half. The best thing was the loser's check—$6,800.

I was back in town in the real estate and insurance business in 1971, and coach Bryant called me and said, "It's stupid for you to be living here and me not utilize you." And he offered me a job as a part-time coach working with the kickers. I didn't go to meetings or anything, just met with the kickers at practice and worked with them. He would introduce me as his "shoes coach," because I just wore street shoes to practice. Or sometimes his "downtown coach." I could go to games. But between the 1978 and 1979 Sugar Bowls, they changed the rules where I couldn't be on the sidelines at games.

I love everything about the university and do anything I can for it. I go to football games, but I also go to basketball, baseball, gymnastics, everything.

Tommy Brooker was a member of the 1961 national championship team as a tight end, defensive end, and kicker, and was one of two senior members of that team drafted to play pro football. He was an Academic All-American. He is president of the "A" Club Foundation and a member of the board of the First and Ten Club, a support group for athletes and former athletes.

BILLY NEIGHBORS
OFFENSIVE AND DEFENSIVE TACKLE
1959–1961

Coach Bryant and I both got to the university prior to the 1958 season. I'm sure he had never heard of me until maybe when I signed. I had never heard of him until he got here. I didn't know anything about him. But it didn't take me long to figure out he was different.

I remember my freshman year hearing some of the other players talking about Junction [Texas A&M's training camp], about how he'd tried to kill all his players at Texas A&M.

I was from Tuscaloosa County and a lifelong Alabama fan. My father was a big fan. He had gone to the Rose Bowl to see Alabama play. And my brother Sidney was on the team under [coach J. B.] Whitworth. Alabama was the only place I wanted to go. I never even considered any other school, never visited any other place.

The first conversation I had with coach Bryant was when I went out to practice that August. He walked up to me and told me I needed to get out in the sun and lose some weight. He was unbelievably imposing.

I made it a point not to have too many more conversations with coach Bryant. Other than practices and games, I only talked to him twice one-on-one when I was in school. I stayed out of his way. I didn't want to fool with him.

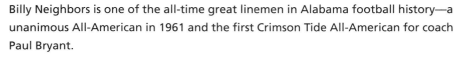

Billy Neighbors is one of the all-time great linemen in Alabama football history—a unanimous All-American in 1961 and the first Crimson Tide All-American for coach Paul Bryant.

Even after I finished, I felt that way. After my senior year, I lacked six hours to graduate. I was playing pro ball and wasn't going to fool with it. But he made me graduate. We all graduated. He called me up and chewed me out. I never knew how he got my telephone number in Boston.

I came back in the spring of 1963 and earned my degree while working as a graduate assistant coach. I was a flunky coach. He'd send me off to speak to civic clubs and things like that.

When I was playing pro ball, I'd get letters from him and he'd ask me to call him. I never did. It's hard now for people to believe he was that imposing. I stayed away from him for years. I probably didn't see him until after I had been gone at least seven years.

I think we had more than one hundred freshmen in our class. About half left before the season ended. Only eight of the original group finished four years later. He worked us pretty hard that first fall. He took some of us out and practiced us with the varsity, even though we couldn't play as freshmen. The next spring he started getting us ready to play. As soon as football was over, we started workouts in the upper gym. We worked all year, really.

I think I may have been on a track scholarship. I guess in those days you could do that to get extra football players. I know in the spring when we had home track meets, they'd send me over to the track to put the shot. I'd come in third every time and earn one point. In those days, a track team just traveled with one shot-put guy, so I'd come in third behind our guy and their guy. I never went to a road meet. Then after I did the shot put, I'd head back to football practice.

On Sundays we'd watch his television show, and even then he was coaching us.

You can't argue with the results. Alabama had been horrible the year before he came—didn't win a game. They had been bad for several years. He turned it around in a year with a winning record. In the first meeting we ever had with him, he told us we were going to win the national championship. I don't think any of us knew anything about the national championship. I know Auburn had won it in 1957, but back then nobody made anything of it.

He told us to stay in school and study, to make sacrifices, and to get ourselves in great shape to play 60 minutes. He told us we could never give up and that we had to be unselfish, to play as a team.

He was absolutely teaching us for life. He sort of boxed it up as a way to live your life, to be dedicated to whatever you are going to do—to try to do it right.

The mood of the campus changed while I was there as we got better each year. Even the teachers seemed to treat us a little better. Some of the teachers didn't want football players in their classes. Every now and then a teacher would ask us to raise our hands if we were football players. I'd get up and leave. There was no sense staying in a class where that mattered.

I played both ways, like all of us did. Sometimes you'd never leave the game. Coach Bryant told me after I finished that I had averaged 58 minutes per game for three years. I never missed a game, although I only played a little bit in the first Georgia game when they beat us in Athens. I had a hip pointer.

I remember the games we lost. That game at Georgia in 1959; the Liberty Bowl at the end of the year because I played awful up there; and at Tennessee in 1960. We were 26–3–4 my three years.

I also remember Auburn never scored on us. We beat them 10–0, 3–0, and 34–0. One year they never got across our 40-yard line. Coach Bryant said they'd beat us if they did. They had that great kicker, Ed Dyas, who is a great guy, too. They only got across the 50 one time.

I was lineman of the week in the nation against Tennessee. We didn't read the papers, but somebody told me. But we had lost the game, and when we got back to practice, the coaches crucified us. And I graded 3 on offense and 5 on defense—out of 100. I'd made 12 or 14 tackles. But after I got that grade, that lineman award didn't mean anything.

Pat James graded me. He hated penalties and I don't think I ever got one. I might have been called for one. But I never graded over 50 or 60 at Alabama. But by the time I was a junior, I had figured out that the grade didn't mean much.

But I thought about it when I went to the NFL and graded 90-something in my first game. And I never graded under 90 in eight years in the NFL. I told coach James about that later. He just laughed.

Coach James actually took me and made a movie about how to block.

I didn't like bowl games. We voted against going to the Bluebonnet Bowl, but coach Bryant made us go. He let us vote, but that didn't mean anything. I never knew of anyone who voted to go. We went out and played Texas and it ended in a 3–3 tie. I blocked a guy into the end zone and Pat Trammell fell on top of me with the ball, but the officials didn't give us the touchdown. Coach Bryant asked me if I had blocked the guy into the end zone. I said I had. He said, "Next time block him out of the end zone." It was a bad call, but that happens.

The last game I played at Alabama was against Arkansas in the Sugar Bowl to complete our 11–0 national championship season. Coach Bryant told me later it was the best game I ever played at Alabama.

I was invited to go to New York to be on *The Ed Sullivan Show* and *The Bob Hope Show* for All-Americans. Coach Bryant and Pat Trammell went to Washington to meet President Kennedy. Pat was the offensive captain and I was the defensive captain. They asked me to go meet the president, but I couldn't go because of those television shows.

That's a pretty big deal for a kid from Northport.

I'm like a lot of people who went to the university to play football. I wouldn't have been worth a damn without it. I wouldn't have gotten an education. I wouldn't have traveled anywhere. I wouldn't have become a broker. It got me name recognition.

I got to play eight years of pro football, four in Boston and four in Miami, on four good teams and four bad teams, and made All-Pro a couple of times. Of course, the money wasn't anything like it is now. I think in eight years I might have made a total of $600,000. That was more than the average person, but you certainly weren't set for life.

In the off-season I went to Huntsville, where my wife Susan is from, and I've worked for Wachovia Securities there since 1968. We raised our daughter, Claire, and our sons, Wes and Keith, in Huntsville. Wes and Keith also played at Alabama. My boys were full of Alabama and they were going to Alabama. But they were recruited by coach Bryant like he didn't know them. He went to their games, came to our house. By then I had become much closer to coach Bryant, and I'm glad I did.

I was on his first team and Wes was on his last.

67

Billy Neighbors was All-America in 1961 and won the Jacobs Award as the best blocker in the SEC. He was selected as a member of the Alabama Team of the Century and was selected to the Team of the Decade for the sixties on both offense and defense. He was defensive captain of the 1961 national championship team and was inducted into the National Football Foundation Hall of Fame in 2003.

JACK RUTLEDGE

OFFENSIVE GUARD AND LINEBACKER

1959–1961

I WAS ONE OF THOSE WHO WERE AT THE UNIVERSITY waiting for coach Bryant to arrive in 1958. I had been signed by coach Whitworth and played freshman football in 1957. I had heard the rumors for a couple of years that Alabama was going to hire Bear Bryant, but it really didn't mean anything to me. I had grown up an Alabama fan because my daddy was an Alabama fan. I grew up in Hokes Bluff, then moved to Gadsden, then went to Birmingham where I played at Woodlawn High School.

I was big and strong, a 200-pound guy, and played fullback and halfback at Woodlawn. I was back of the year in my senior season, gaining more than 1,000 yards, averaging 9.1 yards per carry, and leading the state in scoring. We won 29 straight games and two state championships. And what that got me at Alabama under coach Bryant was a chance to play right guard. I got a little work at fullback, but he needed linemen more than he needed backs.

There are a lot of stories about that first spring practice. It was not fun. You were trying to survive. I'd get back to my dorm room, just lean against the wall, slide down to a sitting position, and stay that way for an hour. In the winter workouts, we had wrestling bouts in the gym. And you learned the death hold because it was about more than conditioning. It was about making it out.

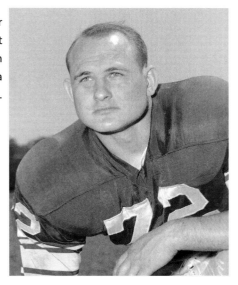

Jack Rutledge was the back of the year in Alabama as a high school senior, but was converted to an offensive lineman at Alabama. He later coached 'Bama offensive linemen.

After spring practice, coach Bryant made a list of 14 men who had made it through and on whom he was counting next fall. I was on the list. He called me into his office. He told me what we were going to do and how we were going to do it and that he was counting on me. I thought that would be a good time to bring up another subject. I told him that when I had been signed, I had been promised that I could get married after my freshman year. He said, "Forget everything I just told you. A married man can't do it."

I guess he thought I couldn't do it because I didn't play in the first three games in 1958. I asked coach Bryant if he'd just hold me out that year, let me be redshirted, and that's why I was on the 1961 team.

I played a lot in 1959 because I knew all the offensive line positions. I didn't start, but I played 15 to 20 plays each game. On the practice sheets, I wasn't on the depth chart. My name was at the bottom of the sheet, and they'd tell me where to go. Don Cochran was a starting guard in 1959, but he had a hyper-extended elbow, so they didn't put him in any contact work in practice. So I got the contact work in practice, and he played in the games.

The next two years I started 16 games, mostly at guard, and also played linebacker. In fact, I played as much defense as I did offense, but because I became an offensive line coach, I think I'm considered an offensive lineman.

Each year we had a few more who could play, and coach Bryant got everyone ready to play. You never knew what color jersey you would have in practice. Red was first team, green was second. In the early years, if you didn't like the jersey you were wearing you could challenge the next guy up. And I had plenty challenge me. The problem was, when you finished the challenge drill, you were so tired that you did a poor job in practice that day. And so the next day you were in green.

It wasn't necessarily about fundamentals in those early days. I think coach Bryant was trying to run some people off. The first day I worked at offensive line, I was up against Jim Blevins, who had been in the Marines and who would fight. The first time I went up against him, he beat me. But coach Pat James showed me some technique, and the next day I knocked Blevins back. On the play after that, he tried to rip my helmet off because if we were going to fight he didn't want me to have a helmet on. Somehow I got him down and was on top of him. The players were chanting, "Hit him! Hit him!" But I wasn't going to hit him because I knew he'd get me back when we got to the dorm. That was the atmosphere we were living in.

But it really paid off in 1961. And the turning point was probably in the 1960 Georgia Tech game, when we were down 15–0 at halftime. That's when coach Bryant came into the dressing room and we all expected to get chewed out, and he said, "We've got 'em right where we want 'em."

In the second half he benched Bobby Skelton as his quarterback, told him he would "never play another down." Pat Trammell came in and did good, taking us to a score. But we had a play where someone jumped, and when he did, a Georgia Tech man ran right past me and hit Trammell—a cheap shot that hurt him. That's when coach Bryant called Skelton up and told him he was going to give him one more chance. Digger O'Dell kicked a field goal, and we won 16–15.

That 1960 team probably had only seven or eight guys who had made it through the first spring training. But we had coach Bryant's first recruiting class—Trammell, Tommy Brooker, Billy Neighbors, and that bunch—and the second—Lee Roy Jordan, Bill Battle, Jimmy Wilson.

And in 1961 we went out and practiced just in sweats. What a change.

Every Sunday all the players would watch coach Bryant's television show because he was telling us what we were going to be doing that week. He was telling the fans, "I did this," taking the blame, but he didn't take the blame when practice started.

One of the things he did on the program was show photographs of the players and tell where they were from or something about them. One Sunday my picture came up and he said, "Jack Rutledge, the Governor." I had a resemblance to Governor John Patterson. In fact, he came to our homecoming game one year and stopped by the dressing room after the game. The players were saying, "Hey, Governor! Meet the Governor!" And he said to me, "You mean you're as ugly as I am?" That nickname sticks with me today.

I had planned to be a heavy equipment salesman after college because that was my family's business. But they needed a coach at Demopolis, Tommy Brooker's old school. Coach Bryant told me I wouldn't make any money in coaching, so I needed to be sure if I wanted to do it. I decided to take it, and Tommy Brooker and John O'Linger went down and helped me in spring practice. I stayed three years, went to Sheffield for a year, then came back in 1966, and stayed with coach Bryant until the end. I also worked under coach Stallings as director of Bryant Hall, the players' dorm. I lived in the dorm for 18 years. I was offensive line coach—coach Bryant always had two, so it was first with Jimmy Sharpe and then with Dee Powell after Jimmy went to Virginia Tech as head coach in 1974. I also worked with Clem Gryska on the junior varsity team and with Sam Bailey on the kicking game. And I was also in charge of the dorm and in charge of films. The toughest thing was not being able to make all the coaching meetings because of other responsibilities.

I coached some great players, and I've got five national championship rings and about 15 SEC championship rings. But mostly I have great memories.

One of the things I cherish is my time as dorm director. Naturally, there were discipline problems, which coach Bryant handled, and I had to keep a lot of secrets. Coach Bryant believed that was between him and the player. Coach Bryant was more interested in the cause of problems than he was in just handing out a penalty. He really didn't want to penalize a player if he could fix the cause. Every result wasn't the same, but everyone always believed his decision was fair.

I worked hard as a player and as a coach under coach Bryant, and I'm still going strong, working a small farm and keeping up with my family, which is all still in Tuscaloosa. I've been battling on another field for the past few years since I was diagnosed with cancer in 1999, and hopefully, I'm winning.

Jack Rutledge was a three-year letterman on Alabama teams that went 26–3–4 and won the 1961 national championship. He coached on three 'Bama national championship teams in the seventies.

DARWIN HOLT
LINEBACKER AND FULLBACK
1960–1961

IF YOU PLAYED FOOTBALL AT ALABAMA, PEOPLE KNOW YOU. And if you were involved in controversy like I was, people really know you. I've traveled all over the country and had people ask me if I'm the Darwin Holt who played football at Alabama. And they are reluctant to bring up the Georgia Tech incident . . . but they always do.

I don't regret what I did. It was a legal play. I resent the fact that I'm 65 years old, and it's still there. The press just won't let it rest. I love the reputation I had of being one of the toughest guys who played at Alabama. But that's not the same as dirty, and I was not a dirty player. In two years at Alabama, I had two penalties—an offside on a blitz and a late hit when I went into the pile after the whistle. I actually hit my own man, but I got the penalty.

The incident, of course, is in 1961 when we were playing Georgia Tech.

It was late in the game and we were leading 10–0. There wasn't a chance we weren't going to win. Georgia Tech was having to punt, and I called a right return because that was the wide side of the field. All we wanted to do was maintain possession. If I had called left return, it would have been Lee Roy Jordan blocking on Chick Granning. There was no secret about the way they covered punts and how we would block them.

Everything we did was choreographed—which way the toes were turned, which shoulder you were lined up on. Every detail mattered. I was three

Darwin Holt was signed by Paul Bryant to play at Texas A&M, then followed his coach to Alabama, where he was an outstanding linebacker on the Tide's first national championship team under Bryant.

yards inside, two yards behind, and I knew he'd turn 90 degrees, then I would block him out. I was supposed to drive inside his arm and take him the way he wanted to go. It was a legal block and there was no penalty on the play. I was to hit him high, so I didn't leave my feet and could turn and go.

At first, Chick handled it well. I went to Atlanta to see him, and he took me around and introduced me to everyone. He said, "Hell, Darwin, if I hadn't been looking up in the stands, you wouldn't have got me." You can see in the film that he dropped down so the forearm that was to hit him in the chest got him in the face. Later Chick decided it wasn't in his best interest to defend me.

Bobby Dodd, the Georgia Tech coach, probably made a mistake by not putting Chick in the hospital right after the game instead of taking him back to Atlanta. I only hit him. They nearly killed him because his head swelled up because they waited a day to hospitalize him.

My teammates supported me. Coach Bryant and I agreed we wouldn't talk to the press about it. I got a call from a guy claiming to be a reporter at *Sports Illustrated*. He said that coach Bryant was going to talk to them about it and coach Bryant had told him to tell me it was all right to talk about it. I called him a liar and hung up on him.

Later I made the decision I could be a fool and not discuss it, or I could discuss it and make it a meaningful experience. I don't mind talking about it because I didn't do anything wrong. It was a good hit. That was my job. I've suffered the wrath, but at the time I would have thought that missing the guy I'd get the wrath of coach Bryant.

I know the incident, as it has been called, cost me at least one thing, and it may have cost me another. It may have cost me being an All-American. I had some preseason publicity and I had made Lineman of the Week a few times— back then linebackers were considered linemen. But after that, I wasn't going to make All-America. Lee Roy made it, of course. That would have been something if we had had two All-America linebackers.

And I know it cost me a chance to be a football coach, which is what I wanted to be. Alabama was a coaching mill. Coach Bryant turned out coaches like gangbusters. And that was because he taught you so much. Not just what to do, but why you did it. People wanted you as a coach if you had played at Alabama.

I called all the plays, so I had to know everyone's assignments. They didn't send in the plays or even signal them in.

I went to Canada to play after I finished, but then I wanted to coach, and coach Bryant got me a job under Bob Shaw, who had been with the Colts and the Giants when they won world championships. I went to New Mexico Military in Roswell. I'd coach the high school team in the first half of practice, then coach the junior varsity team. We thought coach Shaw was going to get the Stanford job, but he didn't get it. Instead he got Saskatchewan in Canada. But I realized that if one of my players ever hurt anyone that I'd be blamed. I decided I had to get out of coaching. Maybe I didn't really have to, but that was the way I felt.

I originally signed to play for coach Bryant at Texas A&M in 1957. They had been trying to recruit my brother, Jack, who went to Oklahoma. I was told coach Bryant was looking at the film of my brother and said, "I want that No. 64." That was me and I was a junior. They told me if I didn't get hurt as a senior, I had a scholarship. So I went there that fall, and that Christmas coach Bryant had left for Alabama. I stayed at A&M through spring training, but I was dropping further and further down the depth chart until I was just a blocking dummy. One thing I liked about coach Bryant was he didn't worry about how much I weighed. Every other coach was always talking about how to put weight on me. I was 150 when I went to A&M. My senior year at Alabama I was 167.

75

I called coach Sam Bailey, who had been my freshman coach, and told him I wanted to go to Alabama. He told me to go to junior college and then I could come. So that's what I did. The junior college at Gainesville, Texas, where I was from, didn't have a football team, so for the first time since I was a small child, I didn't play football. When I got to Alabama I found out that if I hadn't graduated from junior college, I would have had three years of eligibility. But no one told me that so I had only two.

I hurt my knee in 1959 and didn't get to play. After the season, coach Bryant showed me a letter from the NCAA. A guy at Northwestern had been hurt, and the NCAA had given him back a year of eligibility. So coach Bryant wrote and got one for me. I was the second player in the nation to get a medical redshirt. That meant I could play in 1960 and 1961.

Somehow I knew we'd win the national championship in 1961.

When I lined up that year, I always reached out and tapped Billy Neighbors on the butt. I never wanted to be more than an arm's length away from him. He protected me. He played that year with a split sternum and made All-America. He was some kind of special.

We had great coaches and great players. And it was sort of like the Marines. Coach Bryant wanted only a few good men. Not everyone can be a Marine, but those who are, are the best at what they do and they thrive on the challenge to be tough enough every day. Playing for coach Bryant wasn't for everyone, but the only ones who ever said anything bad about him were the quitters.

He did it primarily with defense. I did a little research on coach Bryant. He was head coach in 425 games. He won 323 of them and tied 17 others. And in those 425 games, the opponent scored 7 points or fewer in 235 games. His teams had 93 shutouts. Goose eggs, he called them.

One of the things I learned from coach Bryant was not to give up. When I had my problems, I could have turned and run or become an alcoholic or whatever. But I didn't.

I'll never forget the first time I saw Tuscaloosa. I was raised in Gainesville, and the nearest thing to a river we had was the Red River, which was just a little ditch unless it flooded. When I came to The University of Alabama in 1959, I drove all night and came across the Black Warrior River the next day. I thought there must have been a flood. Coach Bailey told me, "That's the way a river looks here. You're in Alabama now."

Although I was out of the state for awhile, I loved Alabama so much I couldn't wait to be back here and make this my home. And I appreciate the way the people of this state have supported me.

Darwin Holt was Alabama's starting linebacker in 1960 and 1961 when the Crimson Tide went 19–1–2. The Tide won the national championship in 1961, allowing only 25 points in 11 games, and had only two games in two years in which the opponent scored more than 7 points.

LEE ROY JORDAN
LINEBACKER AND CENTER
1960–1962

IT'S FUNNY HOW PEOPLE CAN REMEMBER DETAILS of football games. I don't really remember that many. That's probably because I don't talk about them much. I have good friends who can recall minute details of games they played in, but they like to rehash them a lot so it refreshes their memories. There are a couple of plays and one game that I have heard a lot about from people who saw them.

One of those plays was after my Alabama career. In those days they had a College All-Star team play the defending NFL champions in a game at Soldier Field in Chicago. We played the Green Bay Packers and actually beat them, the last time the All-Stars beat the pros. Green Bay had a great fullback, Jim Taylor from LSU. We had a moment to meet head-on and I drove him back, maybe for a loss. The announcers must have made a big deal out of it because so many people have told me about it.

Another play people have in their minds was against Georgia Tech. I was a center on offense. We had a pass intercepted, which meant I turned into a defender and I was chasing the guy who had intercepted the pass. Near the sidelines, he just dropped the ball. Coach Bryant made something of that on his television program the next day and said, "If they stay in bounds, old Lee Roy will get them." He had a way of saying things that made people remember.

I always thought I had a pretty good memory of the Orange Bowl game at the end of our senior year. It was an important game for the seniors because we had lost one game by one point earlier in the year, but we had finished with a respectable season the way we beat Auburn and then Oklahoma. The reason I say I thought I had a good memory of that game is that I always thought they kicked a field goal just before halftime. But we won 17–0. I knew I was making a lot of tackles because I was getting sore, but I had no idea I would make 31 tackles. Our objective was to stop Joe Don Looney, which we did. And they hadn't made many turnovers, but we got two fumbles, which helped us control the game.

I grew up in a small community, perhaps 350 people in Excel, Alabama. My family farmed. We raised about everything—cotton, corn, peanuts, and anything you could grow in a garden. And we had cattle, horses, chickens, and turkeys. We raised almost everything we ate and then hoped to have enough to sell. And everyone had responsibilities. I was taught very early about work.

I went to Excel school. I started at one end in the first grade, and went down the school through middle school or junior high, and graduated from high school at the other end of the school. Every male had to play football. If he didn't, he had a hard time in the community because we needed everyone to play 11-man football. We dressed everyone who could play from about the seventh grade on up so we'd have about 22 to 25 boys. We had a fine coach in W. C. Majors, who went on to coach at Fairhope.

I had a growth spurt between my sophomore and junior year in high school, about 3 inches and 31 pounds. I left a runt and came back a pretty big dude. I was one of the bigger boys, about 190 pounds. We ran the single wing, and I was a fullback and tailback. I got my hands on the ball a lot. Jerry Claiborne was scouting a boy at W. S. Neal in Brewton and I had a pretty good game against them as a junior. After the game he came to the dressing room and told coach Majors that someone would be watching me next year. And Bobby Drake Keith watched me on a regular basis as a senior. It was exciting to have college coaches watching you. I was also getting interest from Auburn and Southern Miss.

Coach Bryant had taken the job at Alabama my junior year in high school. My coach told me that coach Bryant would like guys like me. Not necessarily the biggest, but quick and with good stamina. He said the most important thing to coach Bryant was "want to." And that impressed me.

I was part of his second recruiting class. Billy Neighbors and Tommy Brooker and Pat Trammell were the big names in the first class, and we had

Lee Roy Jordan is considered the finest linebacker in Alabama history, a Hall of Fame member who set an Orange Bowl record with 31 tackles in a win over Oklahoma.

guys like Bill Battle, Richard Williamson, Charley Pell, and Jimmy Wilson. It was hard work that freshman year in 1959. We were fresh meat for the varsity to practice against. But we competed against them.

We had a pretty good run in 1960, beating Georgia, Georgia Tech, and Auburn. And then in 1961 and 1962, we had about 10 shutouts. We had six in 1961. We gave up 25 points, went undefeated, and won the national championship.

Coach Bryant believed in defense. Put a kicking game and a little running game with defense and you'll win a lot. I played both ways, center on offense and linebacker on defense, and if I ever got a break, it was sitting out on offense a few series. Our defense was kind of a 5-2 that would be a 3-4 today. Darwin Holt, Ed Versprille, and I could move around to about anywhere, but I was usually one of the inside linebackers.

We had great support from Alabama fans and students. When we'd come back from away games, there would always be a nice crowd to meet us at the airport. Alabama fans had been supportive in the bad times, and they were certainly appreciative that we were doing a good job and winning.

My first game was against Georgia in Birmingham. I had a minor injury, and it was a few days before the game that I learned I was going to start. So I started every game in my Alabama career.

I can't imagine anyone being any luckier than I was. I played in college for coach Bryant and then in Dallas for coach Landry, one of the top franchises in the NFL. I live and have a business in Dallas now, but spend five or six months a year in Alabama. And we're going to be retiring there to our house in Point Clear.

A year after I graduated in June 1964, I married Biddie Banks, who I had met in a biology class. Her mother was good friends with Mrs. Bryant. So we got married at Biddie's grandmother's house in Eutaw, and Dr. Frank Rose, the president of the university and one of the greatest men I've ever known, married us. Coach and Mrs. Bryant were there. Mrs. Bryant made Biddie's veil.

It may be that the best lesson I learned from coach Bryant was to be first. If he called for a drill, I'd run over people to be first in line to do it. And that's the way I've been in everything. I didn't wait on others. I wanted to be first.

But everything I've ever done is because of a big boost I got from attending The University of Alabama. And I feel very fortunate that people still recognize me and think good thoughts about the teams we had. I've tried to be a good ambassador for the university because I am very proud to be an Alabama graduate.

One wonderful relationship I have had is with Gene Stallings. He was a young coach, but a very, very good one and a confident one when I was playing at Alabama. And we were so fortunate to have him with the Cowboys. We lived in the same neighborhood in Dallas, and I was very fond of his whole family. And when we beat Miami and won the national championship, I think I remember more about that game than any I played in. He is a great man, the epitome of class, a person who really cares about other people. And that couldn't have happened to a better guy.

Lee Roy Jordan was a two-time All-American, selected Player of the Decade for the sixties, named to ESPN's all-time college team and to Alabama's Team of the Century, inducted into the College Hall of Fame in 1983, and selected for the NCAA Silver Anniversary Award in 1987.

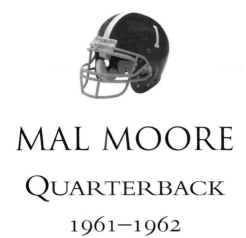

MAL MOORE

QUARTERBACK
1961–1962

No one would suggest I got off to an impressive start in my Alabama football career. It was actually before the freshmen were to report in September 1958, coach Bryant's first year at Alabama. I went to Tuscaloosa for the Alabama High School All-Star Game, which was always played in August at what was then Denny Stadium. I wasn't playing in the game, but some of the guys who would be my teammates at Alabama were playing in it: Billy Neighbors, Tommy Brooker, and Pat Trammell. In fact, after the game I went and introduced myself to Pat.

I got there in the afternoon, before the game, and went to the coaches' offices, which then were in Moore Hall. Coach Gene Stallings was there and he took me down the hall to meet coach Bryant. I guess back then everyone in Alabama was talking about Bear Bryant being back at Alabama. And when I shook his hand, I said, "I'm glad to know you, Bear." Pure ignorance. I know it made coach Stallings uncomfortable because he hustled me away from there.

I had actually been recruited by coach J. B. Whitworth's staff. Dorsey Gibson, who had come from Oklahoma State, was the assistant coach who had recruited me. When coach Bryant took the Alabama job after the 1957 season, two of his assistants, Jerry Claiborne and Elmer Smith, came to Dozier to see me. We just talked for a few minutes in the driveway—I didn't even know enough to invite them into the house—to confirm that I would be at Alabama.

That had not been a hard decision for me. My father was a huge Alabama fan. He had loved Alabama going back to the Rose Bowl days. And so I grew up pulling for Alabama. I can remember Saturday afternoons around a dove field listening to Alabama games on a truck radio. We'd pull for Alabama like the devil.

Alabama had some tough times my last three years in high school, but we were still Alabama fans. I was looked at by Georgia, Auburn, and Alabama, and there was no question where I was going. And I am so thankful the opportunity came my way.

I'm sure there were days when we didn't recognize the opportunity we had. My freshman season they were short-handed on the varsity because so many had quit in the spring, which was coach Bryant's first spring practice. So they put us right to work helping get the varsity ready for games.

We did have some freshman games. Sam Bailey was the freshman coach. I remember when we were getting our uniforms for the freshman game, he told us that the uniforms were the ones the varsity had worn the year before when Alabama went 0–10. He said, "They are in perfect condition, except the butts might be worn out."

I remember we played a freshman game against Tulane on a Saturday night in Denny Stadium when the varsity had played in Knoxville that afternoon. We had lost to Tennessee 14–7. I don't remember how we were doing in the freshman game, but I remember we were in the dressing room at halftime, and coach Bailey was about to put something up on the blackboard. Just then the door slammed open and there stood coach Bryant in a big topcoat. We hadn't expected to see him. One of the guys sitting there clapped his hands and said, "Let's go, guys, let's go!" Coach Bryant said, "I don't want to hear that phony stuff." Then he said he had seen all the bad football he could stand in one day. And he said, "Come Monday, if you don't love it, you'll never make it." And about 12 or 13 guys quit, including two who had started the Tennessee game.

I really think it was just a normal practice, but the expectation was terrifying. He was helping the players make up their minds. We were probably all thinking about quitting.

I've always felt that we didn't know it at the time or understand it at the time, but we were witnessing and participating in a change of 180 degrees in a group of men becoming a unit, becoming a team. He changed the way we thought, the way we handled ourselves, the way we conducted ourselves.

Mal Moore has spent most of his lifetime at Alabama, as a quarterback and then an assistant coach and offensive coordinator under coach Paul Bryant, as quarterbacks coach under Gene Stallings, and then as athletics director.

83

And that was all part of his way of getting a team to think right, to believe in him, believe in everything we did, believe in perfection, believe in the little things that make the difference.

It couldn't be just taught. It had to be experienced. We had to be put through some tough times to have the sense of pride in accomplishment. We had survived, and that gave us an air of confidence. Everyone on the team had that twinkle in his eye and played with great confidence. That's what made the difference in his teams when we got against great teams that may have been better than we were, man for man. But we had the edge in confidence. Our players always saw themselves as special because they had paid the price, like Marines in a lot of ways. We were brainwashed in a positive way.

And that pride extended to the student body, to the alumni and fans, and at that time to the citizens of the state of Alabama. And across America in the sixties and seventies, Alabama football was respected. Everyone expected Alabama to always win. It was a privilege to be around it. It was accomplished by a great football coach who had the ability to make so many people believe.

Participating in the atmosphere we did in those first few years under coach Bryant prepared those players for any adversity. You faced tough times on those teams, then were exposed to great success for going through it, hanging in there. It gave us a sense of purpose and a belief that we could accomplish anything. There is no question we gained from the experience of playing for coach Bryant.

I was redshirted in 1960 and played behind Pat Trammell on our 1961 team. I played in most every game, I think, but some not as much as others.

In 1962 I was a fifth-year senior, and Joe Namath was a sophomore. I introduce Joe as the man I brought out the very best in. He really had to strain to beat me out. I think I was first team until he learned the snap count in the spring of 1962.

One of the things I'm noted for is having seven Alabama national championship rings. I was very, very fortunate. I played on the 1961 team, was an assistant under coach Bryant on the 1964, 1965, 1973, 1978, and 1979 teams, and an assistant on coach Stallings' 1992 team.

Beginning in 1971, I was coaching quarterbacks at Alabama, and we started something new. Changing to the wishbone offense was a strategic move in coach Bryant's coaching career. We had gone two seasons with 6–5 records. The wishbone offense fit coach Bryant perfectly because he was such a strong believer in winning games with good defense and a sound kicking game. And the wishbone fit that philosophy. He told us we were going to open the 1971 season against Southern Cal with the wishbone, and we were going to close the season against Auburn with the wishbone. There would be no changing our minds. We had success by going undefeated with the wishbone, and it was a great time in our history. We were the first team to win 103 games in a 10-year period.

84

It was a total team effort. The wishbone is a team-oriented, ball-control offense. Everyone gets hit, everyone is involved in blocking. It takes 11 people. You're not counting on one player having a great game. It fit coach Bryant at that time in our history.

We taught it and ran it for about 12 years. Then the pro influence started, so we probably ran it at just the right time, getting the most out of it in the nick of time.

One thing coach Bryant liked was that we weren't blocking two men, so you could put your best players on defense. You needed good guards and a good center to block at that point. You needed guys with agility, speed, and quickness.

We threw the ball out of the wishbone more than anyone else, but that was partly a matter of necessity. We never did have the speed of an Oklahoma in our backfield. But we had good receivers, we had quarterbacks who could hit them, and we learned to put them in formations to disguise what we were going to do while keeping our wishbone features.

Getting the job as the athletics director at The University of Alabama on November 23, 1999, was certainly a high point in my career, and I take great pride in it. It has been a challenge because we were in some awkward times with the NCAA. I feel that we've gone through this, and if I have a strength, it has been that I have been able to hold a lot of factions together and headed in what I believe is the right direction. And we have done that through the Crimson Tradition Fund, which has been our focal point in raising money for the enhancement of our facilities.

I knew coming into this job that this had to be done. And I knew we couldn't wait until NCAA probation was over or wait to see how coach Dennis Franchione did. None of that regarding these facilities mattered. We had to do this now in order to help bring us out of tough times quicker and stronger.

One thing that has excited and pleased me most has been how our fans and alumni and friends have responded. They have stepped up and made a difference. It is something they can all be genuinely proud of. I know I am.

We have a great name, the Crimson Tide, and a great tradition, which comes from great success. There's a line in the fight song, "You're Dixie's football pride, Crimson Tide." We brought fame not just to the university but to Southern football. That kind of tradition is something you can't buy; you have to earn it. And, brother, we've got it, and that makes me proud.

85

Mal Moore was a quarterback on Alabama's 1961 national championship team, an assistant coach on six other Crimson Tide national championship teams, and is now director of athletics at the university.

JOE NAMATH
QUARTERBACK
1962–1964

WHEN I WAS A KID IN BEAVER FALLS, PENNSYLVANIA, my father and his friends played football pools, betting a dime or a quarter on pro games. And they'd let me pick a few games. So I'd watch the pro game on a black-and-white television set that Sunday, and I started trying to call the plays, learning from them. I was dreaming about being on a football field.

And who would have dreamed I would play on football fields for Paul Bryant, the greatest coach ever, and Weeb Ewbank, who had already coached the Baltimore Colts and Johnny Unitas to a world championship?

I learned that to be a quarterback you had to have a lot of qualities, including confidence. I always felt I could play and that I never had to talk about it. One reason was growing up the youngest child. If I played a baseball game and went three-for-four, my brother would say, "What happened?" He wanted to know about the out.

At Alabama, the quarterback got to see coach Bryant more than players at the other positions. One of the things I enjoyed was the walk the quarterbacks made with him the morning of every game. We'd walk down the street and talk about the game plan. On one of the first walks we made, he said, "Joe, you got the plan?"

I said, "Yeah, I think so."

"You *think* so?" he said. "You *think* so? Boy, it's time to *know*."

That was the last time I made that mistake.

I didn't want to go through the "A" Club initiation. I had earned my letter my sophomore year, but I didn't want to get whipped, I didn't want to get shaved. It was a pretty tough initiation.

I got a message that coach Bryant wanted to see me, so I went to his office. He said, "I hear you're not going through 'A' Club initiation. Why not?" I told him I didn't want to go through all those things; that I had earned the letter. He said it was tradition. I still didn't want to do it. He said if I didn't go through "A" Club initiation, I couldn't be elected captain. I said OK to that, too.

Then he said, "I want you to."

I said, "Yes, sir."

You knew he was right, even when it wasn't the way you wanted it to be, or the way you saw it. He was the man. If he said, "I want you to," we all would have done it.

How did I become an Alabama football player? I was lucky.

Coach Bryant and Tom Nugent, the head football coach at Maryland, were friends, and when I failed the college boards at Maryland, I was still available. I really didn't want to go to college. I wanted to play baseball. I don't remember ever studying at home in high school. My mother had graduated from high school, but my father had finished only the third grade. When he came to America from Hungary at age 12, he went right to work. It was always work, work, work. Math came reasonably easy to me, and it's a good thing, too, because over the years I've had a great relationship with numbers.

I got by as a student. All I wanted to do was pass. Everything was football, baseball, and basketball, and the odd jobs—caddying or working for the city. So I didn't score high enough on the college boards for Maryland, although I was eligible for most schools.

There were deals out there. The first coach who ever came to my house to recruit me took me outside after he had talked to me and my family. He told me if I would sign with him that I would have a vehicle and a certain amount of money each month. I've forgotten now if it was $100 a week or $300 a month or exactly what it was, but I know at the time it was an astronomical amount. But my brother Frank said, "What kind of people do you want to be with? If they're cheating now, they will cheat you later. Or they will have you becoming a cheater."

Frank had gone to Kentucky on a football scholarship and was a catcher on the baseball team.

I heard later that coach Nugent said that Alabama wasn't on his schedule, and that's why he called coach Bryant. This was in August, and I was at home in Beaver Falls. The guys were already in Tuscaloosa practicing.

Coach Bryant sent coach Howard Schnellenberger to Beaver Falls. My mother liked coach Schnellenberger tremendously, especially when she found out he was at Kentucky when my brother Frank was at Kentucky. She went upstairs and packed a suitcase—a small suitcase—and came back down and said, "All right, Joey. Take him, Coach."

Coach Schnellenberger and I flew through a terrible storm into Tuscaloosa. We got there after practice had started. I remember the movement, the crispness, a lot of players out there hustling around on both sides of the track. Coach Bryant was up in the tower. Coach Bryant said something to coach Schnellenberger, and I couldn't understand anything he said. Coach Schnellenberger said, "Go up there. He wants to see you." I said, "What?" And he repeated, this time with some urgency, "Go on up there. Coach Bryant wants to see you."

So I went up. I wasn't thinking about being on his tower, that it was an important place. It was just a matter of getting up there, and thinking about getting down. And I didn't understand a word he said, except for one word, "Stud," and I didn't know what a stud was.

I was one player who did not know about coach Bryant. I didn't know about his history. I didn't know about this legacy he was working on. But one day at practice he got through to me very well and taught me a good lesson about respect and about how men need to look one another in the eye when communicating. I think that's when he and I really started to connect. At least I did.

Once in practice I was throwing passes and he was standing next to me, watching me. And for some reason I wasn't throwing a good, tight spiral. He said, "Give me the ball." And he took the ball and was manipulating it around and saying, "I think if you'll . . ." and he paused and said, "Oh, hell, why am I telling you about passing. You know more about it than I do." And he flipped the ball back to me.

The Vanderbilt game in my sophomore year was the only time I ever got benched for poor play. I was having a bad game and got taken out of the game in the first quarter. This was when the quarterbacks called all the plays and ran the offense from the field. Now it came after a lot of preparation with coach Bryant and coach Phil Cutchin and coach Elwood Kettler, but the quarterback called all the plays.

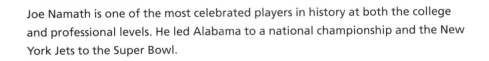

Joe Namath is one of the most celebrated players in history at both the college and professional levels. He led Alabama to a national championship and the New York Jets to the Super Bowl.

I knew I was messing up, and that was the reason I was pulled. I went over to the sideline by the bench, took off my helmet, and threw it on the ground. I sat down on the bench with my head in my hands.

Coach Bryant came over and sat down beside me and put his arm around my shoulder. Then he put his hand on my neck and started squeezing. And it was hard, like one of my big brothers squeezing me. It told me what he thought of that kind of behavior, and how fast he'd kick my ass back to Beaver Falls, Pennsylvania, if I ever displayed that kind of selfish attitude again.

I looked coach Bryant right in the eye—I had learned that—and told him I wasn't upset with him or the coaches. I was only upset with myself.

Coach Bryant told us early, when we were freshmen, that we would remember the tough times—the games we lost, the bad times—longer than we would remember the good. And that is true. Except for the championships, a championship game or a championship season, it is the failures you most remember.

One of my greatest disappointments came in the Orange Bowl in my last game. We had already won the national championship, but we lost to Texas in the Orange Bowl. Late in the game we had an opportunity to win, and I fouled up on the goal line. We had first and goal at the six and gained four yards on a first-down run. And I guess we gained about a yard on second and a little less than a yard on third. On fourth down we went with the surest play, a quarterback sneak. It wasn't disrespect of Texas. It was a belief that we could knock them off the ball and get it in. We were taught around here that if you couldn't blow someone out for a yard, maybe you didn't deserve it.

Over the years people have asked, "Joe Willie, did you score a touchdown against Texas?" My answer is that I did not because it was not ruled a touchdown. But I did get over the goal line. So many times over the years have I wished that I had had enough brains instead of being caught up in the situation to call time out on third down to go over to talk to the man, to talk to coach Bryant.

But you know how lucky I am? Jim Hudson, George Sauer, John Elliott, and Pete Lammons were four of the guys on that Texas team who came to the Jets when I did and helped us win the World Championship.

The pain of losing that game was awful. But the next day I signed a contract with the Jets. The pain doesn't go right away, but signing that contract helped ease it a little.

My first season at Alabama in 1961 was frustrating because freshmen couldn't play. We sat in the stands and watched Pat Trammell lead us to the national championship. It may have been a good rule at the time for freshmen not to be able to play, but I couldn't wait to be a sophomore.

My first game as Alabama quarterback was the Georgia game in 1962. I had a terrible headache, just one of those throbbing headaches. We went out on the field, the band started playing, and my headache disappeared. I got so caught up in it that my headache just went away.

The first play of the game. I called a quarterback sneak behind Lee Roy Jordan. I just wanted to get hit to settle down. We didn't make the first down and punted. And I think we may have intercepted a pass, but on the first play after we got the ball back, Richard Williamson broke open on an out pattern, and we scored and went on to a 35–0 win.

After the game in the dressing room, we were having a big time, a lot of jubilation. And the newspaper guys came in and started interviewing us. And I heard coach Bryant say, "Get away from the Popcorn Kid. Talk to the guys who did the winning." Well, I took a little offense at coach Bryant calling me Popcorn Kid, and I must have showed it with my body language. I was standing next to Lee Roy, and he kind of popped me with his forearm and said not to let it bother me. Coach Bryant had a way of keeping your head on straight.

Later the *Saturday Evening Post* would write an article saying the game was fixed. Now, I was the quarterback and the quarterback called the plays. The coaches didn't call the plays.

When the article came out, we had a team meeting and coach Bryant read it to us. He got to the part where it said, "Georgia gained only 35 yards." He stopped and said, "That's too many yards." It was a tense situation, but that broke us up.

To be Crimson Tide is an honor because of the history and tradition. I never felt I did anything except be with a great bunch of guys. But being any part of it makes you humble because of the greatness that was there. And to be a small part of it makes you want to know about it, to learn about it. And you appreciate what other people have done.

The tradition of the university is about people. And other people associate you with your university.

I've always felt at home at the university, coming back to visit. Mal Moore is a special guy, and one of my former teammates, and that has a lot to do with my coming back more frequently in the past few years. He has made me feel welcome, inviting me to be a part of what is going on here.

And now my daughter Jessica is in school at Alabama. I have another daughter, Olivia Rose. People ask me if I want her also to go to Alabama. I tell them she's 14, and right now all I want her to be is 15. Those years, 12 to 18, are interesting, to say the least.

And I've always had some unfinished business. I had made a promise to my mother I would have a college degree. I always said I was going to do it. And then Jessica inadvertently gave me the final push. We were talking about her going to the university, and she said, "Daddy, I'll be the first one in our family to finish college."

It may have taken a beat. Not two beats. And I said, "Want to bet?"

So that's what gave me the impetus and why I'm now finishing my degree. And it's not in basket-weaving. It's not in journalism, either.

When I was a rookie in training camp, the writers from around the league would come into different training camps. We would sit in bleachers, and they would call you out to talk to the reporters. And one of them was a smart-ass. He said, "I heard you majored in basket-weaving at Alabama." I said, "Yeah, but that was pretty tough. So I dropped it and went into journalism."

I don't know if that was the right way to start out with the writers.

Joe Namath was an All-America quarterback in 1964 and was MVP of the Orange Bowl. He and Kenny Stabler were named quarterbacks on Alabama's Team of the Century. He was a 1985 inductee into the Pro Football Hall of Fame.

PAUL CRANE
CENTER AND LINEBACKER
1963–1965

WHEN I WAS A FRESHMAN, LEE ROY JORDAN WAS A SENIOR. He was a great player. I admired him greatly, and still do. We were going out to spring training prior to my sophomore year and the equipment manager gave me jersey No. 54, the number Lee Roy had worn and made famous. I was very proud to be awarded that number and put it on and went out to the practice field.

When coach Bryant saw me he said, "What are you doing with that number on?" It was embarrassing. I said the equipment manager had given it to me. And he said, "Well get in there and take it off." And I think I've made coach Bryant sound a little nicer, more subtle, than he sounded to me.

I turned and started back toward the dressing room and he called to me. "No," he said. "Leave it on."

And that's how I got the opportunity to wear the number that Lee Roy made famous. It was an embarrassing beginning, but a thrill nonetheless and very positive. And after me a number of players have worn No. 54 and done very well with it.

That jersey was symbolic of what a great honor it was to play for Alabama.

Not too long ago someone gave me a little music box with the Alabama fight song. It reminded me of when I went to Alabama. I had gotten a little wind-up toy in the shape of a football that played "Yea, Alabama!" and I'd go to sleep at night listening to it. Even today, the Alabama fight song—which I think is great—means something to me. It represents my time at Alabama.

Paul Crane was an All-American center and linebacker who was named SEC Lineman of the Year as Alabama won the 1964 and 1965 national championships.

I am very appreciative for having had the opportunity of playing for Alabama and for coach Bryant. It was a great time to be at Alabama. Because of the players we had and the coaches we had, it was a great experience.

Alabama practices were memorable in those days. We had a little three-on-three drill, three offensive linemen, a quarterback and a back or two, against three defensive players. It was in a very confined area and a high-energy situation. A coach would stand behind the defensive players and signal where the ball was to be run. The defenders couldn't see it, of course. The rest of the players circled around and cheered until it was their turn.

One day Creed Gilmer and Tim Bates, who were defensive players and good friends, kind of got together. While Creed was on defense, Tim would very subtly signal which way the ball was going. He was cheating for the defense, or at least for Creed. And Creed did pretty well in the drill.

But when Creed went out and Tim was on defense, Creed didn't reciprocate, for whatever reason. So Bates had a lot tougher time of it and got pretty mad at Creed. I think they can finally laugh about it now.

I considered some other schools when I was being recruited out of Vigor High School in Prichard. But I flew up to Alabama and met coach Charley Bradshaw, who was a very smooth recruiter. And coach Dude Hennessey also helped recruit me. Then I met with coach Bryant, and that confirmed my decision to go to Alabama. It turned out to be a great decision for me.

Playing at Alabama has given me a reference point. Part of it is that people remember you, even that far back, which is nice. But the personal reference point is the hard work, commitment, and dedication it took to play for coach Bryant and Alabama. Each of us has a period in his or her life that has a profound effect or results in a huge change. For me that period was my time as a player at Alabama. It has served as the reference point for the rest of my life.

After my Alabama playing career I was signed as a free agent by the New York Jets. I was there from 1966 through 1973. That meant I got to play in the Super Bowl with Joe Namath when we won the World Championship against Baltimore in Miami. That was a case of being in the right place at the right time. So I got a Super Bowl ring to go with my 1964 and 1965 national championship rings.

And after my playing career I got to come back to Alabama and work under coach Bryant coaching linebackers in the midseventies. Coach Bryant was really interesting on the sidelines. If it was a really tough game, he was very calm. But if we were playing a game we were supposed to be able to win without much trouble, he would be a bear over there.

I left Alabama after the 1977 season, just before Alabama would win two more national championships, to go to Ole Miss. We weren't very successful, so I got out of college coaching and moved to Mobile where I'm the director of the Catholic Youth Organization.

95

Paul Crane was an All-America center and linebacker for Alabama in 1965 and was named Outstanding Lineman in the South that year. He was captain of the 1965 team. He played on teams that went 28–4–1 and won two national championships, then won a Super Bowl playing for the New York Jets.

STEVE SLOAN

QUARTERBACK
1963–1965

P LAYING FOOTBALL AT ALABAMA IN THE MIDSIXTIES was sort of like being in the brotherhood of coal miners. You didn't know if you were going to get out of that mine or not. It was a tough process. But the winning made it fun.

Both at the time and ever since, I felt honored to be a part of the team and to play for coach Bryant and the assistant coaches. They were all so dedicated, and I was fortunate to be a part of it.

I grew up in Cleveland, Tennessee, not far from Knoxville, and I was a Tennessee fan. I also liked Georgia Tech and Vanderbilt. Alabama never entered my mind until the recruiting process started. Coach Clem Gryska, coach Howard Schnellenberger, and coach Gene Stallings seemed to be there all the time. They just did a better job of recruiting than anyone else. And, of course, Alabama was doing well. I always felt fortunate to get a scholarship to play football at Alabama.

I'm not sure how much of a factor it was, but we were a T formation team in high school, and Tennessee was still running the single wing. I had played defense all through high school and thought I could play defense at Tennessee. But I was sold on quarterback and Alabama.

When I got to Alabama in the fall of 1962, we had about 65 freshmen, and it seemed to me that a lot of them were quarterbacks. Mal Moore was a senior; Joe Namath was a sophomore and the starter; and they had Jack Hurlbut, who was kind of like me, a guy who could play offense and defense.

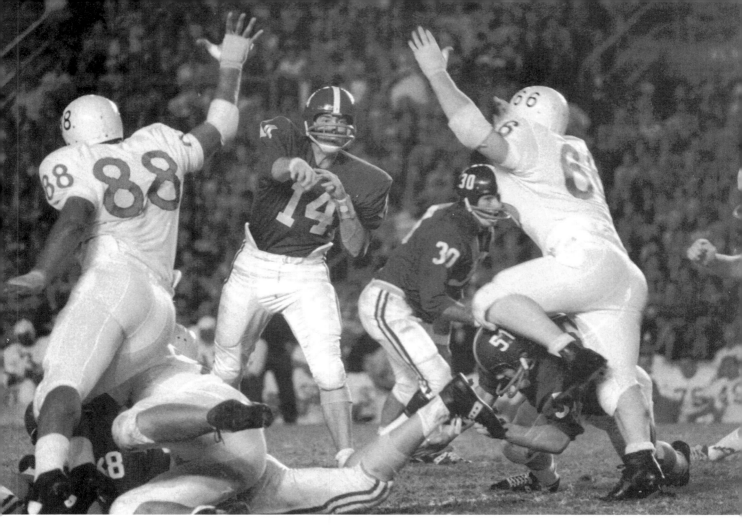

Steve Sloan (No. 14) was MVP of the 1966 Orange Bowl, passing for two touchdowns and leading Alabama to a 39–28 victory over Nebraska as the Crimson Tide won the national championship.

I played on the freshman team in 1962, and then in 1963 played nothing but defense until the Sugar Bowl game at the end of the season. I only started a couple of games on defense, but I played on kicking teams. And then near the end of the season, Joe was suspended for the rest of the season. Only Joe and coach Bryant know why. I think Jack played all or most of the Miami game. We went to Biloxi to practice for the Sugar Bowl, and at some point coach Bryant decided I would start at quarterback. He may have thought Jack would be better on defense than I was. In any event, that's a heck of a time and place to get your first start at quarterback. I think I got a little older that week.

It snowed in New Orleans, which is unusual, and we played Ole Miss, a team we rarely played in the regular season in those days. We did play them my senior year in that 17–16 win. They had a very good team, but our defense played well, and Tim Davis kicked four field goals and we won the Sugar Bowl 12–7.

I remember one play in particular. I was running a down-the-line option and went the wrong way. I made a nice pitch, but the only one there was the referee, and he didn't catch it. I was able to recover the ball, but coach Bryant wasn't very happy about that play.

It was good to win the game, although I didn't have much to do with it. But I did get some experience. The hard thing was we called our own plays, and because I had worked so little on offense, that was difficult.

Joe was back in 1964, but he got hurt in the North Carolina State game, which was early in the season. I was starting in the secondary, but I was the back-up quarterback. I had broken a finger in practice and hadn't gotten much work on offense. But I played the rest of the game at quarterback and we won 21–0. Roman Gabriel was quarterback for North Carolina State. One funny thing that happened was I guess the coaches forgot I was playing in the secondary, and they left me in, playing both ways until halftime, when they got that changed.

After the game, in the dressing room, coach Bryant came over to me and said, "How do you think you played?" in a way I thought he didn't think I'd played very well. I said, "We won the game." It was the first time I remember seeing him laugh.

I started the rest of the games, except Florida. Joe came in and got us wins against Georgia Tech and Auburn, and we were 10–0 and national champions. We both had bad knees when we played in the Orange Bowl and lost to Texas.

It was an enjoyable year playing offense and defense, especially since we got all those wins.

Coach Bryant had a way of making things work out. I don't know how he did it, but I'm convinced he was able to make things come around to the way we needed. We started out slow on offense in 1965, but we were good on defense. And by the time we got to about mid-season, we were a good offense and a good football team. In our last three games, we scored 30 or more points against LSU, South Carolina, and Auburn, which was a lot of points in those days. And so we made it to the Orange Bowl against Nebraska.

They were waiting until after the bowl games to choose the national champion, and we were ranked about fourth. But a couple of teams in front of us lost that afternoon in bowl games, and that night we were playing Nebraska for the championship.

The quarterbacks called the plays then, but coach Bryant told me to open the game with a tackle-eligible pass to Jerry Duncan. That was a lot of fun. Jerry had been a running back and he was fast, and the tackle-eligible, which was later banned, was like getting the ball to a halfback on a screen. We won the game 39–28 and another national championship.

Back then we had so many good players that the quarterback may have looked better than he was. Nobody dropped a pass and nobody got to the quarterback.

I played with the Atlanta Falcons for a couple of years but had a bad shoulder. I came back to Alabama with the intention of going to graduate school. I was in the library, and someone told me coach Bryant was looking for me. Ken Meyer was leaving to take the San Francisco 49ers head coaching job, and so I was hired to work with quarterbacks.

The quarterbacks were closer to coach Bryant than any other segment of the team. As a player, you don't know everything that goes on behind the scenes. As a coach, it was a different perspective.

99

When I was a junior or senior at Alabama, I took a management course that focused on four basic principles: organization, leadership, planning, and control. I had a great teacher in that course, and I realized that those four principles were utilized by coach Bryant. I'm not sure he would have known of those four principles, or that he was aware he employed them. His organizational skills were extraordinary, which I appreciated more when I became an assistant coach. I don't know where he got that. And his planning skills were great. And he was an all-time motivator.

I certainly admired what he did. Even though we might have different thoughts about some things, I regard him as an extraordinary man.

I know that everyone who had the opportunity to be exposed to coach Bryant has thought about ways in which he affected their careers, and that may be more frequent for those of us who remained in athletics. He had a stronger personality than I have. He was a little tougher than I can be. But his planning and organization and all those things have really helped me out in my career in athletics. People like coach Bryant don't come along very often. He's in a class with people like General Patton—forceful, charismatic. I always think of him fondly.

I think the driving force for him was that he had grown up poor and he never wanted to be poor again. He was exceptional in a lot of ways.

In 1987 I had the privilege to return to Alabama as athletics director when Ray Perkins, who had been coach and athletics director, left to go to Tampa Bay. In the interview I was asked who I would hire as head coach. Bobby Bowden had let it be known he would take the job. Whoever was interviewing me told me coach Bowden was too old. They asked me about Bill Curry, who was a good friend. I didn't think the Georgia Tech thing would pose the problem it did.

It was a tough situation to come into. I really didn't have any choice on a lot of the issues. We were going to have to go to Auburn, and they were going to come to Tuscaloosa eventually. I think Ray had said we would never go to Auburn to play. And coach Bryant never would have. It was a tough issue, but there was no other way to do it. We couldn't terminate the game. It was a really complex issue. I thought I did the right thing. I got hundreds and hundreds of letters, and only one supported me.

And there were some other problems that proved sticky.

Because I've always been in athletics, I've missed a lot of the reunions and things with my former teammates, but we still keep up with one another. I keep up with Alabama, and not just football. I follow all the teams. I got to be good friends with Sarah and David Patterson, and I follow gymnastics, and really everything. It's interesting to me that so many people still remember me as an Alabama football player.

100

Steve Sloan was All-America, Academic All-America, led the nation in passing efficiency (153.8), and was MVP of the Orange Bowl as a Crimson Tide senior in 1965. He is now athletics director at Tennessee-Chattanooga.

JIMMY FULLER
Offensive Lineman
1964–1966

IT'S NOT EASY TO GET A NATIONAL CHAMPIONSHIP RING. When I was being recruited in 1962, coach Sam Bailey came to my house. He was wearing his ring from Alabama's 1961 national championship season. I remember him pointing out that whether you looked at it right side up or upside down, it said 1961.

I said I sure would like to have one of those. He took it off, and I thought for a second he was going to give it to me. But he just held it out for me to see and said, "If you come to Alabama, you'll have a chance to get one." I went to Alabama and got two.

The first one was great. The second one I gave to my father, and I think he was happier to have his than I was to have mine. He was so proud. And I think I was happier for him than I had been for myself.

We probably deserved another one in 1966 when we went 11–0, while Notre Dame and Michigan State were playing a tie game, but that's just one of those things.

I never thought about getting another national championship ring, but I was lucky enough to be on coach Stallings' staff in 1992. And so I got my third national championship ring as an Alabama assistant coach. That one made me so happy for the players. I was so proud of them, and you could see the pride they had in themselves.

Jimmy Fuller (No. 73) was an offensive lineman on two national championship teams under coach Bryant in the midsixties, then returned to Alabama as an assistant coach and earned a third national championship ring in 1992.

All of the rings were different and all were special.

I was an Alabama fan growing up in Fairfield. Neither my father nor my mother had gone to Alabama, but they were Alabama fans. And it was mostly because of coach Bryant and what he was doing.

I played football at Fairfield, and we also had a good wrestling program, and I enjoyed wrestling. I thought about going to Auburn because they had a good wrestling program. And then Alabama got a program started, although I think it was just a club program, nothing like what Auburn had, and that helped convince me to go to Alabama. I really thought I was such an athlete that I could compete in multiple sports at Alabama. Little did I know that I was barely able to compete in one, much less two. Wrestling dropped by the wayside.

Back then things were different. When I was being recruited, the players from that 1961 national championship team and the 1962 team would come by my house, guys like Bill Battle, who was from West End, and Billy Richardson, from Jasper. I think the players and ex-players made the biggest impression on me because they had so much class. They were the type of persons I wanted to be.

And that was a time when coach Bryant was signing guys who weren't particularly big, but who were quick and who played hard. The step from Fairfield High School to The University of Alabama was a huge one. In the fall of 1963, we had a freshman team that played three or four games, but that wasn't the most important thing we did. We couldn't play for the varsity, but they did let us practice against them. That was an eye-opener. You realized pretty quickly that the expectations were high and the competition was stiff.

I think we had 66 freshmen that year. That's six football teams, although we were coming in at the time when you were playing just offense or just defense. But we had a lot of players to start with, not nearly as many as when we finished four years later.

We were thrown into the mix with that opportunity to practice against the varsity each day. I had been an interior lineman in high school, and that's what I was throughout my career. After a brief look on defense, I played offensive guard and tackle. And I think I was on every kicking team.

We weren't very big. Just recently someone gave me a program that had me and Jerry Duncan on the cover. I checked out the roster, and we had no more than eight guys who were over 200 pounds. And I don't mean 250 or

260. I mean 205 or 210. About 100 pounds below what the average offensive lineman is today. I was about 193, although I was hurt, and while I was recuperating I got fat, up to about 220. Some of our biggest guys were running backs, like Les Kelley; and Wayne Trimble, a quarterback, was one of the biggest.

But coach Bryant convinced us that while the other side might be bigger, we were better.

And one reason we were so successful was that, in my three years playing, we had three of the finest quarterbacks imaginable—Joe Namath, Steve Sloan, and Ken "Snake" Stabler. They were outstanding.

I don't think there is a man alive who was in that first meeting we had with coach Bryant who didn't recognize that he was different. I think as the years have gone by, I have come to realize more and more what a special person he was. I couldn't put my finger on it in that first meeting, but he was laying out exactly how things were going to be for us. He could talk about the plan for practice that day, but years later you would realize he was talking about so much more than that. And in 40 years in athletics I have taken almost everything from my time at the university and with coach Bryant.

Anyone who was ever around him will tell you that his lessons weren't just about football. I was aware of his influence when I was in business. But it really comes into focus in athletics.

I really didn't realize my life was going to be in athletics. I was preparing for a career in the transportation industry since I had been able to work for freight companies in the summer. That was my father's field. But after a talk I had with coach Bryant about coaching, I decided that was where I needed to be. And I was lucky. I was able to go back to Fairfield High School and coach under my former coach, Harold "Red" Lutz, who had played at Alabama. And when coach Lutz left to go to Tuscaloosa High School, I became head coach at Fairfield.

One thing coach Bryant had told me was that you had to coach with your own personality, that you couldn't be someone else. But that didn't stop me from getting a houndstooth hat and leaning against the goalpost before the game. But I only did that once. That wasn't me.

My coaching career was always linked to Alabama. I went to Jacksonville State under Charley Pell, who had played just ahead of me at Alabama. Then I went to East Carolina under Pat Dye, who had been a coach at Alabama. And when Charley Pell left Jacksonville, I got that job. Then Ray Perkins, who I had played with at Alabama, got the head job after coach Bryant, and I came back to Alabama as an assistant.

Some people have a hard time going from head coach to assistant coach, but it didn't bother me. I have always been able to close a door when I leave and go to the next thing. After Ray left, Bill Curry came in and brought his entire staff. But Jack Fligg, who was one of his offensive line coaches along with Mac McWhorter, was moving into administration. Sylvester Croom and I were the offensive line coaches under Ray. Bill was going to decide between us, and I told Sly to take it. But he said he wanted to try his hand at pro coaching and had a chance to go with Ray to Tampa Bay, so I got to stay.

Of course, I didn't even think about going to Kentucky with the Curry staff. And when coach Stallings got the job, he decided to keep me. At first there were just the two of us, and we were going full bore recruiting. I finally said, "Coach, I know I can recruit. And I know you can recruit. But we need some help." And he promised me we'd get it, which we did with a great coaching staff.

After coach Stallings retired, I did too. Or so I thought. I dabbled in some business things. And hunting and fishing weren't bad. But all my life I've had people who helped me out. So I didn't go back to Jacksonville State as athletics director for the money or because I just had to get back in athletics. I did it because I feel I owe so much, and if I can help, I want to give something back.

105

Jimmy Fuller was on Alabama teams that went 30–2–1 and won two national championships. He also won a national championship as an assistant coach and coached three consecutive All-SEC centers in Wes Neighbors, Roger Shultz, and Tobie Sheils.

RAY PERKINS

SPLIT END

1964–1966

I CAN GIVE YOU A SHORT ANSWER AS TO WHY I chose Alabama to play football and go to college. Alabama was the only school that offered me a scholarship. Dude Hennessey recruited me for Alabama. He came to a game on Friday night, and following the game he offered me a scholarship.

Alabama was the only school that recruited me. Alabama was the only school that invited me for a visit. I went to Alabama when they played North Carolina State in 1961. Roman Gabriel was North Carolina State's quarterback. I had a great visit. I got to meet coach Bryant and talk with him for a little while. They made me feel like I was wanted.

It worked out great that Alabama would be the only school that recruited me because Alabama was the only school I was interested in. I had wanted to go to Alabama since I was a sophomore in high school.

One of those odd things is that I had a cousin who was a good friend of a nephew of coach Bryant. All he could talk about was coach Bryant and winning. And he told me if I went to Alabama to play for coach Bryant, that I could play for anyone—that if I went to Alabama, I would win. Winning was a big thing to me when I was young. I wanted to win.

I grew up in Petal, Mississippi. Across the river, in Hattiesburg, was a guy named Andy Anderson who was a big fan of coach Bryant and Alabama. I met him when I was a sophomore in high school, and he gave me an Alabama

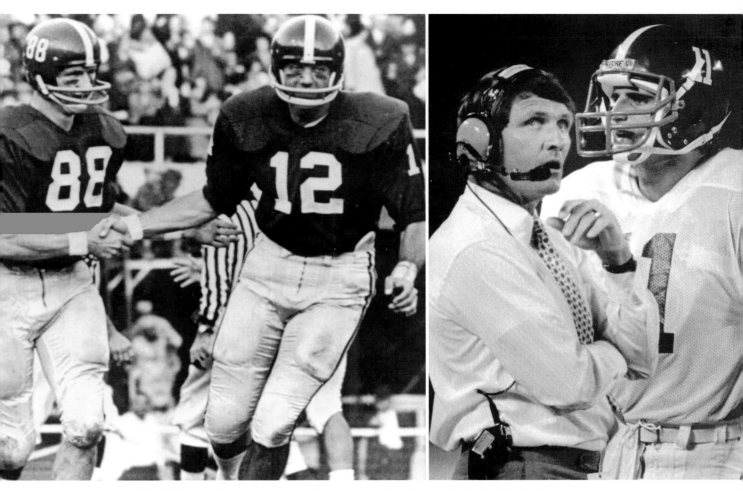

Ray Perkins (No. 88) was an outstanding receiver for quarterbacks like Joe Namath (No. 12) in the midsixties at Alabama. In 1983 he replaced coach Bryant as Alabama's head coach. Among his players was quarterback Mike Shula (No. 11).

press guide. I read through it, all the tidbits about Alabama and coach Bryant and the players, and got it in my mind I wanted to go to Alabama.

One good bit of information I got from coach Bryant's nephew through my cousin was that we did win at Alabama. The five years I was there were five of the greatest years of my life. And what made it that way was the football success—the winning.

We won two national championships and three SEC championships during the years I played in 1964, 1965, and 1966. Our record was 30–2–1.

The players from that era still have a great bond. We meet somewhere every year to go hunting or do something, 20 or 30 of us. I enjoy that little reunion because my time as an Alabama player was a great time, a very memorable time.

After I left Alabama I played for the Baltimore Colts and coach Don Shula from 1967 through 1971. I spent one year coaching receivers at Mississippi State, then went back to the NFL. I coached receivers at New England (1974–1977), was offensive coordinator at San Diego in 1978, then was with the New York Giants from 1979–1982.

Being head coach at Alabama was a dream come true. I had thought about that job for a long time before I got it. Every year coach Bryant came to the National Football Foundation Hall of Fame banquet in New York, and he would always call me and ask me to sit with him at his table. He did that in 1982. He had already announced that he was retiring at the end of the season, and it had already been announced that his last game would be the Liberty Bowl.

The next morning he called my office. "Raymond," he said. He was the only one who ever called me Raymond. "Raymond, are you interested in this thing down here?"

I said, "Coach Bryant, I would walk to Tuscaloosa for it."

He said, "Well, I didn't think you would be interested. I thought you were making so much money up here you wouldn't be interested."

I assured him I was interested.

That afternoon I got a call from Joab Thomas, the president of the university. He invited me down for an interview in Birmingham. The rest is history.

The most meaningful thing about my time as a player at Alabama were the people I played with, the coaches I played for, and of course, coach Bryant. I love the memory of coach Bryant because he meant a lot to me as a coach and later as a friend.

The most meaningful thing about my time as coach was the players. And I still hear from a lot of them and keep up with a lot of them. That is rewarding.

Having my quarterback, Mike Shula, back at Alabama as head coach means a lot to me.

So the most meaningful thing is the people I met and played with and had associations with—and still do. I made a lot of great friends with those two experiences.

One of the things I'm asked most about is whether I wish I had turned down the Tampa Bay opportunity after the 1986 season and perhaps stayed at Alabama for a 15- or 20-year career. I can't say I have never thought about that, but it has been very little. I don't dwell on it. In the coaching business you make decisions based on the information you have and try to do what is best. And just as I don't think about making the decision to go to Tampa Bay, I've never dwelled on the question of whether I should have stayed in New York and not taken the Alabama job. There's no use in playing that game.

I did go to Tampa Bay for four years and then I thought I was retired from football. But in 1992 Charley Thornton, who had been sports information director at Alabama when I played, called from Arkansas State, where he was athletics director. That was not a great job, but I went back into football. I stayed just one year at Arkansas State, then went back to the NFL as offensive coordinator at New England, then offensive coordinator at Oakland, and finally spent a couple of years at Cleveland before retiring from football for good.

Ray Perkins was an All-American in 1966 and was captain of Alabama's undefeated team. He set an Alabama bowl record with nine receptions in the 1966 Orange Bowl as Alabama defeated Nebraska 39–28 to win the national championship. He had an Alabama bowl record 178 yards in the 1967 Sugar Bowl. He played in two Super Bowls. He was Alabama head coach, 1983–1986, and in the NFL was head coach of the New York Giants and Tampa Bay Buccaneers.

JERRY DUNCAN
OFFENSIVE TACKLE
1965–1966

I WAS A HALFBACK IN HIGH SCHOOL, AND THAT'S WHAT I EXPECTED to be at Alabama. It wasn't the happiest day of my life when I was moved to the offensive line. As it turned out, it was probably the best thing that ever happened to me.

The guy I have the most memories about is Howard Schnellenberger, who was my offensive line coach. I still stay in touch with him. He's athletics director at Florida Atlantic. It was a great challenge for him to take a guy like me who had been a halfback and try to make an offensive lineman out of him. And it was challenging for me, too. He was very tough, a disciplinarian of the first order. He forced you to learn good technique. And that meant a lot of preparation—practice and watching films. He was constantly trying to make you a better football player. And you also knew if you weren't doing the best you could, he was going to get the next guy.

That probably was the reason coach Bryant chose my name when he decided to start making some awards to give players incentive to do well in spring training, which is not a very fun practice time with no game to look forward to.

In the early seventies, he started the awards, and in the first batch was the "Jerry Duncan I Like to Practice Award." I didn't know anything about it until after it was announced, and I haven't really talked to too many of the players who won it.

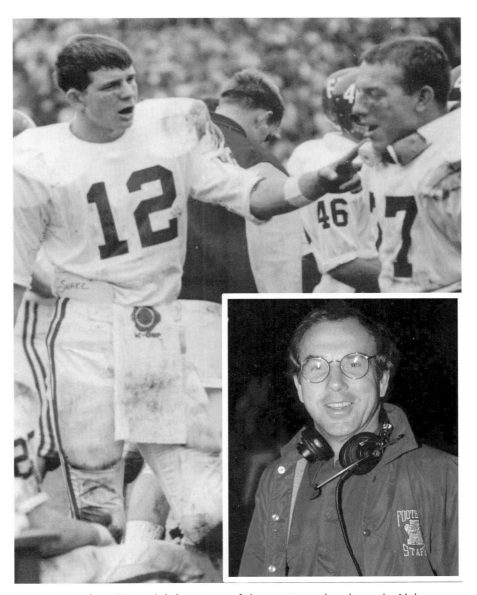

Jerry Duncan (No. 67, on right) was one of the most popular players in Alabama history. He was a small offensive tackle whose success as an eligible pass receiver from the likes of quarterback Kenny Stabler (No. 12) forced a change in college football rules. Later Duncan was equally popular as a color man for Alabama football radio broadcasts.

I've had plenty of old teammates who questioned whether any of us liked to practice, and that's a good point. I'm sure none of us enjoyed it. I guess a lot of players wonder why anyone would want to win that award. But we went about it in different ways. Some people are great players and might not have to practice as hard. Nothing ever came easy for me, and particularly after I was moved from halfback to tackle, which was done in the spring before my junior year in 1965.

I had to really focus. Sometimes I was a little banged up or I might have a headache. But I felt I still had to go. When I was playing, if I missed a couple of days of practice, there was a guy right behind me who was probably better than I was anyway, and if I gave him the opportunity, he was going to get my position. So I had to act like I enjoyed practice whether I did or not. And the truth is I did enjoy it, or at least that's the way I remember it now. Practice was tough. Coach Bryant was a taskmaster, but I think that 1964–1966 group had a lot of fun. And I guess part of the fun was going as hard as I could to let him know I wanted to play.

I don't know how I was picked out for that award over all the great players who have been at Alabama, but I'm mighty proud of it.

I was extremely fortunate to come along at the right time to have the opportunity to play for Alabama. I wasn't really a very good football player, although I was probably a decent athlete. I played at Sparta, North Carolina, a very small program with 25 or 30 guys on the team in the smallest county in the state. And I found out later that coach Gryska was sent up to sign me without even talking to my coaches or looking at film. I never did know what coach Bryant had heard about me. It was an extraordinary time to be given the opportunity to play for coach Bryant and the great assistant coaches we had. It was a fantastic journey.

Back then they could sign quite a few guys. After they had taken what they wanted from the state of Alabama, they went out and got whatever else they needed. And because they could sign a large number, they could take a chance on a guy like me. And then I had to prove to coach Bryant that he hadn't made a mistake. I think there were times that he thought he made a mistake before I finally came around and started playing.

I played with three or four great players. The rest of us were a bunch of average ragtags. But we didn't know we were average. Coach Bryant just worked us and worked us and molded us into a unit that could play with anybody in the country.

Now some of those who were above average were our quarterbacks. It was fun to block for Steve Sloan, who looked like he was stumbling around but who was turning upfield and gaining yards. And Ken Stabler could run the option as well as anyone ever, and he could pass, too. Joe Namath was quarterback my sophomore season, so you'd say we did have some pretty good players.

And it was fun to block for them, but since I never weighed more than about 180 pounds, it would have been a lot more fun if I had been about 40 pounds heavier.

It was fun to be a part of those teams. We won the national championship in 1964 and again in 1965 and then went undefeated in 1966 while Notre Dame and Michigan State tied. But when the polls were in, we didn't get that third national championship. It was really disappointing because we thought we could beat Notre Dame or Michigan State, and we thought we had done all we could do. I'm sure I was extremely disappointed then, but looking back it's insignificant.

I have very good memories of winning the 1965 national championship because we had to beat Nebraska in the Orange Bowl to do it. We were outmanned. Nebraska had better players than we had, and they were a lot bigger than we were. That was probably the best team I ever played against. But coach Bryant changed our offense for the game and decided to throw the ball a lot. And in those days, you could line up so that the tackle (me) was an eligible pass receiver. In fact, they would change the rule later because of the success we had. We ran three or four tackle-eligible plays, including one on the first play of the game, and we used three or four onside kicks. By the time we got to the fourth quarter, our offense had kept their defense on the field so long they were exhausted. We won 39–28.

It was funny. We'd win the national championship, and it was great, but there weren't any parties or parades or anything like that. Three or four days after we won one, coach Bryant was back trying to figure out how to win it again. I've never known anyone like him. He refused to rest on his laurels.

After I graduated, I became a stockbroker in Birmingham, which I have done for 35 years. I'm sure having played at Alabama opened some doors for me. It

113

may have closed a few by fans of other schools, but I feel that I've had an opportunity to deal with some of the finest people in the state of Alabama.

I also had another wonderful opportunity. For 24 years I was part of the Alabama football radio broadcasts, first with John Forney and Doug Layton, then with Paul Kennedy, and finally with Eli Gold. That was a pleasure and it gave me a chance to be around coach Bryant for another 10 years.

Jerry Duncan played on teams that won two national championships and had a record of 30–2–1. Rival coaches insisted on a rules change because of Alabama's success in using Duncan as a tackle-eligible receiver. He was later the sideline color man on Alabama radio broadcasts. He's senior vice president with Smith Barney.

KEN STABLER

QUARTERBACK

1965–1967

FROM THE DAY YOU FIRST PULL ON THAT CRIMSON JERSEY to the end of your life, you reap the reward of playing football for Alabama. That reward is in being remembered. It may be for something specific, or it may be just for being a former Crimson Tide player.

It still amazes me the number of people who will tell me about seeing the run in the mud. The details of the rain and wind, umbrellas turned inside out, clothes ruined, and yet they stayed to watch as we beat Auburn 7–3 in 1967. And I hear this virtually every day from some Alabama fan. I listen to the whole story because it is a thrill for them, and it is a great feeling for me that they remember. And we old Alabama players like to talk about Alabama football, too, particularly a win over Auburn.

A lot of people think the Alabama-Auburn game is the most emotional rivalry in college football, and it is gratifying to have been part of a play that will live forever because it was Alabama-Auburn and a game-winning play. I go through airports, and inevitably someone will yell, "Roll, Tide" or "Hey, Snake."

I have two teenage daughters, and it's great for them to see where Dad fit into the mix in the legacy of Alabama football, to see people ask me for autographs or talk to me because I am a former Alabama player. They can look at the photographs or even the old films, but it is the people who make it real.

Ken "Snake" Stabler (No. 12) was a masterful quarterback as a runner or passer in leading the Crimson Tide to a 34–7 victory over Nebraska in the Sugar Bowl for an undefeated 1966 season. After a fine professional career, Stabler joined the Alabama football radio broadcast team.

To have been an Alabama football player is, as coach Bryant said, to be part of a family. And no matter your role, you were a productive part of that family.

And more than anything, Alabama football was coach Bryant. I don't think I realized what he was doing for me until I was old enough to look back on it. In my case, I was young and dumb and wild, and when I became a disciplinary problem, coach Bryant disciplined me. At the time I couldn't see it, but he was teaching me a life lesson. I was close to throwing everything away, and he saw something worth saving. He suspended me, then gave me the opportunity to get back. Don't think I got off light. I got the hell beat out of me at practice, but he didn't let me throw it away.

Coach Bryant had a knack for treating everyone fairly, and in a way that everyone thought was the same. You believed that he was as polite to the janitors cleaning up the stadium as he was to the president of the university, that he treated the fourth team guard the same way he treated the All-American.

He was taking care of me. He saw I needed a kick in the pants. I was just about to throw away my college career, which led to a 15-year career in the NFL and to a lot of other good things in my life. Without coach Bryant saving me, I guess I'd be a bartender somewhere.

He gave me two opportunities. The first was when he offered me a scholarship to the university. The second was when he saved me from myself with his discipline. He prepped me for the next level, the next level of football with his teaching of fundamentals and understanding, and the next level of life with lessons that seem to come back to me all the time.

The greatest disappointment was an excellent season. We were two-time defending national champions going into the 1966 season, and that year we went 11–0 and outscored our opponents 267–37 in the regular season. We had six shutouts. And then we beat Nebraska 34–7 in the Sugar Bowl. Yet we finished third in the nation.

I had watched as a kid as Pat Trammell won a national championship, then watched Joe Namath and Steve Sloan win national championships, and I thought 1966 was my turn. We made a pretty good run, but we didn't get there. It was disappointing, but I believe we did all we could do.

I was around a lot of winning football. In high school under coach Ivan Jones at Foley, we went 29–1 in my three years. Then at Alabama we were 28–3–2. And then I went to Oakland, where I played for John Madden, who was like a big brother. We made it to the championship game five times, then finally beat Pittsburgh to get to Super Bowl XI, where we beat Minnesota 32–14. And then I finished my career in New Orleans for Bum Phillips, who was like a grandfather. I always played for someone I respected and wanted to please.

I wasn't highly recruited out of high school. Dee Powell recruited me for Alabama, and Lee Hayley recruited me for Auburn, and I think I got some letters from Mississippi State and Tulane. I was a typical small-town athlete, playing football until it was time to play basketball and then playing basketball until it was time to play baseball and on and on.

My father was a huge Alabama fan. He would really get excited on Saturdays as we got ready to listen to Alabama games when Pat Trammell and Billy Richardson were playing in the early sixties. Being around him and listening to Alabama football on the radio sold me pretty early.

I did consider going straight to pro baseball. I threw hard and had a good overhand curve and good control. A Yankees scout offered me $50,000 and a college education. I had to take a pretty hard look at that. In 1964 in Foley, $50,000 was a lot of money, and it could have been a help to my family. My father was a hard-working mechanic for automobile dealerships, and we were probably lower-middle class. But we had the essentials and didn't absolutely have to have the money. My parents left it up to me and were genuinely supportive. They wanted me to be happy.

I loved baseball. But I also had a love of football and of Alabama.

Coach Bryant came to my house and had dinner with us and told me he wanted me to come to Alabama and play football. Alabama was winning; I wanted to follow in the footsteps of Trammell and Namath; I wanted to play for coach Bryant; I wanted to win a national championship; and I wanted to be a part of the Alabama football lore that my father loved.

Looking back, I made the right decision to be a part of the Alabama family. And I always thought I would have a chance later to make some money as an athlete.

I love my relationship with the football program now, being able to participate as a member of the radio broadcasting team. It is a thrill to be close to the program where I played.

Ken Stabler was an All-American, SEC Player of the Year in 1967, and MVP of the Sugar Bowl as he completed 12 of 17 passes for 218 yards and one touchdown, and rushed for 40 more yards and another touchdown. In 1992 he and Joe Namath were selected as quarterbacks on Alabama's Team of the Century.

The
SEVENTIES

JOHNNY MUSSO

RUNNING BACK

1969–1971

When I was 11 years old, I knew what I wanted to do, and I was able to live a childhood dream. I never lost the wonder of it. The reality of playing for Alabama never left me. I couldn't believe I was lucky enough to be wearing that crimson jersey and playing for coach Bryant. It never lost its magic. Every time I slipped on that jersey, it was a wonder.

I grew up in a state where there was a great appreciation for the football tradition of Alabama, and for Auburn, as well. My sister went to Auburn, and they won a national championship while she was there. I think maybe because she was at Auburn my brothers and I became Alabama fans just to irritate her. But it stuck.

Coach Jordan had quite a presence at Auburn, but coach Bryant was larger than life. And there were Auburn players I admired, Tucker Frederickson and others.

I saw my first Alabama game when I was 11 years old. I snuck into Legion Field in Birmingham to see the 1961 Alabama-Auburn game. I saw coach Bryant get off the team bus. And then I saw Lee Roy Jordan. He looked like granite, a face carved from stone. I was really taken with that.

And then I watched Alabama win the game. Alabama played great, clearing the last hurdle to the national championship. If I was ever conflicted about my favorite team, watching Alabama play that day solidified my loyalty to Alabama.

Johnny Musso (No. 22), "the Italian Stallion," was Alabama's leading running back from 1969 to 1971. In 1970 he rushed for 221 yards against Auburn. The next year 'Bama went to the wishbone, and he was the leading rusher on a team that went 11–1.

I had started playing football the year before, YMCA ball. I was pretty good at it, and having success probably helped me develop a love for football. As I played, I had a goal to one day wear that red jersey. I wanted to play at Legion Field and be a part of Alabama football tradition.

A lot was going on at college campuses in the late sixties. There was the Vietnam war, the long hair, the pot, and the rebellion. It was a crazy time, and that extended to dynamics in college football.

When you play at Alabama you are linked to the past, the present, and the future. You carry a torch that others carried quite well before you, and there is a great responsibility on your part as an Alabama football player to carry it and pass it to the next generation of players. That can be weighty.

After playing freshman ball in 1968, we were in an I formation offense that was primarily a passing offense in 1969 and 1970. In those two years, there were only a couple of exceptions that the other team did not have better talent. And you found out real quick that representing Alabama was a burden because teams that had been beaten by Alabama for decades would beat you as bad as they could. There was no mercy, no calling off the dogs. We would be in the fourth quarter and playing for no other reason than pride.

But then we had the experience of doing it right, winning them all, getting back-to-championship caliber, and carrying the banner when things were going well. I can say now that I probably gained from both experiences. And I think most Alabama players have handled the responsibilities well because they have a genuine love for Alabama football.

Football is a great place to learn, a great environment for the other disciplines, life lessons. They can be learned in other places, but I don't know any place better than the football field. There is the toughness demanded of a physical game. And it is the ultimate team sport. It has to be 11 or it doesn't work. In basketball you can have one guy carry the load. Certainly, there are positions on the football field that can have a greater impact, but nothing like where you put four off to the side and let one player go one-on-one. I believe there are lessons that are unique to football.

And I think coach Bryant at the heart of things was a teacher. He wanted to impact young men, and I think he understood the greater worth of the game. His motivation was to win. That was his highest motivation. But his second was to have a positive impact on players, and I think he did a good job of that.

He confirmed what my mother taught me. She was a tough lady who went through a lot of hard stuff. As much as I admire coach Bryant and as much as he impacted my life, I think my mom taught me those lessons and he reinforced them. And he gave me the environment to test it.

In 1971, my senior year, coach Bryant made the decision to switch to the wishbone. I think the team received that very positively because Terry Davis was our best quarterback. He was a really good athlete and a great competitor, but he wasn't a great passer. But the players were excited about a player who could make things happen, who could make quick decisions, who could do things on the run. Our imaginations were sparked by having an athlete like Terry who could run the option.

I think he was the best wishbone quarterback ever. As the wishbone was developed at Alabama, it got much, much more sophisticated. In that first year, it was a true read, triple option with just a few other plays.

It took players being unselfish. The best example was David Bailey, a marvelous wide receiver who is still in the Alabama record book. He didn't have blazing speed, but he could get open and had great hands. He could have become frustrated, but he didn't. He became a great blocker. He put every bit of effort into helping the team.

For me personally, it was a little harder to direct the ball into my hands than it had been in the I formation. I'm glad I got to play in both. There wasn't a lot of variety in the wishbone, and there was a lot of blocking.

I think everyone stepped up to make it work. And, of course, it helped to have John Hannah and Buddy Brown at the guard positions and Jim Krapf at center.

And it was fun because we kept it stealth. When the Skywriters—a group of sportswriters from throughout the South who visited every SEC team during August practices—came through, we had to waste a day of practice to run our old stuff. But we thought we had an edge. The last practice we had in Tuscaloosa before leaving to go to Los Angeles to play Southern Cal was at night because we were going to play at night. And it was the last practice we'd have on the wishbone because when we got to Los Angeles we would again practice the 1970 offense.

While we were practicing, the students were having a pep rally on the quad. The practice field was surrounded by curtains, but the pep rally moved to our practice field, and coach Bryant allowed the curtains to be opened and eventually opened the gates to let the students in to see their team. And they saw we were doing something new, and you could tell they were excited, that they had the same hope we did.

We went out to Los Angeles and scored the first three times we got the ball and then held on to win. It was a great game, a great moment, particularly after the way they had beaten us the year before, and it was great to be part of it. I think that gave us the confidence to go through the season undefeated.

The players certainly believed in coach Bryant. I thought back to the 1965 season when Alabama went to the Orange Bowl with a conservative offense to play Nebraska. Steve Sloan threw the ball all over the field, and Alabama won the national championship. Coach Bryant showed he had something up his sleeve, and he showed us he still had it. He could make things happen. It gave us confidence that coach Bryant was back fully engaged, and that set the tone for the year.

Our last game of the year was against Auburn. We were both undefeated. And I didn't know if I was going to get to play. My Auburn friends think we staged the injury, but it was real. In fact, it still hurts. I dislocated my toe against LSU and didn't play against Miami. It was the most painful injury I ever had; you couldn't put an ounce of weight on it.

There is no way I can adequately express my admiration—my love—for coach Jim Goostree, our trainer, for the work he did in those three weeks between the time I was injured and the Auburn game. He did a lot of experimenting with different types of plastic molds and lambskin and light foam to make a light cast. It had to have support, but it also had to have flex, or I wouldn't be able to run. I had treatment three times a day. And for an hour each night he would come to the dorm and rub cortisone onto my foot. We didn't want to inject it because that can cause damage, but it could be absorbed through the skin. He went beyond his job, and I'll never forget it. He was determined to give me a chance to play.

124

I wore a 10½ shoe on one foot and a size 12 on the other to accommodate the light cast on my toe. It was a little awkward. I couldn't run on Thursday before the game. We went to Birmingham for a walk-through Friday, and I didn't do anything. Then Saturday in pregame warm-ups it felt better.

I learned later there was some question about whether I would start. I always thought I would start, but I also thought after a play or two or three that I would be hurt.

I did start, and as I got more and more confident, the awkwardness of the big shoe and the pain seemed to be less of a problem. And it worked out great with us winning 31–7.

Johnny Musso was an All-American in 1970 and 1971, and SEC Player of the Year in 1971. He was also an Academic All-American and National Scholar-Athlete. He was named to the Alabama Team of the Century and was inducted into the College Football Hall of Fame in 2000.

TERRY ROWELL
NOSE GUARD
1969–1971

COACH BRYANT WAS JUST ABOUT TO MOVE FROM THE SMALL, quick men that he had been so successful with in the sixties to the bigger guys—still quick, but bigger. I was one of the last little ones to play on the line. I was about 5'10" and 175 to 180 pounds, and had been a running back in high school. But when I got to Alabama, I saw Johnny Musso and realized I wasn't going to be Alabama's running back. If I was going to play, I had to listen to the coaches to figure out how and where.

My motivation was the bench. I couldn't imagine not playing. In fact, I had decided if I wasn't going to play that I was going to quit and go join the Marines. I did go into the Marines Officer Training Program. I was 19 years old and bulletproof. The funny thing is, after I did finish at Alabama and went to go into the Marines, they wouldn't take me. My vision wasn't good enough.

I had actually played on the defensive line in high school at a nose position. I really didn't think about size, but I know coach Bryant thought about it. We were practicing blocking punts, maybe before the Auburn game. coach Donahue had me in. And we heard coach Bryant from the tower: "Keno, if you get that little man hurt, your ass is fired."

Coach Donahue—coach Bryant called him "Keno"—grabbed me by the belt and pulled me back. He said, "Turry Rowell"—he always said "Turry" not "Terry," and he always said both my names together, like one name,

"Turryrowell"—"Turry Rowell, get out of there." As if it were my idea to be in there.

One thing we players knew was that from that tower coach Bryant could see everything. He knew what was going on over every foot of the practice fields.

I had a special relationship with coach Donahue. I say special because I was probably a little more of a free spirit than he would have preferred, but we both knew when it was time to work. We stayed in touch up until he died. Long after I had played and after coach Donahue had finished coaching at Alabama, I was at a spring practice scrimmage at the stadium, and he was there. We sat up in the end zone to watch, and he was into it like he was still coaching and getting the team ready for a game. He was pointing out things about technique and alignment that I couldn't begin to see.

I can still remember how excited I was the first time I heard from Alabama. I was at Heidelberg High School, which was really Heidelberg School—grades 1–12 and about 600 students—and I was having some success as a running back and in track. I ran about a 10-second 100-yard dash. We ran in yards in those days. I tried to play basketball, but I usually fouled out in about three minutes.

126

At first I started hearing from the Mississippi schools. In those days Ole Miss was pretty good, and Mississippi State and Southern Miss were pretty weak. And then I got a letter from Alabama. It may have been a letter they sent to hundreds of high school players, but it was special to me.

We didn't have much in the way of facilities at Heidelberg, but I had gone up to Meridian a few times to work out there. Bob Tyler, who would later coach receivers at Alabama and would also coach at Mississippi State, was at Meridian. That's where I met George Ranager and David Bailey, who would be great receivers at Alabama.

My mother had gone to school at Ole Miss. But she went with me on my recruiting trip to Alabama. On the way home she said, "You'd be crazy to go anywhere but Alabama." And it was actually closer from my home to Alabama than it was to Ole Miss or State.

I have nothing but fond memories of my time at Alabama. I know they have had great teams at Alabama, national championships before I came and national championships after I was there. But I wouldn't swap places with anyone. With the exception of two or three players—Johnny Musso and John Hannah and Jeff Rouzie when he was healthy—we didn't have anything

At about 175 pounds, Terry Rowell (No. 57) was running-back size. But—motivated by not wanting to be on the bench—he was a fine nose guard, playing alongside the likes of 240-pound tackle Jeff Beard (No. 77).

resembling an NFL player. But we played hard. We were motivated. And we had the greatest coach of all time.

I think for the most part we did more than we were likely to have been thought capable of. That was because of our coaches, coach Bryant and, in my case, coach Donahue.

I remember beating Southern Cal to start the 1971 season and then beating Auburn at the end of that year. I was one of those guys who was always scared to death we were going to lose a game. I think the Auburn game that year was the only time I ever went into a game when I knew we were going to win. And that was when they had the Heisman Trophy winner (Pat Sullivan) and we didn't know if Johnny Musso was going to be able to play.

With the exception of the Nebraska game in the Orange Bowl—my final game and playing for the national championship—I thought we played with one heartbeat, which is not easy. We were all on the same page except for that one night. I have thought and thought and thought about that game. I've always wondered if we had played 10 times what would have happened. I know one thing. We couldn't have beaten Tuscaloosa High School that night. The losses stick with you.

I also remember the 1970 game against Southern Cal in Birmingham. It was bad enough that we lost the game badly. But what has made it worse is this myth about coach Bryant bringing Sam Cunningham to our dressing room and telling us, "This is what a football player looks like." That just didn't happen, and I don't know why anyone would say it did. I can imagine that coach Bryant went to Southern Cal's dressing room and congratulated them, and he may have said something to Cunningham there because Cunningham had a great game. But can you imagine coach Bryant bringing another player into our dressing room and telling John Hannah and Johnny Musso, "This is what a football player looks like"? Of course not. I will say that Cunningham doesn't say it happened. But he kind of dances around it. He doesn't deny it, either.

I lived in Tuscaloosa for awhile in the oil and gas business, but now I'm back in Heidelberg. Both my son and daughter are Alabama graduates, too. And I remain a big, big fan of the Crimson Tide.

Terry Rowell was a top performer for Alabama's undefeated 1971 team as he tied for the team lead in tackles for losses (9) and fumble recoveries (3) and led the Tide in primary tackles as a junior with 45.

JOHN HANNAH
OFFENSIVE GUARD
1970–1972

IT'S FUNNY HOW THINGS WORK OUT SOMETIMES. When I was in high school and being recruited, I gave serious thought to going to Southern Cal. My uncle, Bill Hannah, who had played at Alabama, was coaching at Cal State–Fullerton, and I thought if I went out there that I would have family. And the pro-style offense that Southern Cal ran appealed to me because my goal was to play in the NFL.

My brothers and I were aware of my father's career at Alabama and with the New York Giants, and we were proud of him for that, even though he never talked about it. He was and is a big Alabama fan. I'm not sure it would be fair to say that he pushed me to Alabama, but I'm also not sure it would be fair to say the decision was completely mine. Maybe it was a joint thing. But I had grown up an Alabama fan, and I think I went with that loyalty.

I had gone to Baylor School in Chattanooga my first three years, then transferred back to Albertville High School in my hometown for my senior year. Before I did, I checked with Steve Sloan, who had been recruiting me, to make sure I would still be recruited if I was at Albertville, and he assured me I would be.

But things go around. I didn't go to Southern Cal. And the two games Alabama played against Southern Cal are two of the most memorable I have. The first in 1970 was awful when they shellacked us in Birmingham. The

John Hannah is considered the finest offensive lineman in the history of football. After an All-American career at Alabama, he was an All-Pro performer for the Patriots. He is the son and nephew of former Tide players, and both his brothers were Tide football players.

second was in 1971 in Los Angeles when we beat them and got Alabama's program turned back around.

Now I am back at Baylor as director of football development. This is something I always wanted to do but didn't feel that I could afford to do until my children were grown. And it's great to be back in the South. My son, Seth, is in the Highway Patrol in Alabama. There were nice things about Massachusetts, where I stayed after my pro career ended in 1985, but you are pretty much isolated from former Alabama teammates. I did enjoy the opportunity to work with some high school football teams there.

Steve Sloan, who recruited me when I was at Baylor and who is one of the finest men I know, is also in Chattanooga now, athletics director at Tennessee-Chattanooga.

All during my playing career, I had the opportunity to be around a lot of great coaches, and they taught me important lessons. Everything I learned in football allowed me to achieve success in other areas. It's not just athletics, of course. I believe in the Greek philosophy of mind, body, and spirit. If one part is missing, the others don't work. You've got to have all three to be a winner.

When people discuss accomplishments, I tell them I trace all of mine to Major Luke Worsham. He's deceased now, but his wife is still in Chattanooga. He was my mentor at Baylor. He coached me in football, wrestling, and track and field. He decided to turn me into something.

I think I flourished as an athlete under Chuck Fairbanks with the Patriots. He was a quiet kind of guy with a different leadership methodology. He had an open door policy and he would listen to your point of view.

I never had a comfort level with coach Bryant. Even after I was in pro ball, I wasn't one of those who was close to him. We had an arm's length relationship because I was so scared of the man. I didn't talk to him much except when I needed his permission to do something. My relationship with him was mostly just looking up in the tower and knowing he was there.

That is not a criticism of coach Bryant. I know it was special to play for him. The biggest thing he gave me was the ability to see what I could do, which was more than I thought I could. He drove me to play harder, to practice harder than my opponent. I needed that experience. I needed coach Bryant to give me discipline and hard work. I respect, honor, and love what coach Bryant did for me.

131

But I had to get out of that environment of fear to become the best athlete I could be.

When I was growing up, my father encouraged me and my brothers, Charley and David, in athletics, but he didn't push us. In fact, he never coached us. I was four years older than Charley and six years older than David, which is a lot when you are a teenager, so we were never able to play together. When I was in the pros, I got to play against Charley once when he was at Oakland and once when he was at Tampa Bay.

When I was at Boston, David got to come up for training camp and work as a ball boy. He got a lot of instruction on offensive line play from us players and coaches. But then he went back to Alabama and they moved him to the defensive line.

I wasn't able to get to any Alabama games when they were playing except for a couple of bowl games, but I did get to watch them on television.

Jimmy Sharpe was my position coach at Alabama, and he was always a real positive coach. He gave us a lot of confidence. I had a good relationship with him. It's funny because he was still coaching from the perspective of the little offensive linemen that Alabama had used in the sixties. Jim Krapf and I were in the first era of the big offensive linemen, and coach Sharpe's technique was still based on guys who were 190 or 200 pounds. That wasn't negative; just different. I weighed about 255 when I went to Alabama and played at about 260, which would be small by today's standards. We weighed every day. Coach Bryant wanted us lean and mean, and there's a lot to be said for that.

We went to the wishbone offense my junior year, which was great for winning. It's hard for me to say if I would have gone to Alabama if they had been in the wishbone when I signed. Although a lot of good college teams were in the wishbone about that time, and there were some offensive linemen going from the wishbone to the NFL, I never did feel comfortable in pass protection in pro ball because I hadn't learned it in college. It was a big transition. I was behind all the other guys who had come from pass-oriented teams. On the other hand, there is no doubt it helped me in run blocking.

We won a lot of games my last two years. You don't really remember the games you were supposed to win and did win. You remember the games that were really good or really bad. The bad ones were the Southern Cal game in 1970, the Nebraska game in 1971, and the Auburn and Texas games in 1972.

I think the Nebraska game in the Orange Bowl is a game we might have won if it had been played a day earlier. You have to learn from the losses, and I think a lesson from that game was that you have to be consistent in the approach, not have highs and lows. I think we learned in the Auburn game that you can't play not to lose, or you probably will. I think if we had attacked, kept our offense wide open, those blocked punts would have been of no consequence.

But you have to look at what caused you to lose. If you were doing the best you could and the other side just has better players, that's one thing. But if it's something you could have done to change the outcome, you have to learn from that.

We had disappointments, but we also had huge victories. The win over Southern Cal was the biggest. But I also remember the Auburn game when Pat Sullivan was the Heisman Trophy winner and we were both undefeated, and we beat them pretty good. Also, the Tennessee game in Knoxville when we came back to win with just a couple of minutes to play and Steve Bisceglia had a big game is one I remember.

132

But the biggest thing you remember is the relationships you developed and the friendships you made with your teammates. Even though I may not stay in touch that much, there is still that bond. I hope now that I'm back in the South, I will be more in touch.

We had great players like Johnny Musso and Jim Krapf and real characters like Bearcat Brown, Wayne Hall, Steve Bisceglia, and Joe LaBue. It was just a great bunch of guys like John Croyle and Steve Sprayberry and on and on and on. I think about them all the time and what they meant to me.

John Hannah has been called the greatest offensive lineman of all time. He was a two-time All-American, selected to Alabama's Team of the Century and ESPN's all-time college football team, was a nine-time All-Pro selection, was inducted into the Pro Football Hall of Fame in 1991 and the College Football Hall of Fame in 1999. He also lettered as a heavyweight wrestler and as a shot-put and discus man in track and field.

JOHN CROYLE
DEFENSIVE END
1971–1973

MAYBE IT WAS BECAUSE I HAD JUST SEEN THE MOVIE *They Shoot Horses, Don't They?* that I had a little moment of panic. I had been working at wide receiver in practice my freshman year. I was running a drill and planted my foot. My knee started to separate about the time Robin Parkhouse hit it. When everything was over, my leg was just swinging. Every ligament but one was torn. Coach Bryant came over and looked at it and said, "What a waste." I thought they were going to shoot me.

Most people would say that was a bad time. But when I remember the good things about playing football at Alabama, I also remember the bad parts as being good. After that injury, I went to work. And I kept working and working. And then one day I knew I was going to make it back. Coach Goostree [trainer Jim Goostree] was watching me work out. He said, "It looks like you know what you're doing." That's when I knew I would make it. And I was lucky to play on football teams that won a lot of games. We just lost one regular season game and we were 32–4 and won a national championship.

As bad as the injury in 1970 may have seemed at the time, it taught me how to work. And that has helped me as I have carried on with children, including my biological children. It made me learn to persevere. And the rewards were getting back up and having a chance to play, and having coach Bryant say, "Good job." That's a rush.

I know I'm only known now as Brodie's father. But I took positive experiences out of my Alabama playing career. And with Brodie having been injured, I have seen how he has learned to work. One day when he's grown, he'll know he has to get up and go to work.

Before every ball game, coach Bryant would look at us and say, "In this game there will be four or five plays that will determine the outcome. You never know when they are coming. It's up to you if you'll be a winner or the goat on those plays." And that's the way it is in life. There are four or five plays in your life. One of mine was God using coach Bryant to mold me into a man and making me a part of his family.

I knew for a long time I wanted to play for Alabama and coach Bryant. When I was a sophomore in high school and on the basketball team for coach John Bostick at Gadsden, we went to the state tournament in Tuscaloosa. At that age I was already about 6'4" and 195. A family friend, Dr. John Duncan, told me he wanted to introduce me to someone, and took me to the athletics offices. There was coach Bryant. He said, "Hey, son," and that was the beginning of my devotion and commitment to him and to the university. I was immediately aware of his charisma, his mystique, and it only grew with the passing of time.

Three of my high school football coaches—Gerald Stephens, Clark Boler, and Ingram Culwell—had played for coach Bryant, which helped sell me, too. And I was recruited by Dude Hennessey.

135

But it was coach Bryant. He had "it." Alabama had a couple of down years in 1969 and 1970. Coach Bryant admitted later he had some distractions in that time. But we could just tell that things were about to get better. Think about the coaches—Ken Donahue, Dude Hennessey, Pat Dye, and Bill Oliver on defense; Mal Moore, John David Crow, Richard Williamson, Jack Rutledge, and Jimmy Sharpe on offense. Coach Bryant talked about surrounding yourself with winners, and he did.

He also had a gift. Not motivating people, although he was good at that, but finding motivated people and directing them. The great ones— Namath, Stabler—were strong characters, and it took a strong character to lead them.

In our first meeting he told us, "Don't tell me how good you are. Just go with me and win championships." And in September 1971 we went to Los Angeles and beat No. 1-ranked Southern Cal. Everyone knows we surprised

John Croyle was an outstanding defensive end who had to overcome severe injuries. His son, Brodie, was an Alabama quarterback, and his daughter, Reagan, an Alabama basketball player and homecoming queen. John is best known now for his work with abused children.

them with the wishbone, but it was coaching and those intangibles you can't measure that made it possible.

We feared coach Bryant. But I think you sometimes fear a person before you respect him. And he certainly had everyone's respect. He had an ability to get average guys to believe they could beat anyone in the country. I was just average, but he'd say things to me that would convince me I could run through a wall.

And he genuinely cared about each of us as a person. I had talked to him about what I wanted to do with my life, having a ranch for kids. He said, "When I left Arkansas, I tried to forget everything I knew about farming. I can't help you." But, of course, he did help.

I was 19 when I came up with the idea for a farm or ranch or something to help the children that no one else will help. I had worked at a summer camp in Mississippi. I met a boy whose mother was a prostitute in New Orleans and he handled her business. I taught the boy how to become a Christian. And he did. And he came back and told me; and I realized I had been given a gift to help kids who are hurting—to be a father figure, to guide them.

One year the Skywriters came to Tuscaloosa, and I was one of the ones being interviewed by these writers from all over the South. Someone asked me what I wanted to do, and I told them—build a home for kids. I remember Clyde Bolton of *The Birmingham News* was very skeptical. Now he's one of our staunchest supporters.

After my Alabama career was over, I told coach Bryant I wanted to play pro football so I could earn the money to have the ranch. He knew I wasn't good enough to play pro football. But he told me not to do it unless I wanted to be married to it. He told me to follow my dream.

You don't really know how you are going to do something sometimes. I had gone with Woodrow Lowe on a speaking engagement. When we got back, my father said he wanted me to see something. It was 140 acres for sale for $45,000. Dr. William Buck, an oral surgeon in Birmingham, gave me $15,000, and John Hannah took his signing bonus and gave me $30,000. Our first house was the John Hannah Home. We would not be where we are without John Hannah.

Originally, the only plan was for a boys ranch. Then we met a 12-year-old girl whose mother had held her down while her father raped her. We wanted to keep her, but we had to send her home. She was murdered.

Now we have the girls ranch. And we were given a school that is midway between the boys ranch and the girls ranch. We operate without state or federal funds, and we are debt-free. We have more than 100 children who call the Big Oak Ranch their home. In 31 years we have had more than 1,500 children. A number have gone to college. These are people who just needed a chance. Our first child is now more than 50 years old.

When I was 24, I went to coach Bryant and asked for three things: I wanted him to write a letter of endorsement; I wanted him to serve on our advisory board; and I wanted to build a Paul Bryant Home that was going to cost $70,000. He said OK to one and two, and "let's see" to number three.

Six days before he died, I went to see coach Bryant. He wanted to know if a guy had sent me $1,000. I said he had. The man had asked coach Bryant to sign a sweatshirt, and said if coach would do it he would send $1,000 to the Big Oak Ranch. That check was the last $1,000 we needed to build the Paul Bryant Home.

There is not a day that goes by that I don't use something I got from him. In business, or dealing with a boy who is being cantankerous, or hugging a little girl who just needs a chance. In your life you are going to impress, impact, or inspire. He was master of all three and best at the last. And that's the one that lasts. That's the one that lasts when you are gone. That's anywhere—on a football field, in business, or in a children's home.

I wanted to be someone in football. But I know if you are a great football player, but a loser inside, you haven't done anything. Coach Bryant was one who molded football players into men. I wasn't a football legend, but I wouldn't trade places with anyone I know. Being a legend might have been fun, but I would rather have helped a 10-year-old boy who had no other chance.

I have never been depressed and never had a second thought or second guess about what I do. And coach Bryant saw that for me before I did.

When I was at Alabama, we all lived together in Bryant Hall, and I think that made us a family. And I see and talk to my former teammates often. I know the guys today have more freedom, but I think there was something to be said for living in the dorm and building team unity.

I can't tell you how many of those men I played with have helped us in our efforts to save children. And if you want to help, you can do so by contacting Big Oak Ranch, P.O. Box 507, Springville, AL 35146.

John Croyle was winner of the "Jerry Duncan I Like to Practice Award" in 1972 and went on to earn second team All-SEC the following season at defensive end.

WILBUR JACKSON

HALFBACK

1971–1973

IT SEEMS TO SURPRISE EVERYONE THAT NO ONE EVER MENTIONED to me when I was being recruited that I would be the first black football player to sign with Alabama. If it ever came up, I don't remember it. I remember a few years ago talking to Chuck Strickland, who was captain with me on our 1973 team, and telling him that it had been tough on me, so tough that I thought about quitting. He laughed and said, "We all thought about quitting because it was so tough."

I felt as though I was treated just like everyone else, and I also felt that is how it should have been. I didn't want anything given to me because I was black, but I didn't want anything taken away from me, either. As far as I could tell, I was treated no differently than any other player. It was a tough experience on the field, but it was tough on everyone. But when I had success, it meant everyone on the team had success. And when someone else had success, so did I.

I guess the closest thing anyone ever said about me being first was during a recruiting trip to Tuscaloosa. I came up for three games, and each time there were 75 to 80 guys on the sidelines. After the game we'd go to the dressing room. On one of those trips, coach Bryant had all the prospects at his house. He pulled me aside, took me into a separate room, and told me if I would come to Alabama, he'd make me the best wide receiver in the nation. Alabama wasn't running the wishbone yet, and I was recruited as a wide receiver.

He said if I ever had any problems to go see him—no one else—and he'd make sure everything was taken care of. I guess that might have been about me being black.

When we were growing up, we had two channels on television, and on Sunday afternoons we watched the Alabama and Auburn highlights. So I was watching *The Bear Bryant Show* each week, and I knew he was very well known nationally, as well as in the state, of course. So when he told me things were going to be fine, I believed they were going to be fine.

I played at an all-black high school, T. A. Smith, in Ozark until my senior year. Dexter Wood and Ellis Beck from Carroll High in Ozark had signed with Alabama in 1969, and I signed in 1970. We hadn't played together in high school, but it helped me that they were here. And we had guys from Dothan and Troy and Elba. They were all white, but we were all from the same area and had a good connection.

I didn't have a car, but if I needed to go somewhere, I could always catch a ride with a teammate or even borrow a car. And when I see one of my old teammates now, even if it has been years since we've seen each other, it is like we were just together.

When I played pro football, I found out I had a lot of other teammates, too.

I never thought about playing professionally until my junior year when I got a letter from the Dallas Cowboys. But my goal was to play football for Alabama and to get an education. As it turned out, I did get that professional football opportunity. One thing I learned is that it was a lot easier to play pro ball than it was to play at Alabama. The Alabama practices were a lot tougher than the games. And we were winning. I wondered sometimes what the practices would be like if we were losing. But, of course, it paid off.

The other thing was the camaraderie of former Alabama players, coach Bryant players. When we'd finish a game, guys on other teams like Lee Roy Jordan and Kenny Stabler, who had played before me at Alabama, would make it a point to come and talk to me after the game. And later I'd talk to guys who came after me, Barry Krauss and E. J. Junior and Curtis McGriff, who was from the same area I was, but I didn't know him until we were both in the NFL.

What we talked about was what was going on in Tuscaloosa. We had all played for coach Bryant and we were tough. We all have our own story to tell, but ask anyone who played for coach Bryant and ask about poise and pride and you'll get the same answer. We have a common bond based on

Wilbur Jackson (No. 80) was recruited as a wide receiver, but became an outstanding running back in Alabama's wishbone offense. This 80-yard touchdown run broke Tennessee's back as the Tide scored three fourth-quarter touchdowns in a 42–21 win in 1973.

what we had gone through and what the university and coach Bryant had meant to us.

And I'm sure the guys playing now have that Crimson Tide bond.

I was recruited by coach Dye. Because the guys at T. A. Smith were going to move over to Carroll the next year, my senior year, we went through spring practice at Carroll in 1969. Coach Dye had come down to check on Ellis and Dexter, I believe, and the coach at Carroll, Tom McClendon, showed coach Dye a jamboree film of me. Coach McClendon brought coach Dye over to T. A. Smith to meet me. He checked on my transcript.

The next year we opened the season against Montgomery Lee, and coach Dye was there. He was also looking at some Lee guys, Paul Spivey and John Rogers, who both signed with Alabama. He talked to me after the game.

Coach Dye had the recruiting area, but Joe Kelley, who was from Ozark, was a graduate assistant, and he came down a lot, too.

All our teams at Alabama were good, but the 1973 team my senior year was really good. We lost to Notre Dame in the Sugar Bowl 24–23, which was a shame. Notre Dame made the plays to win and you have to credit them, but we were probably the best team in the country. We didn't lose many games, and I certainly remember the big wins over Auburn and Tennessee and Georgia.

After I finished playing pro ball, I came back to Ozark, where I have owned a commercial janitorial service for the past 20 years. And even in that I think about coach Bryant's lessons. His pregame speech might change a little, but it was always the same in talking about pride and poise and confidence. He said to have a plan for everything. He said, "If you get behind, are you going to fight back, or are you going to fold your tent." Those things have stuck with me about always doing my best.

Wilbur Jackson was an All-SEC halfback in 1973 and was captain of the national championship team as a senior. He is the Alabama career leader in yards per rush, 7.2 yards per carry with 1,529 yards on 212 rushes. He was one of four backs to rush for more than 100 yards in the same game for one team, an NCAA record. He played professional football in San Francisco and Washington. The 1983 Super Bowl was his final game.

JOHN MITCHELL

DEFENSIVE END

1971–1972

GROWING UP IN MOBILE, I KNEW ALL ABOUT ALABAMA and the great foot-ball stars like Joe Namath and Lee Roy Jordan. I knew all about the great wins and the national championships. I watched Alabama when they were on television and listened to the games on radio and watched *The Bear Bryant Show* on Sundays. Any kid would have wanted to go there.

But I couldn't go to Alabama. Alabama was not recruiting African-American players when I finished high school at Williamson in 1969. And if they had been, I probably would not have been the one they would have taken because I was kind of a skinny kid.

I did have a chance to go to Alabama. I was part of the science fair team at our school, five little African-American kids. And we won our local and state competitions and went to South Carolina for a competition and won there. And all five of us had academic scholarship offers to Alabama and to Auburn. And none of us accepted. Two went to Tuskegee and two to Alabama State.

I wanted to play football, so I went to Eastern Arizona Junior College, where I got bigger and better. And I had my choice of a lot of schools when I finished after the 1970 season. I finally decided on Southern Cal. I made a recruiting visit there, and my hosts were Sam Cunningham and Charles Young. I met O. J. Simpson. And I really liked it. Coach John McKay had a great program, and I was excited about playing there.

Alabama didn't cross my mind. I didn't know Alabama had signed Wilbur Jackson in 1970. I thought Alabama was still all-white. I graduated in December and was back in Mobile when I got a call from Judge Ferrill McRae, an Alabama alumnus in Mobile. Alabama was interested in me. It seems that coach McKay had told coach Bryant they were going to sign an Alabama boy who was playing at Eastern Arizona. Coach Bryant got on the phone to coach Gryska and told him to recruit me. They never even saw a film of me. Coach Gryska and coach Riley recruited me strictly on the basis that, if Southern Cal wanted me, I must be good enough.

I also realized my family had never seen me play in Arizona and would probably never see me play if I went to Southern Cal. But by my going to Alabama, they could drive up to Birmingham or Tuscaloosa and see me play. I really thought about that later when, after the first home game, I walked out of the dressing room and saw my parents waiting for me. It was one of the biggest moments in my life, and I know they were so happy to be able to see their son play for Alabama.

It's ironic that my first Alabama game was at Southern Cal. As it turned out, I played in the game before Wilbur did, so I became the first black player to play football for Alabama. I never felt like anything except a part of the team. I had to work my way up the depth chart to get a chance to be a starter. Coach Bryant got on me the same way he would any other player. And I was certainly aware that Alabama had been good before I got there, and I knew that Alabama would be good in the future. Whether John Mitchell played and whether John Mitchell was the first black player was not a major effect on Alabama football.

Southern Cal had beaten Alabama badly the year before, and for us to go to Los Angeles and beat them was very, very big. I can still remember when we recovered a fumble late in the game to clinch the victory. That was about as happy as I had ever been.

Lynn Swann was a great player on that Southern Cal team and a great player for the Pittsburgh Steelers. We live in the same neighborhood and see each other. I never let him forget that game.

Richard Williamson was my position coach. His father died that week, so he didn't go to Los Angeles with us, and I didn't know if he would be there. He was a great coach and I really relied on him. I had come from a junior college where we had three or four coaches total. At Alabama every position

John Mitchell could have gone to Alabama on an academic scholarship, but 'Bama was not signing African-American football players when he finished high school. He went to junior college, then played and coached for Alabama.

had its own coach. About 15 minutes before we were to go out, coach Williamson stuck his head in the dressing room. That says a lot about him and how much he cared for his players. I still see him because he's coaching at Carolina and I'm coaching at Pittsburgh, and we play each other.

I got to Alabama in the summer before all the players checked in, and they put me in a room in Bryant Hall. Later my roommate, Bobby Stanford, showed up. Bobby was white and from Georgia, and we became and remain the best of friends. His parents would come up, and if they brought him something, they brought me something. His father is gone now, but his mother, Frances, is still the same wonderful woman who kissed her son good-bye and then kissed me good-bye when they left.

Every player has memories of his favorite game. Mine has to be the 1972 game in Knoxville. We were not playing well and Tennessee had a 10–0 lead at halftime. Luckily, we had played well on defense or it would have been worse. But we scratched out a field goal and our defense kept playing well. Finally, we broke through for a touchdown and tied the game with a minute or two to play. A few plays later, Mike DuBose knocked the ball loose and I recovered it. Terry Davis ran it in and we won 17–10.

146

One thing that makes that game so memorable is the halftime. Coach Bryant never ranted and raved at halftime. When he came in, we had long faces and he just said, "Get those frowns off." Then he let the coaches teach us. And before we went back out he said, "You're Alabama. They have to beat you." No one beat us very often.

I had graduated in December after the 1972 season. I was in Mobile and called coach Bryant to see if my scholarship would extend to going to graduate school because my parents couldn't afford it. He said he wouldn't talk to me about it on the phone. So I drove up on a Wednesday to talk to him. I hoped he would give me some little graduate assistant position and pay for my school. Instead he said he was offering me a full-time job on his staff and asked if I would take it. I said, "Yes, sir." And he said, "Well, then, get to work."

I got a room in the dorm and had to wash the clothes I had worn every night because I hadn't brought any more clothes. That weekend I went back to Mobile for my clothes. Every day I look at my 1973 national championship ring that I got while coaching.

Back in the midnineties, we started a little reunion of players who were on the 1971 and 1972 teams. It started with Bobby Stanford, Jimmy Rosser,

Ed Hines, Johnny Musso, Jack White, and me in Jacksonville, Florida. Now we meet every other year in Gulf Shores and have about 50 guys show up.

I don't know if any of them have a greater appreciation for Alabama than I do. I was a little African-American kid who knew nothing and who was nurtured by and learned from coach Bryant. He gave me my opportunity. Any success I have had I owe to him. There is no way I could ever repay The University of Alabama.

John Mitchell started all 24 games in his Alabama career as the Tide compiled a 21–3 record and won two SEC titles. He was a two-time All-SEC player and All-American in 1972 and captain of the 1972 team. He is defensive line coach for the Pittsburgh Steelers.

WAYNE WHEELER

SPLIT END

1971–1973

ITHINK THE MOST AMAZING THING ABOUT HAVING PLAYED football at Alabama is the recognition. Alabama people never forget. I was on a ski trip in Aspen, Colorado, a few years ago when someone came up to me and said, "Didn't you play football at Alabama?" It was amazing. And I think most Alabama people remember me for one play, the opening play of the 1973 game against Tennessee in Birmingham. We were both undefeated, and it was a big game.

Coach Bryant set the play up. We had opened every game that year with a dive play out of the wishbone. Gary Rutledge was our quarterback, and before the game coach Bryant told him and me that we were going to throw it on the first play of the game. I was wide open, and we had an 80-yard touchdown to start the game.

We went on to an 11–0 season that year and won the UPI national championship. But then we lost a one-point game to Notre Dame in the Sugar Bowl. That was a heartbreaker. That was the best team we had while I was there. Losing that game left us with kind of a hollow feeling. You don't feel like national champions when you don't win the last game.

Playing football at Alabama was the best experience of my life. I never had one regret since the day I chose Alabama. My family and everyone else didn't really want me to go out of state, so I kind of went against everyone when I

Wayne Wheeler had an outstanding career as the wide receiver in Alabama's wishbone offense.

signed with Alabama, but for me, it was the best decision I've ever made. It was everything I expected it to be, and I played with the greatest players and coaches I could have ever asked for.

I grew up in Florida and always thought I would be going to the University of Florida, but a guy who played on my team the year before, Robin Parkhouse, went to Alabama, and then they recruited Steve Dean and me. As soon as I made the trip up there, I decided to go to Alabama. I didn't even make any more trips. Parkhouse told me, "If you want to win a championship, come here." I was sold. That's what I wanted to do, and that's why I went to Alabama.

At that time I really didn't know about the Alabama tradition. I learned it as I was there. But I could tell it was the type of program that I had been accustomed to playing in. What I thought was important was what they thought was important. I came from a high school program that was relatively successful. We had some good athletes. Basically, anything but first was not good enough.

Those of us who went to Alabama from the Orlando area had been raised a bit different than the Alabama boys. We were probably a little more liberal and a little more into freedom. We were more free-spirited and less conformist, but that wasn't going to cut it at Alabama. Coach Bryant wanted us the same. We might not have wanted to accept that at first, but I think that had a lot to do with us winning. We didn't have any individuals. Johnny Musso, for example, could have been a Heisman Trophy winner, but he wasn't left in the game if he wasn't needed.

At the time, I didn't always agree with everything coach Bryant did, but he was probably right, and I respected the man. I felt like he was doing what he felt was best for us. I think coach Bryant was like a father. He expected things of us that our own families would expect, and I think that carries over into life after football—in what's important to you, how you look at things morally, and everything else. I think as you get older, you realize it more and more. It's kind of funny because I was a kid when I signed with Alabama, and I didn't start to realize I had been learning life lessons at Alabama until probably 10 years later.

During my redshirt year in 1970, I practiced on the scout team. We had a pretty decent team to go against the varsity. One day I was running a deep post route, and I caught the ball and literally did get the post, meaning I ran into it full speed. When I came to, coach Bryant was down there with me, and he had been in his tower when this happened. That said something to me because he could have very easily had other people take care of that, but he was down on the field himself. Not all coaches will do that. Not all coaches will care about you that much.

I always felt like Alabama was kind of the underdog in the eyes of the country, even though it shouldn't have been that way. I always felt like we were underrated compared to some of the teams like Notre Dame and Ohio State and Southern Cal, and maybe they did have some bigger name players. But we got the job done as a team. I think that's a big factor in Alabama football having always been so good.

We never felt like we were going to lose. That's how it was the whole time I was there. It wasn't because we were so good. It was just an attitude. I can remember playing against Kentucky. They were beating us at halftime by a couple of touchdowns. We came out after the half, and you could just see it on everyone's face, "Well, we've got to go to work." We ended up beating them by a couple of touchdowns. It was an attitude that we just couldn't be beaten. It didn't always hold true, but it did for the most part. That's probably a feeling that very few people get to experience in a lifetime, that kind of total confidence.

I tried pro football for a while after finishing at Alabama, but I don't have a very pleasant memory of it. I was at Tampa Bay, where John McKay was the coach. One of the wide receiver candidates was his son, J. K. McKay. They cut me and kept the coach's son.

Coach McKay was nothing like coach Bryant. Coach Bryant may have been hard, but he cared for his players and wanted us to do well.

Maybe I wasn't cut out for pro football. I played football because I liked it. Playing for money is a whole different game. The motivation is different. I'm a teacher now, so obviously money is not a big issue with me.

I'm pretty much out of athletics except for helping coach a girls high school track team and teaching physical education. I fell out of a deer stand a few years ago and broke my ankle. All those years of football without a major injury, and I fell out of a tree. But I still hunt and fish and play golf.

I haven't been able to make it up for any Alabama games in a few years. My wife has had health problems, and I do a lot of caring for her. But I will never forget those wonderful years as a Crimson Tide football player.

Wayne Wheeler was an All-American on the 1973 national championship team and was selected to the Team of the Decade. He averaged 22.7 yards per reception for his career on 55 receptions, including 27.9 yards per catch as a senior.

WOODROW LOWE
LINEBACKER
1972–1975

When people ask me why I went to Alabama instead of Auburn when I lived in Phenix City, just a few miles from Auburn, I have a simple answer. We had a flat tire. Auburn had invited me to a game, and I was going over with a buddy. But we had a flat tire, didn't have a spare, and had to hitchhike back to Phenix City to get help. I never made it to the Auburn game, and I never even met the Auburn coach who was supposed to be recruiting me.

I was being recruited by Pat Dye and Dude Hennessey for The University of Alabama. But I really wasn't that highly recruited. I didn't sign until about a month after everyone else had signed.

When I first started hearing from Alabama, my coach told me about Lee Roy Jordan. I went to the library and was able to do some research and found out what a great player he had been at Alabama, and that motivated me to want to be an Alabama linebacker.

And, of course, I knew what a great coach Paul Bryant was. And when I got there, I found out he was a lot greater than I suspected. One thing he talked about was character, and looking back, I can see we didn't have any players who weren't of high character. He talked to us about hard work, sacrifice, having confidence. He really stressed believing in yourself and how putting on that crimson jersey epitomized confidence. And he talked about

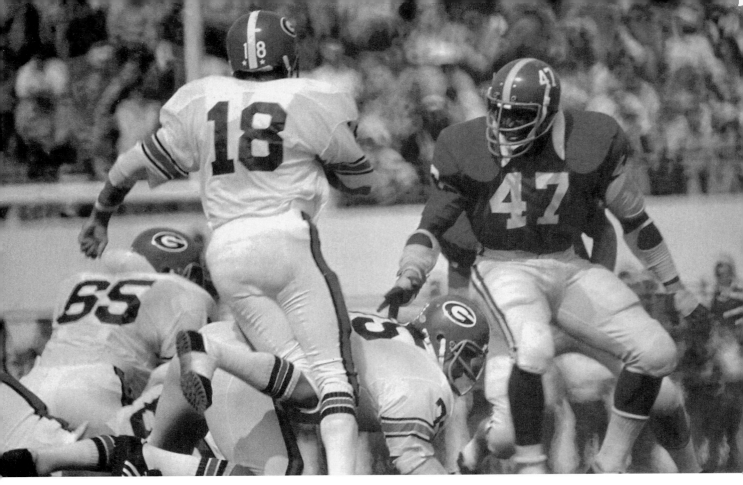

Woodrow Lowe (No. 47) earned his first of three All-American citations as a sophomore in 1973 as the Crimson Tide went undefeated in regular-season play and won a national championship.

team, that no one person was bigger than the team. We had some stars, but I don't think even they knew it at the time.

I think it says something about Alabama that there has never been a Heisman Trophy winner, but there have been 12 Alabama teams that have been national champions. That speaks to team.

I think another key to success was that we never were down for long. If we had a setback, we bounced back. And we did it with sacrifice, hard work, and discipline. You're never far off from getting back on your feet if you know how to tighten your belt and get back to work.

It wasn't easy. It was an ordeal. But when you succeed, you have pride. I knew that I had been given the training and preparation to do whatever was necessary. That isn't conceit. But I was made to be confident that I was as good as anyone. We all know people who talk a good game. Coach Bryant and his staff taught us to play a good game. He told us when we made a good play to act like we were used to doing that. We didn't have to show out. We didn't have to tell anyone about it. If we were good enough, someone would tell us about it. And that is true.

I also believe I developed another trait. I didn't make much of an effort to get to Auburn after we had that flat tire back in 1971. But at the end of my career when we were about to play Penn State in the Sugar Bowl, I had to display great effort. And not in the game.

I went down to the lobby of the hotel to pay my incidentals because we checked out before the game. The university paid for our rooms and meals, but if we had phone calls or something like that, we had to pay for it ourselves. It was just a few dollars, but we had to take care of it before we left the hotel.

I could see the bus outside as I stood in line to pay my bill. Suddenly the bus started to move. I knew my bill wasn't very much, but I had a twenty dollar bill in my hand and just gave it to the cashier with my key and took off running. Some of the players and even a couple of coaches saw me, and I could see they were laughing. I thought I would be in trouble, but I knew I would be in more trouble if I was late getting to the stadium. I just kept running. I was wearing my crimson blazer and a tie and felt like O. J. Simpson running through the airport in that television commercial that was popular at the time. Except I was running through the streets of New Orleans trying to catch the team bus. The bus would stop for a light, but just as I thought I might get to it, the light would change and off it would go again.

Fortunately, it wasn't very far to the Superdome. When the bus pulled up, I was pretty close to it. The players started coming off the bus, and I just mingled in with them. And I went out and played one of my best games, and we defeated Penn State. I don't know if coach Bryant ever knew about me missing the bus. I think he probably did.

I had a lesson reinforced that day. I knew there were two time zones at Alabama. Central Time and Coach Bryant Time, and Coach Bryant Time was 15 minutes earlier.

I was fortunate enough to play 12 years with the San Diego Chargers. I have coached at the high school level and at the pro level, and I'm now coaching special teams at UAB. In everything I've done, I've taken the lessons I learned at The University of Alabama. My brother, Eddie, followed me to Alabama; my son, Woodrow, was a student coach there.

One thing that was unique about coach Bryant was the way he stayed in touch with his former players. Each year before the start of the season, I'd get a telegram from him, a little note to let me know he was thinking about me and wishing me and the team good luck and reminding me to show class. I've got one of them framed and hanging in my house. I've talked to other former players like Joe Namath and Bob Baumhower, and he sent all of us those good luck notes at the beginning of every year. He never forgot his players, and no one who played for him will ever forget him.

Woodrow Lowe is one of two Alabama football players to be a three-time All-American, and he was also named Freshman All-America. He had 134 tackles for the 1973 national championship team. When he was drafted in the fifth round, coach Bryant said, "That's like getting a fifty-dollar gold piece for fifty cents." Lowe played 12 years in the NFL.

MIKE WASHINGTON

CORNERBACK

1972–1974

OVER THE YEARS I'VE HAD A LOT OF PEOPLE TELL ME THINGS that coach Bryant supposedly said, and a lot of them are things I never heard him say or say anything like. But I can tell you one thing he said. In our first meeting with him as freshmen in 1971 when there were only a few black players on the team, he told us that he didn't care who we were, he didn't care who our mama and daddy were, and he didn't care what color we were. He said we were going to get an education and we were going to play football—in that order. And he stuck to his promise. If you did what you were supposed to do in the classroom and on the football field, everything was fine. And, as I found out one day, if you didn't do the right thing, you found out about it.

I didn't think anything about it, but I've heard since that people were wondering how coach Bryant would treat a black player who needed his personal attention. They found out one day at my expense.

We all knew that if coach Bryant came out of the tower, he was coming to get someone, either a player or a coach. I was on the scout team, and we had Johnny Musso and John Hannah and all those big guys out there. They had run a sweep, and Steve Ford, a defensive back from Tuscaloosa, was playing cornerback. Hannah hit him and broke his leg. That moved me up to corner. Here came that sweep again, and when Hannah got close to me, I gave him one of those olé moves like a bullfighter, getting out of the way. And Musso ran for a touchdown.

There was a chain across the steps at the top of the tower, and when coach Bryant came down, the first thing you heard was that chain drop. We heard it and looked up, and he was coming down. And he could move. It seemed like he was going about 40 miles per hour. Everyone wondered about the victim. I was at right corner, the farthest of anyone from him. In a minute, he had passed everyone but me. I was the only one left.

I looked at coach Bryant coming. And I looked behind me where there was a fence separating me from the railroad tracks. And something was telling me, "You'd better hit that fence, because he's coming at you." But I also knew if I ran, my mama and grandmother would be waiting at home and that wasn't going to be too good, either.

He got to me and grabbed my facemask. And he was really strong. He twisted my little head like it was a pretzel. And every time he twisted he had something to say. The bottom line was that I had better get my butt in gear or I wouldn't have to run away. He would send me home. But he also told me I had too much talent to let it go to waste by wasting time in practice.

I had tears rolling down my eyes. And I know everyone who was there remembers the day. If there was ever any question about whether coach Bryant was going to treat everyone the same way, he answered it that day.

We had just integrated the high schools in Montgomery prior to my senior year in 1970, and I had been in a white school for only one year. Before that I had never thought about having the opportunity to play at Alabama or any other SEC school. To play for coach Bryant was far-fetched. But Richard Williamson started recruiting me for Alabama.

I had been at Booker T. Washington High School for two years and then moved to Robert E. Lee High School, and it was a big change, particularly in culture. One of my teammates, Ralph Stokes, was also recruited by Alabama, and we signed along with Sylvester Croom. They had signed Wilbur Jackson the year before; he was the first black football player, so we were breaking some barriers. We considered it an opportunity, not a chore. We thought we would have the chance to prove that we could perform athletically and academically with the white guys. That was important.

I had black people who told me I wouldn't have a chance at Alabama and white people who said we should go to a black school. It was a lot on a kid of 17.

Ralph and Sylvester and I got a head start because we played in the all-star game in Tuscaloosa a few weeks before the freshmen were to show up. Ralph

157

Mike Washington (No. 34) was an All-American cornerback who turned in eight career interceptions as 'Bama won one national championship and three SEC titles.

would be one of my roommates, and Sylvester would be another, and we are all still close. I'm an SEC official now, but I don't call Mississippi State games because of my friendship with Sylvester.

When we finally showed up at the dorm as Alabama students, we were out in front of Bryant Hall with guys like Jim Krapf and John Hannah, who were huge. And I weighed maybe 165 pounds soaking wet. Well, soaking wet were the operative words, I guess. One of the players said something to me and I kind of smarted off. It taught me you don't talk to upperclassmen like that. They threw me in the fountain that was in front of the dorm. And Ralph ran upstairs and locked the door to our room.

A few years ago, ESPN had a movie about coach Bryant at Texas A&M, *The Junction Boys*. People asked me if I saw it, and I did, but I told them I didn't have to see it. I lived it. He didn't take us out in the woods, but practices were tough.

Coach Bryant told us when we got there that a lot of us wouldn't make it, that guys would go to the bathroom and not come back. And I saw that happen three or four times. There were a lot of days I wanted to go home, but I felt a responsibility to take advantage of the opportunity the university had given me. I didn't want to disappoint my mother and grandmother and all the people who were rooting for us to make it.

As much as I wanted to leave sometimes, there were many more times that I was glad to be there. We were having a great time. We had a great run of winning football games. If I had it to do all over, I'd do it the exact same way.

Every year I was there, we won the SEC. We lost three bowls. I played in the Cotton Bowl, the Sugar Bowl, and the Orange Bowl. And other than in the Cotton Bowl, we were playing for the national championship. We were fortunate that they picked the national champion before the Sugar Bowl game in 1973 so we at least won one national championship. We had really good teams those three years.

I played pro ball after my Alabama career, but I never had the same feeling. At Alabama we always felt we were going to win. I was a good player, but we had a lot of great players. We had guys who didn't play much who would have started a lot of places, but they would rather have been at Alabama and playing for coach Bryant.

I started out at Baltimore in pro ball, but I was hurt my first year. I remember the first time it snowed, I called in and said I couldn't drive in the snow. They were upset with me. I wanted to be traded to Tampa Bay, which was an expansion team, but the Colts didn't put me on the list for the expansion draft. Later my lawyer called and said I had been traded to Tampa Bay. I was very happy to get out of the snow.

It was tough to win, especially as an expansion team. We finally made it to the NFC Championship Game, but lost to the Rams. I retired in 1985. I enjoyed playing at Alabama much more than I ever enjoyed pro football.

> Mike Washington was an All-American in 1974 and All-SEC in 1973 and 1974. He had eight interceptions for 98 yards and made 80 tackles. He blocked three field-goal attempts in 1973. He played nine years in the NFL.

RICHARD TODD

QUARTERBACK

1973–1975

WE HAD A REUNION OF OUR 1973 NATIONAL CHAMPIONSHIP TEAM a few years ago, and Randy Billingsley, who was a halfback on that team, greeted me by calling me "No Pitch Rich." That's funny, but I don't think it's true. I pitched the ball.

We just had so much talent. Coach Bryant substituted a lot and played so many people. That's why none of us built up a lot of individual statistics. But we didn't care. I'm sure that's why those teams had so much camaraderie.

It's a different time now. Teams just don't have that kind of depth. Our second-team players back then were as good as a lot of other teams' first-team players. And the reason is pretty simple. A lot of men wanted to play for coach Bryant.

That's the reason I was at Alabama. I first committed to Auburn. But after I thought about it, it just didn't make sense not to play for coach Bryant. He was the best coach in the country and had developed a lot of quarterbacks who had been successful. Plus, Alabama had one of the best teams in the country.

Alabama was running the wishbone, and other schools recruiting me said I wouldn't develop as a passer. But coach Bryant showed me how the wishbone could be a good passing offense.

As an example, when we played in the Sugar Bowl at the end of the 1975 season, Penn State was determined to stop the run, stacking the line. They were daring us to throw, and we did. It was a tough game. In the fourth quarter, we had a sweep called to the left, but I didn't like the play for their defense and called time out. I went over to coach Bryant. He kind of winked at me and called a pass. Ozzie Newsome was getting single coverage, and we threw a slant-and-go, a play we had used earlier in the year against Tennessee. It gained 55 yards, setting up the only touchdown, a Mike Stock run, and we won the game.

That was a big win for us. It was my last Alabama game, and we wanted to go out with a win. Alabama had lost—or at least failed to win, since there had been a tie in there—every bowl game since the 1966 team beat Nebraska in the 1967 Sugar Bowl. And we heard a lot about that. Also, it was the first Sugar Bowl game in the Superdome.

The previous two years we got to the bowl site just a couple of days before the game. We had lost in the Sugar Bowl and in the Orange Bowl to Notre Dame. So in 1975 coach Bryant decided to try something new. We went into New Orleans about a week before the game. The first couple of nights we didn't have curfew, and then we had a curfew. But nobody checked on us. So we figured when they had curfew the next night that no one would check. It was still two or three days until the game. And I think 26 of us missed curfew and got caught.

The next morning at breakfast, coach Bryant said, "I've been thinking about what I'm going to do. If it was one or two of you, I'd just send you home, kick you off the team. But I can't kick everyone off the team. So what I'm going to do is send your name and the time you were out to your hometown newspaper. So this year if we lose the bowl game, they won't blame me." And he did it. He sent the names of everyone who was late to their hometown newspapers. And it was in all the newspapers.

You think about him being a disciplinarian, and he was. What he did was not cripple the team, which wouldn't have been fair to the innocent players, but he made us accept responsibility for what we had done. That was a typical move for coach Bryant. I think that helped us win the game and break the long Alabama losing streak. We didn't want to be blamed for losing.

One other thing about coach Bryant was that he treated everyone fairly. There was no favoritism for any reason.

We had a lot of fun playing in those days. We had a great bunch of guys, excellent coaches, and we had really good teams. We were the premier team in the Southeastern Conference. We won the SEC championship every year I was there. It was fun to be able to do that at your state university.

Richard Todd (No. 14) was a wishbone quarterback who could hand off to a big fullback like Calvin Culliver (No. 33), pitch to a halfback, or keep it himself for a run or pass.

I think we understood then, and I know we understood later, that we were part of a great tradition by playing football for Alabama.

I think the one other thing that stood out alongside tradition was the emphasis on class, on doing things the right way.

And it was and is nice to be remembered as an Alabama football player.

After I finished at Alabama, I played professionally with the New York Jets and the New Orleans Saints. Joe Namath told the Jets they should take a look at me. He's really responsible for me being drafted by them. In 1983 I was traded to New Orleans. I was a little bitter. I felt they were saying they didn't believe they could win with me anymore. I had sort of been thrown to the wolves my first year, having to play a lot as a rookie, but the last two years I was in New York, we made it to the playoffs. Looking back, I'm no longer bitter about having been traded.

At one time I thought I might like to be a coach, but I realized I don't have the patience for that. I recognized that in watching my son, Gator, in his golf career. We were very proud that he signed a golf scholarship and is playing for the university. So now I'm closely following two Crimson Tide teams.

I live in Florence, but commute to Atlanta where I have been with Bear Stearns since retiring from pro football in 1985.

Richard Todd was captain of the 1975 Alabama team. In his final game, a 13–6 win over Penn State in the Sugar Bowl, he completed 10 of 12 passes for 205 yards and was named MVP. He played in the Senior Bowl and passed for 332 yards and two touchdowns. He was drafted by the New York Jets and played eight years with the Jets and two with New Orleans.

BOB BAUMHOWER
DEFENSIVE TACKLE
1974–1976

A COUPLE OF TIMES AT ALABAMA, I DIDN'T FEEL WANTED. I moved to Tuscaloosa as a senior in high school and had played only one year of football before that, so I wasn't catching anyone's eye. I did get a little better as the season went on and had a pretty good game in the playoffs against Banks, which I think got me my scholarship. But Alabama hadn't paid any attention to me. Auburn had me for a visit, but didn't make an offer. The only scholarship offer I had was from Vanderbilt.

Coach Charley Bradshaw, who had played for coach Bryant at Kentucky and coached at Alabama, was at Vanderbilt. I went up for a visit and decided to sign with them, but wanted to call home first. I called my mother and she said not to do anything, that the coaches from Alabama wanted to talk to me. I told coach Bradshaw what the situation was and that I felt I needed to talk to Alabama before I committed. He said he understood. And he said, "I don't think I'll be seeing you again."

I flew back to Tuscaloosa and there were about six Alabama coaches waiting to meet me. They said coach Bryant wanted to see me and took me straight to his office. He apologized for not having paid more attention to me and offered me a scholarship. Later I learned he had seen me when he was looking at film of an offensive lineman Alabama was recruiting and wanted to know about me.

Bob Baumhower was almost overlooked by Alabama recruiters, even though he played his senior year at Tuscaloosa High School. He went on to a stellar career for 'Bama and for the Miami Dolphins.

I have always been grateful I made that call home from Nashville. That is one of a number of times that coach Bryant affected my life in a positive way. People talk about remembering exactly what they were doing when President Kennedy was assassinated. I have perhaps a half dozen memories of events involving coach Bryant that are that clear, embedded that deeply in my mind.

For some reason, when I was a freshman, I was on offense. My only experience had been on defense, and that's what I wanted to do. I know as a freshman in 1973 I didn't do anything to create anything of value for me or for my team. In a freshman game against Tennessee, I asked coach Gryska for a chance to play a little defense. I did pretty well, and the next spring I was on defense. And I thought I came out of spring number two behind Randy Hall after I had a good A-Day Game.

That summer I had a tough job working for a concrete company. I didn't really work out much, but came back and made all my times in our tests. Coach Bryant had a color system for practice jerseys. On defense, white was first team, blue second, and orange was the bottom of the heap. So I picked up my basket for our first fall workout, and I had an orange jersey. When I still had an orange jersey on the third day, I decided it wasn't right. I threw the basket back to Willie Meadows, the equipment manager, and walked out.

One of my teammates, Andy Gothard, called me, but I told him I had quit. Then coach Bud Moore called and said coach Bryant wanted to talk to my father. I thought now I was getting somewhere, that coach Bryant would tell my father he had made a mistake and welcome me back because he needed me.

So my father and I went to coach Bryant's office. Coach was very gracious in greeting my father. Then he turned to me and said, "What are you doing here?" I told him I thought he wanted to talk to me. "I don't talk to quitters," he said. Then he told me as long as I was there to sit down.

That meeting changed my life. I was all ready with my little spiel about what I had done in the spring. And he said, "What have you done to get better since then?" And he proceeded to tell me about every other defensive lineman and what he had done to improve himself. He told me he thought it didn't mean enough to me and I had to make a decision on whether I was going to give 110 percent.

After that I looked at things in a completely different way. First of all, I was amazed at how much he knew about me and how much he knew about every player. The reason for that is that he cared about his players. He also cared about the team. Everything he did was for the team and his players.

I carry that meeting with me every day. He gave me an opportunity to come back. He told me that coach Donahue would probably kill me, but that if I survived I might be able to play. No one could stop me after that meeting. I was going to prove to coach Bryant that I was a winner, that I was going to be the best I could be.

It wasn't immediate. I didn't start at the first of the year. But I had a good game against Southern Miss. I think Jeff Bower, who is the coach there now, was the quarterback, and I sacked him three or four times. I started the next week against Vanderbilt. I didn't start the week after that, but I got in and did well. Because of that meeting I had, I kept working. I started every game in the rest of my career at Alabama and every game in my 10-year career with the Miami Dolphins.

It all goes back to that meeting. I don't know how many lives coach Bryant influenced, but I know it was a lot. I know mine was one of them.

One of the good things about playing for Alabama was that he taught us to respect our opponent. I think we had good relationships with the players we played against, and I felt they respected us.

167

You hear all the time about his teaching lessons for life, but it is absolutely true. My time at Alabama playing for coach Bryant and coach Donahue—who was also a great part of the Alabama tradition—is the foundation of everything I did in pro football and everything I have done in life. Hurricane Ivan in 2004 wreaked havoc with our business on the Gulf Coast, and as we work to recover, I think back to the tough times on Alabama's practice field.

When I went to the Dolphins, another defensive lineman, A. J. Duhe from LSU, and I were the first two picks. The guys playing our positions had gotten into a little trouble, so we went right to first team, which was sort of like being thrown to the wolves. And while coach Don Shula was tough, I never felt that I wasn't prepared to do whatever it took to get the job done because of my Alabama background.

Over the years, coach Shula had a lot of guys from Alabama. I think he liked the type of men coach Bryant turned out.

I first met Mike Shula there. He was always around, doing everything he could. He immersed himself in football. When Richard Todd and I got our signing bonuses, the first thing we did was go out and buy Eldorado convertibles. We were Joe Namath wannabes. The Dolphins and the Saints did a nice thing every year, meeting at Vero Beach to practice together for a few days. Bum Phillips was the Saints coach. He'd have barbecue and country music, and we had a good time with the Saints. I wanted my car up there. Mike had just gotten his restricted permit. I think he was 15. But I gave him the keys and asked him to bring it up. He put the top down, got his buddies, and drove it up to Vero Beach.

I first got into the hospitality business with Joe Namath and Richard Todd in the last Bachelors III in Fort Lauderdale. In 1981 we started the Baumhower's Wings restaurants, and we have added Calypso Joe's and Mango's. Now we have 11 restaurants. One of the best things is that I'm back in Alabama, in Baldwin County, and we're fortunate enough to have a lot of great times with former teammates and with Alabama fans. I have particularly enjoyed following Alabama the last few years with my nephew, Evan Mathis, doing so well, starting all four years through 2004. And I've got great expectations for Alabama football under Mike Shula, particularly since I heard he had brought back the off-season workouts that we had in the lower gym.

168

Bob Baumhower was an All-SEC performer for Alabama. He was NFL Rookie of the Year, 1983 NFL Defensive Player of the Year, and a four-time All-Pro for the Miami Dolphins.

GUS WHITE
Nose Guard
1974–1976

I'M GLAD I DIDN'T LISTEN TO MY BAND DIRECTOR. I didn't play organized football until I was in the 10th grade. I was a trombone player in the band. My buddies were challenging me to go out for the football team at Dothan High School. The band director told me that all the football players didn't get to make the road trips, but all the band members did. If I wanted to make the road trips, I'd better stick to trombone, he said.

But I wasn't going to pass up a dare. I had played football on the sandlots in Dothan and watched football on television, but I really didn't know much about it. At the first practice I was introduced to the seven-man sled. The coach wanted us to hit it and slide. I got to the back of the line so I could see what everyone was doing. But I didn't realize the sled had a recoil. So when my time came, I laid into it. And then it rolled back at me, and rolled me over two or three times. I can still remember everyone laughing.

But football came naturally to me. I guess I was blessed that a kid my size had a little speed and was strong.

I remember the first time I ever really noticed Alabama football was after my first season at Dothan. The 1970 teamed played in the Astro-Bluebonnet Bowl against Oklahoma. Jeff Rouzie had a great game. And I remember thinking that Alabama was about to be pretty good.

I had a pretty good season the next year, too. I made all the all-star teams and started getting some recruiting information. Florida practically lived at

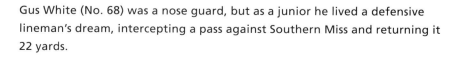

Gus White (No. 68) was a nose guard, but as a junior he lived a defensive lineman's dream, intercepting a pass against Southern Miss and returning it 22 yards.

my doorstep. I knew every night I was going to get a call from someone at Florida. And I started getting letters from schools around the country. Coach Pat Dye started recruiting me for Alabama, and coach Ken Donahue started calling me, too. Then about midway through my senior year, I blew out a knee when I got clipped. I had surgery and was in a cast from my toes to my hip. I thought football might be over.

Florida quit calling. Just about everybody dropped me except coach Dye. He continued to call and check on me. He said he had made a commitment to me, and if I wanted to play football for Alabama, I would have a scholarship.

I actually thought about giving up football. But after talking to my mother, I told coach Dye I would accept his offer. They had made a promise and they had kept their word. I think coach Dye and coach Donahue convinced coach Bryant to stick with me.

I remember the first team meeting we had, and coach Bryant's telling us what he expected of us. He said he would treat us like our mamas and papas would. He said he wouldn't respect our privacy in the dorm if he thought anything was wrong. "I won't knock," he said. "I'm coming in." That was more than enough warning for me.

I wasn't in great shape when I showed up. For one thing, I was still limping. I walked and ran with a limp my whole freshman year.

But I was also pretty big. I wasn't quite 5'10". More than 5'9", but not 5'10". And they joke that I weighed in at 262, but they noticed that I weighed the same before and after practice when other guys were losing four, six, eight pounds in those hot August practices. It turns out the scales only went to 262. They took me over to the student center where they had some meat scales, and I weighed about 278. But I lost weight, down to about 260. (I'll admit I'm over my playing weight now.) Eventually, I got down to under 250 because coach Donahue wanted us quick rather than big.

I was so excited to be playing football at Alabama. But then I found out about something called a "redshirt," where you didn't play in any games. I thought if they were going to redshirt me that I was going to go home. But they didn't redshirt me. Mostly I played in junior varsity games, but then I got into the Vanderbilt game and then played in the Tennessee game. That's when I knew that I had arrived. We opened that game with Gary Rutledge throwing an 80-yard pass to Wayne Wheeler for a touchdown. That was big.

Almost everyone at Alabama had been *the* player at his high school. But when you got to Bryant Hall, you could leave your scrapbook at home. You were a rookie. In fact, that was your name: "Rookie." I can still remember Sylvester Croom calling me Rookie, and he was just a year older than I was.

But you had to earn your way. They had earned it, and we had to.

Alabama had played a four-man defensive front before I got there, but we went to a five-man front, which meant I was a nose guard. And I think one of the highlights of practice every day was Croom vs. White. I always said one advantage I had was practicing every day against the best center in the nation.

Oddly, my roommate was Colenzo Hubbard, who played the same position I did. But we got along great as teammates and roommates and pushed each other to be better. The summer before our senior year in high school, Paul Harris, Colenzo, and I made a pact to come to Alabama. Willie Frye did, too, but he went to Notre Dame. Colenzo is in Memphis now doing ministry.

I learned a nice lesson at Colenzo's expense. Colenzo was on first team one day and had a great practice. The next day he was on second team, and it really bothered him. He went to see coach Bryant to find out why he had been demoted. Coach said, "Well, Colenzo, it's like this. If I told you everything I did and why I did it, you'd be the head football coach of this team." Colenzo said, "Yes, sir," and got up and walked out. I learned not to go up to his office to talk to him about anything. Especially with that sofa that had you nearly sitting on the floor.

I still remember my first class at Alabama. It was an English class. The teacher said, "You football players think you're going to get something. You get nothing." And she was true to her word. It wasn't a cakewalk.

And that's the way it was on the football field. Nothing was given. And I've always liked that. All I've ever asked for is an opportunity, and I think I've made the most of those opportunities.

Our first three years were pretty good. Then in 1976 we lost three ball games, and it was as though we had a losing season. That's when you know that Alabama people are serious about football, when they are upset at 9–3. But we had been 11–1 each of the first three years. I am proud to say we never lost to Auburn or Tennessee in my four years. And then we had a good finish with a 36–6 win over UCLA in the Liberty Bowl.

I didn't play a position that gets a lot of notice from the fans. But I had my moment in the 1975 Vanderbilt game. In those days, a defensive player couldn't run with a fumble unless he caught it in the air. Well, Vanderbilt fumbled, and the ball hit the ground, but it bounced right up to me and I started running for the end zone. I don't think it was but about 25 yards away, but it seemed like 80. And when I got to the end zone, Leroy Cook was going to tackle me in celebration. He hit me dead in the mouth and I dropped the ball. When coach Donahue was going over our grades the next week, he told me he had marked me a minus for the fumble. But of course the play didn't count.

Coach Donahue was something. After I got there, I thought I must have gotten a track scholarship. We'd practice and then everyone would be gone except the defensive linemen. He kept us out there running. Looking back, I would thank him every day if he was here. It was that conditioning that made the difference in a lot of games. He said that fatigue would make a coward of you, and he wasn't going to let that happen to us. He prepared us mentally and physically.

Everyone was doing everything possible to help you be a winner. Willie Meadows in the equipment room. And of course, coach Goostree and Sang Lyda in the training room. I hated to go in there because I hated putting my ankle in those tubs of ice. But they got you up and running.

And of course, coach Bryant reminded us every day that how we performed that day would have an effect on how we performed for the rest of our lives.

173

I went to Tampa Bay's training camp in 1977, and I wouldn't take anything for the experience. But it was never going to work out. The NFL isn't interested in a 5'9" defensive lineman. But I enjoyed it and took satisfaction in knowing that even if I wasn't up to their height expectations, I got the job done every day there.

Coach Bryant told us to get our degrees, and I did that. And I went to work for the Department of Corrections in Montgomery County, where I have been ever since. My wife, Creola, and I have two children and our daughter is going to the university on an academic scholarship.

I don't work in athletics, but it comes up. The older inmates will tell the younger ones, and they'll say, "Did you really play for Alabama?"

And despite what you might think, my job is not physical. You have to be a thinking man and try to avoid the physical.

It's pretty amazing to be remembered as an Alabama football player after all these years. From time to time, someone will say, "You're that Gus White?

I was in the service in Korea and listened to you playing." Or I'll get a card from someone across the country to sign. And that makes you feel good. But that says more about Alabama football than anything else.

Gus White was winner of the 1975 Lee Roy Jordan Headhunter Award in spring practice and played on three SEC championship teams, and in two Sugar Bowls, one Orange Bowl, and one Liberty Bowl.

OZZIE NEWSOME
SPLIT END AND TIGHT END
1974–1977

B<small>Y ALMOST ANY STANDARD, WE HAD A VERY SUCCESSFUL</small> four-year period at Alabama. We won three Southeastern Conference championships; finished in the nation's top 10 all four years; finished second in the nation in both 1974 and 1977; won 11 games three of the four years; won three bowl games defeating Penn State, UCLA, and Ohio State; and went 42–6.

The biggest disappointment is that we did not win a national championship. We could have won it on the field in 1974, but we lost by two points to Notre Dame in the Orange Bowl. And I thought we had won it in 1977, but Notre Dame won it again that year. In 1977 we played our final game in the Sugar Bowl against Ohio State. We were third in the nation going into the bowl games. Both the No. 1 and No. 2 teams lost, and we handed it to Ohio State pretty good, 35–6. That was the Bear vs. Woody game, coach Bryant vs. coach Hayes.

Ohio State was a good team, and that was an impressive victory. I had met Chris Ward, who was the starting offensive tackle for the Buckeyes, at the Heisman dinner in New York. He was a nice guy, and I developed a friendship with him.

After the game we had a van to go to Mobile for the Senior Bowl. Johnny Davis, Bob Cryder, and I, and a player from Ohio State drove over together. While we were driving we heard on the radio they had voted Notre Dame

Ozzie Newsome (No. 82) is in both the college and professional football halls of fame because of his outstanding pass-catching ability, as evidenced by this amazing reception against TCU.

the national champion. It made that trip twice as long. We just couldn't believe it.

I believe that game may have propelled Alabama to two more national championships. 'Bama won it in 1978 and 1979. It could have been three in a row.

My parents didn't realize the significance of me signing with The University of Alabama, but after I started playing, it was brought home to them. Their recognition in the community escalated. They'd go to the cleaners or the grocery store, and people would want to talk to them because their son played football at Alabama.

There were a lot of factors in my choosing Alabama, but unquestionably the number one factor was coach Bryant. It begins and ends with him. I told a story many years ago about other schools recruiting me and telling me that their coach had played for coach Bryant or had coached under coach Bryant. And I thought, I could go to the branch, or I could go to the trunk.

There was also the winning tradition. Alabama was the dominant team in the SEC and one of the best teams in the nation. I enjoyed watching *The Bear Bryant Show* on Sundays, and also enjoyed the *Shug Jordan Show* on Auburn football.

When I made my recruiting visit, the atmosphere was all about team, which appealed to me. There were no huge egos, no individuals. It was about The University of Alabama and the Crimson Tide football team.

Everyone connected with the program in any way was doing whatever he could do to help us win. And I don't mean just the coaches and players and trainers and managers. I mean the cooks and the men who kept the dorm clean. Everyone.

Leon Douglas had signed two years earlier to play basketball. He was close to me, and his brother, John, was in my class at Colbert County in Leighton. I'm still close to them and so happy that Leon is back in Tuscaloosa as head basketball coach at Stillman College.

It was amazing the things that came up in recruiting. Thad Flanagan was my teammate at Colbert County, and he had signed with Alabama a year ahead of me. Coaches at other schools would try to give me a guilt complex, like it would be wrong of me to compete against Thad. And some people thought I should go to Auburn and be reunited with my old high school quarterback, Phil Gargis.

When I got to Alabama, it was even better than I had expected. There was a family atmosphere. Every player cared for the next player. And the students were very supportive of the football players. It was a good feeling.

Alabama had lost a great wide receiver in Wayne Wheeler. I knew that everyone was saying that Alabama didn't have a replacement for him. I don't remember what I thought about that at the time, but looking back I can certainly understand it. The 1974 season was just the second one that freshmen could play on the varsity, and coach Bryant probably wasn't sure if he could count on me.

We opened that year against Maryland. Joe Dale Harris and I alternated, taking plays in and out. Joe Dale started the Maryland game, and I went in on the second play. The next week I started, and I started every game the rest of my career.

We went 11–1 my freshman year and 11–1 my sophomore year. The oddity is that we had a two-game losing streak because we lost the Orange Bowl to Notre Dame at the end of the 1974 season and we lost to Missouri to open the 1975 season. We had 10-game winning streaks in both seasons, not losing a game until the Orange Bowl in 1974 and not losing a game after Missouri in 1975.

I learned a lesson in that Missouri game. I was playing wide receiver and had my head down. The Missouri cornerback rolled up and came up under my chin with his forearm. He whacked me pretty good and busted my lip. I learned then to keep my head up and watch what was going on.

After your career has been over a few years, you can look back and see that you were a part of an historic time. But at the time a place in history was the last thing on your mind. It was just playing football. Every day was a matter of making sure you gave your best effort. We had so many good players that I was just concerned with maintaining my place on the depth chart. It was a matter of that day, that practice, maybe that period of practice.

I can also look back and see how my time at Alabama has been helpful to me. Coach Bryant stressed priorities, which is the team. We learned what initiative is. He encouraged us to be as good as we could be because we wanted to, not because of outside motivation. And we learned that when we win, there is enough for everyone. Everyone can share in the glory when you win.

I learned to let the game come to me. If the opponent wanted to double-cover me, we were going to be able to run the ball. And if they put people up there to stop the run, I was going to get a lot of passes thrown my way.

I also learned that every man on the team had to pull his share, which for me meant becoming a blocker sometimes.

I played most of my Alabama career at split end, but also played tight end. My first day as a pro at Cleveland, I was a tight end. But I was flexed out, the first "hybrid" tight end in the NFL. They told me they were going to throw me a lot of balls, and I caught a few, so I was happy.

It's the nature of my job that I can't make it to Alabama games or reunions. But I still talk to Johnny Davis at least once a week. I see John Mitchell a few times a year. I see Dwight Stephenson at the Hall of Fame events. I see Richard Todd when I go home to Florence, where he lives now. I know his son, Gator, is a heck of a golfer for the Tide now. And each summer we go to Gulf Shores, and I get with a lot of the old guys. And I am making a special trip to Tuscaloosa to see the new facilities Mal Moore has put together.

Ozzie Newsome was an All-America split end in 1977, named the Alabama Player of the Decade for the 1970s, selected to the All-Century Team, inducted into the College Football Hall of Fame in 1994, and the Pro Football Hall of Fame in 1999. He is general manager of the Baltimore Ravens.

BARRY KRAUSS

LINEBACKER

1976–1978

At the end of the 1978 season, we had motivation and we had a second chance. A year earlier, we thought we were going to win the national championship. We had beaten Woody Hayes and a good Ohio State football team in the Sugar Bowl. We thought if Notre Dame could somehow upset Texas—which was ranked number one in 1977—in the Cotton Bowl that we'd win the national championship. Notre Dame did upset Texas, but then jumped over us from fifth to first.

The next year in the Sugar Bowl we had another chance. Penn State was number one in 1978, and their coach, Joe Paterno, decided to play the next-highest-ranked team, which was Alabama, in the Sugar Bowl for the national championship.

We knew we had to play another great game, and we were ready. I can remember how relaxed everyone was before the game.

Everyone played well. Tony Nathan rushed for more than 100 yards. Murray Legg had a great defensive game. Benny Perrin had a big interception. Bruce Bolton had a big touchdown catch. Lou Ikner had a punt return that took the pressure off us. As Murray Legg said after the game, "I don't believe we were a great football team. We were a good football team, and coach Bryant made us think we were great." And that was the difference in the game.

It came down to the goal-line stand. Don McNeal made a great play on a pass, and I think everyone came together after that. It came down to a

Barry Krauss (No. 77) was most valuable player in the 1979 Sugar Bowl primarily because of this fourth-down tackle at the goal line, preserving a 14–7 victory over Penn State and giving Alabama the national championship.

fourth-down play. We were holding hands in the huddle. We knew everything we had worked for was at stake, particularly for the four seniors on defense. And we knew we were going to make the play.

We had just stopped a dive play, and I thought they would probably play action or sweep. But coach Donahue made a great call for us to sell out and crash the corners. The defensive line did an incredible job of reestablishing the line of scrimmage.

So, yes, he [Mike Guman] went over the top, and I was the one who hit him. But that was because of what the defensive line had done. It was coach Bryant's plan that the defensive line would take out the interference and let the linebackers make the play. And then Murray came in and pushed us back, keeping the back from twisting and maybe falling into the end zone. Everyone was involved. It was the epitome of Alabama defense, which was teamwork at its best.

Before the game, coach Bryant had told us he expected the game to come down to a defensive opportunity.

He always said that in a close game it would be two or three key plays that would determine the outcome. And it's the same thing in people's lives. Two or three opportunities.

Coach Bryant taught us to always be ready for the moment you can make a difference and said you never know when that time will come. We learned to condition ourselves to be ready for success. He pushed us until we felt we had nothing left and we had to dig deeper to do the job. We did that every day in practice, and so we were able to do it when the national championship was at stake.

182

That Penn State game was a second chance for our football team. I had a second chance with coach Bryant. My sophomore year I wasn't happy about my place on the depth chart. And we had a quarterback who wasn't happy because they were moving him to defensive back. One night after a game, we went out and we missed curfew. It so happened that this was a night that coach Bryant made room checks himself. I knew we were dead.

I didn't wait for him to call me. I went to see him. And I cried and apologized and begged for mercy. The quarterback didn't do anything. Coach Bryant kicked him out of the dorm and took his scholarship. He gave me a second chance. I kept my scholarship and learned a big lesson. Maybe I wasn't a model citizen, but I straightened up a lot.

My introduction to Alabama was really on the beach. I grew up in Pompano Beach, Florida, and one of my friends, Eddie Blankenship, was a big Alabama fan. We liked to toss a football around on the beach, trying to impress the girls, I'm sure. But Eddie introduced me to the wishbone offense vs. the wave. What we'd do is line up in the wishbone on the shore. And when the wave came, we'd start the triple option. A wave hits at an angle so we could run the option down the sand. The fullback would dive into the wave, then the quarterback would run down the wave until he had to give it up. He'd pitch it to the halfback, who would try to dive over the wave. That kind of made me an Alabama fan.

I was being recruited by Florida, Florida State, Miami, and Georgia Tech. Alabama didn't come in until late. Miami invited me to come when Alabama was playing them in the Orange Bowl. I went to the game and thought that Alabama looked cool. And they beat Miami pretty badly, worse than the final score.

Kenny Martin was recruiting me and invited me for a visit. I went up there, and I fell in love with Alabama. I can still remember going in the locker room and standing in front of Woodrow Lowe's locker and looking at his helmet. That was awesome, because Woodrow Lowe was one of the greatest linebackers ever. I was basically done.

My signing was memorable. I had gone to our football banquet. And when I came home and opened the door, there was coach Bryant. He had flown down, and my family knew he would be there, but I didn't. He had my scholarship and I signed right then. Coach Bryant was not the kind of man you said no to.

I was on cloud nine, but I remember one of my best friends saying, "Why would you go to Alabama? They've got great players. You'll never get to play." And I thought, "Thanks a lot for the confidence." Coach Bryant had promised me an opportunity, and I thought that was all I would need.

I can't begin to tell you how tough it was. It was hot and humid. Byron Braggs, a defensive tackle, nearly died of heat stroke. After that, we started getting water breaks. Even the water breaks were so disciplined. The whistle would blow, and you'd have to hustle to your spot, a hundred or more of us on one knee in one straight line, and the managers would bring the water to us.

At one practice I told our trainer, Jim Goostree, that I was going to throw up and that I should go in. I was trying to get out of practice. He told me to go over by the bushes and throw up and then to get back in the drill.

I really didn't start playing much until midway through my sophomore season when we went to Notre Dame. Somebody missed a tackle, and I went in and had a pretty good game, hitting people and making an interception. Coach Bryant started me the second half. He said for the guys who had started the game to start the second half, "except I want Krauss in there. He wants to hit someone."

I led the team in tackles in that game and again a couple of weeks later when we beat Auburn really badly.

We played UCLA in the Liberty Bowl. There was a fireworks display before the game that got me going. On the kickoff, nobody touched me, and I drilled the return guy at about the 5-yard line. Our defense was all over them and we won big. I had an interception for a touchdown. It was probably the best game of my career.

I didn't realize at the time what I was a part of. We had great football teams at Alabama. When I got to professional football, I realized how great coach Bryant was. The best lessons I learned were at Alabama.

There is no question that the greatest experience of my life was playing football for coach Bryant at The University of Alabama. It is something I am very proud of and something I think about every day.

Barry Krauss was All-America in 1978, the year he was MVP of the Sugar Bowl for his memorable goal-line-stand tackle to preserve Bama's 14–7 win for the national championship. He was also MVP of the 1976 Liberty Bowl. He was selected to the Alabama Team of the Century. He played 10 years with the Colts and one with the Dolphins.

MARTY LYONS
DEFENSIVE TACKLE
1975–1978

WINNING 10 OR 11 GAMES A YEAR WILL GIVE YOU CONFIDENCE. Playing in the national championship game provides an opportunity to exhibit it. Alabama football teams had come up just short of national championships in my freshman season in 1975 and in my junior year in 1977. I was captain of the 1978 team, the last time I would have the opportunity. The Crimson Tide, undefeated and ranked second in the nation, met coach Joe Paterno's undefeated and No. 1–ranked Penn State in the Sugar Bowl.

The game was a classic and turned on one of the defining moments in college football history. Alabama had a 14–7 lead late in the fourth quarter when Penn State drove to a first down inside the 'Bama 10-yard line. Three more plays left the Nittany Lions a yard short of the goal line.

As captains, Penn State quarterback Chuck Fusina and I were standing at the spot of the ball just outside the Alabama end zone. We had met on *The Bob Hope Show* when we were presented as All-Americans a few weeks earlier. After examining the spot of the ball, Fusina said, "Marty, what do you think we ought to do?"

I said, "Chuck, you've got about a yard to go. You'd better pass."

Penn State didn't pass. And the run up the middle was stopped cold, preserving the score and leading to Alabama winning the national championship.

No one prepared like we did. Coach [Ken] Donahue met with the linebackers and defensive linemen every night after we started bowl practice.

Marty Lyons (No. 93) and Barry Krauss celebrated being No. 1 after a goal-line stand against Penn State in the 1979 Sugar Bowl gave 'Bama the national championship.

We watched Penn State film. Then coach Donahue would show us a Penn State formation. He'd have the linebackers call the defense, then test the defensive linemen on what our responsibilities were. We knew everything they were going to do if they stuck to their tendencies. And most teams do stay with their tendencies. When we got in our huddle, we knew what to expect. Everyone did his job. Barry [Krauss] made the play, but it was David Hannah who took the blocker's legs out. It was Alabama at its best. And no player could ask to end his career better than to go out as national champion.

I was the 14th player taken in the following year's NFL draft, selected in the first round by the New York Jets, and I was fortunate enough to have a very successful professional career, playing from 1979 to 1990. But the best thing ever said about me was that I was an even bigger success outside football in the best possible way.

It is commonplace for college players on bowl trips to make a trip to visit sick children in a hospital in the bowl city. I had that experience, but I didn't let it end there. I continued to visit children in hospitals when I went to the Jets. And in 1982 a teammate, Kenny Schroy, and I made a commitment to do more. The result was The Marty Lyons Foundation, which continues to grant wishes to children with terminal or life-threatening illnesses.

One of the things that coach Bryant stressed was how important it was to make a difference. He was the reason I started the foundation. He told us about the opportunities we had. I knew when I was on those hospital wards watching those children pulling IV poles that they weren't going to have the opportunities I had.

The Marty Lyons Foundation has sponsored more than three thousand kids. It has a budget of between $750,000 and $1 million a year. It has two paid employees, but hundreds of volunteers.

I love success stories. In 1985 we had a little girl with leukemia. The doctors said if she was fortunate enough to survive that she would never have children. At the foundation's annual "Celebration of Life" reunion, the young woman was one of 1,300 who returned. And she had her two children with her.

It tells us that what we're doing makes a difference years later.

But every story does not have a happy ending. As much as we try to help the kids, a lot of them don't make it. But they've touched our lives in such a way that when we do lose them, they've given us the strength to keep going.

You can help support The Marty Lyons Foundation, 326 W. 48th St., New York, NY 10036. We also appreciate "in kind" donations, such as airplane tickets. And if you can't help financially, give us your thoughts and prayers. Maybe it will save a life.

The New York Jets have been supportive. And so have my former Alabama teammates, like Tony Nathan and Barry Krauss, as well as hundreds of other professional athletes, such as baseball's David Cone.

And I get a boost from [former Tide teammate] Rich Wingo. I have great respect for Rich for what he has done with his life. His pro career was cut short, but his life is an inspiration, a real role model. And when a child passes away—one of those valleys in the peaks and valleys—I can call Rich, and after talking to him a while, know that everything is going to be all right.

I went to Alabama because of the tradition and because of coach Bryant. At the first Alabama game I went to as a prospect, Alabama won big, and it seemed about 100 Alabama guys played. The first time coach Bryant met me, he shook my hand and told me, "I want you to come to The University of Alabama. I can't promise you anything, but if you're good enough, you'll get a chance."

I frequently thought Alabama was trying to get rid of me. In my freshmen year, the graduate assistant coaches working with me were Mike DuBose and Wayne Hall, and they did everything they could to find out if I was mentally and physically tough enough to make it. During my first year, I got to play a little at defensive end behind Leroy Cook. In my second year, I got moved inside, to tackle. I went from working under Dude Hennessey to playing for Ken Donahue. Although you don't realize it until later, anyone who had the opportunity to play for coach Donahue came out of it a better player and, more important, a better person. We were the last ones off the field every day. I always enjoyed running, and it was a good thing. He stressed the fundamentals, which is probably why I was able to go into the National Football League and play at 245 pounds.

Most Alabama football players say the only thing they are promised in the recruiting process is the opportunity, that everything else is up to them. I was given one other promise, that I would have a chance to play baseball beginning in the spring of my sophomore season.

During my sophomore year, I played in every game behind Bob Baumhower. Then when the lettermen were announced, I didn't get a letter. I knew I had played more than some guys who got letters. So I went to see coach Bryant.

I sat in that famous sofa where I nearly sank to the floor and looked up at him smoking his Chesterfield and looking down at me over those half glasses. I told him I thought I had played enough to letter. He said, "Marty, I'm not sure that letter means enough to you." Well, I thought I had an answer for anything he'd say, but I didn't have an answer for that.

Then I said I had one more thing. I wanted to ask him about playing baseball. He told me he had promised me that I could do that. Then he asked if he could give me some advice. That advice was, "Be good at one thing before you try to be good at two things." That was the end of my baseball career.

In looking back, I think he was right. That letter didn't mean enough to me then. But after that meeting, I was inspired to be an All-American. Coach Bryant knew how to treat men.

I have nothing but fond memories of my days at Alabama.

It starts with the players. There was a closeness that is difficult to describe. We practiced hard, we played hard, and we did things together off the field. And there was accountability. When we were in a big game, we knew we could trust one another.

189

When I went to the NFL, Richard Todd was with the Jets and kind of took me under his wing to shield me a little from the hazing rookies get. And we had guys all around the league, particularly in the East with Barry [Krauss] going to Indianapolis and Tony [Nathan] going to Miami. And Miami had Bob Baumhower and would later get Dwight [Stephenson] and Don McNeal. I couldn't have gone to a better place at a better time unless it was when Joe Namath—another former Alabama player—led the Jets to the Super Bowl championship.

And, of course, we had coach Bryant. He was bigger than life. He was bigger than the government. Every year before the start of the season after I went to the Jets, I'd get a telegram from coach Bryant wishing me good luck and the Jets good luck and reminding me to show my class.

And the Alabama fans could not have been more gracious to a guy from Florida who came to play there. When I was inducted into the Alabama Sports Hall of Fame, it was one of the biggest moments of my life.

I have a lot of sadness that I have to deal with, with our children. But I have never been sadder than the day I learned of coach Bryant's death. I cried like a baby. I had lost my coach and a man who had allowed me to become his friend. There is no man who could have had my greater respect and who could have been more influential other than my own father.

Marty Lyons was All-America in 1978 and defensive captain of Alabama's national championship team. He was All-SEC in 1977 and 1978 and was selected to Alabama's Team of the Century and to the Team of the Decade for the seventies.

DON McNEAL

CORNERBACK

1977–1979

I WAS FORTUNATE ENOUGH TO WIN AWARDS IN FOOTBALL. I played on two national championship teams at Alabama, and I played in two Super Bowls. But the thing I am most proud of is that I was elected captain of our 1979 national championship team along with Steve Whitman. Even though I wasn't a really vocal guy, my teammates told me I was a leader. It was a great feeling to get that honor from my teammates.

And when I return to the university, which I do as often as I can, I go to the quad and see all those great names around Denny Chimes—Pat Trammell, Billy Neighbors, Lee Roy Jordan, Joe Namath, Steve Sloan, Kenny Stabler, Johnny Musso, Sylvester Croom, Ozzie Newsome. And then I peek around the corner and see "Don McNeal."

My daughter is going to Alabama. I told her to drop by every now and then and clean my name off. I've got a lot of pride in that.

A few years ago, one of the youths in my church, Corrie Tucker, went to Alabama. When you are a senior at Alabama, you get a blanket with an "A" on it. She took my blanket to Alabama, and when she came back after graduation she gave it back to me. And now I've given it to my daughter.

I don't take my association with the Alabama football program lightly. I don't brag on many things, but I'll brag on that. I take a lot of pride in having been on the same football field that legendary players played on.

Don McNeal (No. 28) was recruited as a possible wide receiver, but when he made an interception, he became a dangerous return man.

I didn't know a lot about college football when I was growing up in Atmore. I guess I was an Alabama fan more than any other team, but I wasn't a real fan. I just knew about the Crimson Tide and about Bear Bryant. Lou Ikner and I had been on the Escambia County championship team. He was a year ahead of me and had signed with Alabama and was probably instrumental in me going to Alabama. He loved it.

I went to Tuscaloosa and Lou took me out to a fraternity party. I met the coaches and the players and started finding out more about the tradition of Alabama. They had all those pictures of All-Americans. I was impressed, by the tradition and by the people.

I was still deciding. Tennessee called and Auburn called. But then coach Bryant called, and when he called, that was it. You wanted to be a part of that success. It was a no-brainer.

But it wasn't everything I hoped for. I had never been away from home, and before long I was homesick and wanted to leave. Lou said, "Mac, give it a year. If you still want to leave after a year, you can leave." My first year went pretty well, and I was set.

Coach Bill Oliver was my position coach, and he was the Man for a secondary player. He taught me everything. I was successful at Alabama and in professional football because of the techniques he taught.

I was so raw when I got to Alabama. I thought coach Oliver didn't like me. In fact, one day I asked him if he didn't like black people because he stayed on my butt so much. Later he told me he had pushed me because he saw potential and wanted to get it out of me. One day he told me, "Now I know you can do it. I'm going to get off your butt."

I played a good bit as a freshman and was the starter as a sophomore. My four years at Alabama were wonderful, the best anyone could hope for. I met a lot of wonderful people. I had a ball. And we accomplished a lot. We won two national championships, and it should have been three.

As a senior in 1979, I had a lot of contact with coach Bryant. He had Steve Whitman and me come to his office on a fairly regular basis. He wanted to know what the players thought about how things were going and what Steve and I thought. We were sitting on that sofa looking up at him, and I think back about what a great time that was. Coach Bryant was a first-class guy.

We went undefeated in 1979 and repeated as national champions. That was a very good football team. We didn't feel sorry for our opponents that year, but we knew they were at our mercy.

In fact, we made it look so easy in 1979 that no one talks about that team. I hear a lot about the 1978 team, and especially about the goal-line stand. And it's nice when people remember I had a little part in it. On second down and goal, Chuck Fusina threw a little short pass to Scott Fitzkee. I was covering someone else in the end zone, but I saw the pass going to Fitzkee and broke on the ball. This is where coach Oliver comes in. I didn't think. I just knew I had to make a perfect tackle or Fitzkee would fall in the end zone. The play I made was instinct, the result of hours and hours with coach Bryant and coach Oliver. Then Barry Krauss, Marty Lyons, Rich Wingo, Curtis McGriff, and David Hannah kept them out of the end zone on the next two plays, and we won 14–7.

I was fortunate enough to play for the Miami Dolphins from 1980 through 1989. I came back to Tuscaloosa during the NFL strike season, 1982, and went out on the practice field. Coach Bryant called to me from the tower and said, "Come on up." I said, "You want me to come up there?" That was unheard of. But I went up. He invited me to come have dinner with him that night. Billy Varner was the university policeman who drove coach Bryant, and he picked me up and took me to coach Bryant's house for dinner. He showed me around his house. That really meant a lot to me. It would mean more soon after.

We made it to the Super Bowl that year, playing Washington at the Rose Bowl in Pasadena. We were out there preparing for the game when a reporter came up to me and told me coach Bryant had died. I didn't believe it. I think about coach Bryant all the time.

Don McNeal was an All-American and captain in 1979 and was selected to the Alabama Team of the Century. He started on Alabama teams that went 34–2 and won two national championships. He played in two Super Bowls with the Miami Dolphins.

STEADMAN SHEALY

QUARTERBACK

1977–1979

THERE WERE PROBABLY A LOT OF REASONS FOR ME TO NOT go to Alabama to play football. When I signed in 1975, Alabama had Jeff Rutledge and Jack O'Rear and five other quarterbacks. I was one of about five guys who signed that year who had been high school quarterbacks, although I was the only one of the freshmen who worked at quarterback.

I wasn't going to a place to turn it around. Alabama had a record of 54–6 in the five years before I got there. Alabama wasn't even recruiting me as hard as Auburn or Mississippi State or Georgia Tech.

I was sitting in our living room in Dothan with Doug Barfield, who was Auburn's head coach. Vince Dooley of Georgia was out front of the house in his car waiting for coach Barfield to leave so he could talk to me. The phone rang and my mother came in and said, "It's coach Bryant."

I went to the phone and he said, "What jersey have you always wanted to wear?"

Crimson, I answered.

"Then what's the problem?" he said.

To be honest, I didn't think Alabama was all that hot to sign me. My sister was a "Bear Girl," and all the Shealys had graduated from Alabama, and I had always been an Alabama fan. Paul Crane was the first coach to recruit me for Alabama, then Bill Oliver. Years later, after I had finished playing and was helping Mal Moore with the quarterbacks while I was in law school, Dee

Powell and Bobby Marks would dig coach Moore about when they were recruiting me. Coach Moore had said, "We'll take him, but we'll never win any championships with him."

And so Alabama took me over Charley Trotman, and Auburn took Charley Trotman over me.

Arriving at Alabama was unreal. I can remember being interviewed and being asked, "What's it like being in a long line of great quarterbacks?" And then he started naming them: Bart Starr, Pat Trammell, and on and on through Namath, Sloan, Stabler and the rest. And that's when it started sinking in: What an opportunity! Quarterback at Alabama is a long, rich tradition. And I felt God had led me to go there.

I had to prove myself to coach Moore, and it took a while. During my freshman year, I quarterbacked the junior varsity team. In 1977 I went in for the first time in the second game of the year at Nebraska. That was the game where Jeff Rutledge threw five interceptions and we lost 31–24, the only game we lost that year. It was not an auspicious debut. On the first play, I fell down for about a five-yard loss.

I was probably going to be redshirted in 1977, but Jack O'Rear tore up his knee, and I got to play 8 or 10 plays in every game. Even after the loss to Nebraska, we kept fighting back. We went to Los Angeles and upset Southern Cal, which was ranked No. 1. I got to play a lot in that game.

The thing I remember most about that trip came before the game. Jeff, Keith Pugh, and I got together before games to pray. I'd pray for things like for God to keep us safe and help us play our best, that sort of thing. And then Keith prayed and said that he knew that game wasn't that important in the great scheme of things. I had never thought about that.

Our lives revolved around football. It was basically 16 hours a day. All I did six days a week was football, watch film, eat, study, and sleep. That was the commitment you have to have at Alabama.

When we went to the Sugar Bowl to play Ohio State, we thought if Notre Dame could beat Texas, which was No. 1, we could win the national championship. All that happened, except Notre Dame went from fifth to first, and we finished second.

Coach Bryant showed a lot of faith in me in that Sugar Bowl game. The game was on the line, and he put me in at quarterback. Our second unit went on two 80-yard drives.

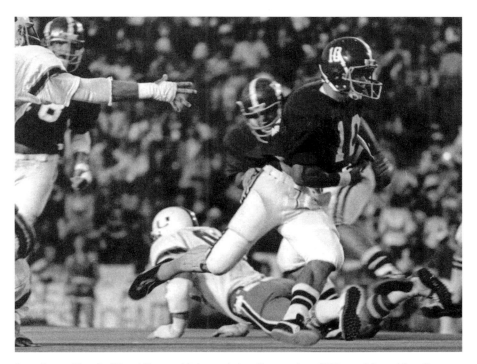

Steadman Shealy (No. 10) was Alabama's leading rusher (791 yards) and leading passer (717 yards) when he quarterbacked 'Bama to a 12–0 season and the 1979 national championship.

I had torn up my knee the next spring, and Dr. E. C. Brock had opened me up for full surgery. Not only that, I got an infection and lost about 30 pounds. I was probably going to be redshirted that year, but I worked all summer with our trainers, Jim Goostree and Sang Lyda. I was having trouble getting my knee bent. They told me if I could get a 125-degree bend that I would have a chance to play. I wanted to play. So the night before I was going to be measured, I tied my knee bent and stayed up all night with it tied at over a 125-degree bend.

The wishbone was really my offense. It wasn't really Jeff's offense. He was an excellent passer. But nobody could run and move like I could, although that might have been in great part because of fear.

I don't think coach Moore wanted to play me very much because I was coming off the knee injury. It had been only four months since the surgery.

I consider it a gift from God that I was able to play. In the first game against Nebraska, coach Bryant put me in, and I ran for nine yards. Coach Bryant realized how I had worked all summer to be able to play and he had faith in me. That's one of the reasons that I love and adore him to this day.

Coach Bryant believed in playing men if they had earned it. I probably played about 10 snaps a game as a sophomore and about 25 snaps a game as a junior, backing up Jeff. And why not play the back-up quarterbacks? Everyone needs to play. I'm convinced that when the back-up gets a chance, he gives about 110 percent effort. I think it's ridiculous the way teams play just one quarterback.

We lost to Southern Cal in 1978, but came back and got back to No. 2, and this time we got to play No. 1 Penn State in the Sugar Bowl. And that win gave us the national championship.

We had been 11–1 my sophomore year and 11–1 my junior year. I made up my mind as a senior we were going to be 12–0. On offense we had nine seniors, and our juniors were Major Ogilvie and Billy Jackson. And some of our guys were fifth-year seniors. And we had smart guys, like Mike Brock on the offensive line, who could call the checks. And, of course, we had another great defense.

The toughest game we had was at LSU. It rained and they had the grass on the field about six inches deep, so it was almost impossible to run. The whole game was played on their end of the field, but we only got a field goal and won 3–0. I was hospitalized after that game. I couldn't run, so I was a sitting duck, and they beat me up pretty good.

We were ranked No. 1 and playing Auburn, and they were not very good. But our offense had fumbled and we'd been benched. We got the ball back on the 18-yard line and we were behind. On the first play, I bounced the pitchout to Major, but he got it. And eventually we drove it on down and I scored the winning touchdown and conversion. We were 11–0 and going back to the Sugar Bowl to play Arkansas.

Coach Moore came up with the double wing offense to run the wishbone in the Sugar Bowl, and we won pretty easily to win the national championship again. A few years later, I got to talk to coach Lou Holtz, who had been at Arkansas, and he talked about that scheme.

The national championship is the standard coach Bryant set for us. We won two and should have won three.

I wasn't allowed to throw much until my senior year. Until then, I'd run the veer, and Jeff was in on the passing plays. But in 1979 I had to pass, because they'd put everyone on the line to stop the run. Keith Pugh and I had a great relationship. We'd stay after practice and work on our own to make sure we knew exactly what we were doing. We'd throw an out-cut, and he always had one-on-one coverage, so we had great success. It really hurt our offense when he missed a few games.

After my playing career, I stayed around as a graduate assistant while I was in law school. I also had some scholarships from the National Football Foundation and as an NCAA Top Five scholar. By then I had a lot of confidence in knowing the offense, and it was then that I recognized what a great wishbone innovator coach Moore was.

I spent a lot of time with coach Bryant, and he would ask me about things as a guy who had been the quarterback. When Charley Thornton left to go to Texas A&M, I got the opportunity to work as host of *The Bear Bryant Show* each Sunday. I may have been the first person to know he was going to retire. He said after the Southern Mississippi game that he wasn't on top of it, that he was allowing his assistants to make decisions he didn't agree with, that he thought maybe it was time to hang it up.

When Ray Perkins came in the next year he asked me to stay and help with the quarterbacks. It wasn't anything like what I had done with coach Bryant. I enjoyed working with Dave Rader and a young quarterback named Mike Shula.

And then I was out of law school and into the real world. And I realized that that is what coach Bryant had prepared me for. He taught me to be competitive and to work hard; that every day was not going to be a bed of roses, and when the down times came, you had to work harder. He was the best teacher I ever had.

Steadman Shealy is a partner in the law firm of Cobb, Shealy, Crum & Derrick in Dothan and Tuscaloosa. He was All-SEC and Academic All-America as a senior.

DWIGHT STEPHENSON
CENTER
1977–1979

I HAVE TO FEEL VERY FORTUNATE TO HAVE PLAYED COLLEGE FOOTBALL for the greatest college coach of all time and then go and play professional football for the greatest pro coach of all time. I had a good career at Alabama, but that doesn't guarantee you anything in professional football.

Don McNeal was drafted in the first round by Miami and I was drafted in the second. We were in training camp and I was working as hard as I could to earn a spot on the roster. I could be a little ornery on the field sometimes. There was a kid who handled the water for us. I had asked him for water and he didn't get it to me as quickly as I thought he should. I shouldn't have said anything—he was only 12 or 13, I guess—but I made a comment. And an offensive tackle next to me whispered, "That's coach Shula's son."

That was the first time I met Mike Shula. And at the time all I could think about was that by jumping him a little I might have jeopardized my chance to make the team.

Of course, that wasn't really the case. Coach Don Shula was a fine coach and just as fine a man. When Mike was a few years older and looking at different colleges, coach Shula asked me what I thought about Alabama. Of course, I told him it was the best possible place. Coach Shula had a lot of Alabama guys on his rosters over the years. I think he liked us.

And it was nice to see Mike go up there and play for Alabama. He's a guy who really wanted to compete and really wanted to be a football coach. One thing you notice about him is that when you are talking to him, he is really listening—he really wants to know what you are thinking. He is a great guy, and I was very happy when he got the job as Alabama's head coach. I know he is going to work hard—give it everything he's got—and I think he will be very successful.

It wasn't just recently I thought about what a blessing it was to play for coach Bryant and then to play for coach Shula. I knew at the time—when I was at Alabama and when I was with the Dolphins—that I was in a special place.

They were much alike in many ways. They were organized. They were disciplined and wanted disciplined people around them. They demanded the best of their players and gave their players their best. They taught us that if we worked hard, there would be rewards. They were class people. And they both gave you tough love at times. I use things I learned from them in everything I do.

I can't say enough about what it meant to play for coach Bryant. I knew a little about him, but once I started getting interested in Alabama, I learned a lot more. I had a fear as to whether I could play for him. I thought the standard was that everyone was Superman. But what he did was instill in us how to handle tough situations, to have Plan A and Plan B, and, as he said, always expect the unexpected.

A lot of people think that I wasn't a center when I first came to Alabama because I was listed as a defensive end. And as a freshman, playing on the junior varsity team, I was a defensive end. But I had also made a little impression as a center. The first day our freshmen group came in, Sylvester Croom took a few of the linemen to the projection room with a football. He had us snap the ball. I must have done pretty well, because he said I had what it took to snap. I have a great appreciation for coach Croom. We stay in close contact.

I wasn't highly recruited. John Mitchell and Ken Donahue recruited me, but they were after a couple of my teammates. The teammates went to North Carolina State, but they took me, anyway. They told my parents that I would have opportunities and that I would leave Alabama a good person. And I wanted to play in the best program I could.

My high school coaches were among those who didn't think I would make it. One of them told me I'd go down there on Sunday and be home by Wednesday. That is not a criticism of them. I was not looked on as a great football player coming out of high school, and they thought I had a better chance to play at a place like Virginia Tech, which was not the power it has become.

Dwight Stephenson (No. 57) is considered the best center in the history of football. He snapped to quarterback Steadman Shealy (No. 10) in the 1979 national championship season during his senior year.

It was odd how I became the starting center in 1977. Terry Jones had been the All-SEC center in 1976, and he was back for his senior year. But that spring coach Bryant moved Terry to nose guard, and I took over at center. And that meant I had to go head-to-head with Terry all spring. I didn't have much size. I was about 216. A lot of the guys thought I'd get killed. Don McNeal was among those.

I had watched Terry very closely when I was a freshman, working against the first offense a lot of the time. Coach Croom wasn't coaching centers, but he had been an All-America center and helped me. And coach Jack Rutledge and coach Dee Powell, the offensive line coaches, helped mold me.

But there is no substitute for doing it, and I had to do it against Terry Jones. Everyone knew that neither I nor Big T was going to leave anything on the field. After our first big scrimmage, both of us graded winners. How could that be? Someone had to lose. I think I probably fell into the "barely a winner" category. Terry had a great attitude about the move, and I will always think a lot of him for that.

We played about the same time in the pros, he at Green Bay and I at Miami, but we didn't play against each other in the regular season. We were going to play an exhibition game once, but he was hurt and didn't play. I was curious how the match would have come out. I know we would have competed. He's my best friend, but we would have done our best to win.

I had a great, great time at Alabama. We really did have fun. Every game was not quite a life-and-death situation, but it was the most important thing at the time. We didn't want to lose a game. We thought if we lost we were personally responsible. And practices after a loss weren't too good. Fortunately, we usually won—34 out of 36 games.

203

It was fun to know when we had the game won, a great, great feeling. And that's because we gave it everything we had. One of the best things about being at Alabama was playing with men who have remained good friends.

I still feel like I'm 22 or 23, but then I look around and see I've got a son playing at Notre Dame. And I see Big T's son, Terry Jr., playing in the league, doing a good job at Baltimore.

I live in Fort Lauderdale and have D. Stephenson Construction Company. I started it in 1994 and, just like coach Bryant wanted to build a good football team, I work every day at trying to build a good construction company. And I still see Don McNeal and Tony Nathan, Alabama and Dolphins alumni, who live in South Florida.

Dwight Stephenson was an All-American in 1979, winner of the Jacobs Award as the SEC's best blocker, and selected to the Tide Team of the Century. He was an All-Pro player for the Miami Dolphins, the NFL Man of the Year, and was inducted into the Pro Football Hall of Fame in 1998.

The
EIGHTIES

E. J. JUNIOR III
DEFENSIVE END
1977–1980

COACH BRYANT ONLY CAME OUT OF THE TOWER for four reasons: practice was over; some dignitary, like the governor, was visiting practice; someone was hurt; or he was going to chew someone out. One day coach Bryant started down the tower steps, and we all looked around to see if we knew the reason. We knew it was too early for practice to be over. We looked over by the tunnel to see if there was a limousine parked outside, and there wasn't. No one seemed to be injured. That left only one possibility. And he was walking my way.

I was a freshman, practicing with the second team defense. And I knew I was about to be chewed out. Coach Bryant looked at me and said, "E. J., go over there and put on a white jersey and get in there with the first defense." I was shocked. I guess I just stood there, because he said, "Did you hear me?"

I said, "Yes, sir," and sprinted over to the manager. By the time I got to the track that went around the practice field, coach Bryant had chewed out the guy who had been in front of me—chewed him up and spit him out.

And I was on first team defense!

Coach Bryant was not happy about the way we had played the week before against Nebraska in Lincoln. The defense had not played well and we had lost 31–24. And he didn't like the way our ends had played, because he told the ends, "I could take two freshmen and do better than what you did." And later that day, I was a freshman moving to first team defense. At the other end, another freshman, John Mauro, got moved up to first team.

E. J. Junior III wasn't sure if he was going to be good enough to hold on to his starting job at Alabama, but he was a first-round draft choice in the NFL.

We were getting ready to play Vanderbilt, and I thought maybe he was just moving me up because we were going to be playing in Nashville, my home town. But that didn't explain Mauro, who was from South Bend, Indiana, going to first team, too. It wasn't about geography.

I started against Vanderbilt and then pretty much started every game the rest of my Alabama career. But you were never comfortable about your position. I turned my knee against Mississippi State, didn't play much against LSU, and watched Dewey Mitchell have a heck of a game. We had John Knox and Wayne Hamilton, too. We were interchangeable, and it was difficult to tell who was the starter and who wasn't.

I think that helped us win games. That was partly because there wasn't much difference—if any—between the first team guys and the guys who gave them a break in games, so that was pretty tough on the opponent. And the other reason is that you had to keep pushing if you wanted to keep your job, and that made us all better. Once you got a taste of first team, you didn't want to go back to second team. I never forgot the chewing out of the guy whose place I took on first team.

It's funny that when I was growing up I hated Alabama. I guess it was because they beat everyone, including the team I wanted to win. It was sort of the way so many people hated the New York Yankees when they were winning all those championships. I was probably for Vanderbilt and Tennessee and Tennessee State. But as I thought about it more, I realized that everyone wants to be a winner, and Alabama was a winner.

As I began to get interested in Alabama football, I discovered that it wasn't just football where Alabama excelled. They were good in basketball and baseball and track. I was going into engineering and discovered that Alabama's engineering program was considered among the best in the country. I liked the social life, which was enough to be good but not so much as to be able to get me in trouble. It was away from home, but not too far away.

And then there was coach Donahue. I made a trip to Alabama on a weekend when there was no football game so I could really see the campus and talk to people. Coach Donahue met with me and my parents, and he sold them when he said, "I can't promise you that he'll start. I can't even promise you he'll play. That's up to him. But I can promise you he'll have the opportunity to get a quality education, and I can promise you that we will teach him about hard work, because we're going to work his tail off."

Playing at Alabama is an experience I'll never forget. It was about the tradition. I learned about character from coach Bryant. Class. How to push yourself beyond your limits. We were the first to hold up four fingers at the beginning of the fourth quarter. Everybody else does it now, but what that meant was that the fourth quarter belonged to us because we were so well-conditioned and so well-disciplined. In the fourth quarter, we were going to dominate. Coach Bryant could take a group of players who were good and make them great. He could take average players and make them good. Everybody had an opportunity to grow. He treated us all the same way.

And he was the reason we played as a team, not like a bunch of stars. Everyone understood his role.

One of the most shocking things I ever heard was from my position coach, Sylvester Croom. Going into my senior year he said, "If you play like you are capable of playing, you could be a first-round draft choice." I had no idea I might be able to play professional football, even though I knew I was getting some mention for All-America going into my senior year.

And coach Bryant had a way of keeping your feet on the ground. One day he said, "You're supposed to be an All-American? I haven't seen him play yet." And that lit a fire under me.

Coach Bryant taught us to be good football players, and it was a special experience to play for him. But I know we didn't get the vintage coach Bryant. He was much more mellow when I was playing for him. Not that he didn't command respect, but nothing like the stories I had heard from guys who played for him earlier. But just because he had changed with the times, the one thing that didn't change was the winning. We were 44–4 over my four years, a record that wouldn't be broken until the nineties by coach Stallings' teams.

We learned to work hard. In fact, the defining moment for everyone who played defense came on the goal-line stand against Penn State in the Sugar Bowl to win the 1978 national championship. When we were in the huddle preparing for that fourth-down play, the leaders of that defense—Marty Lyons and Barry Krauss and Murray Legg—laid it out. They said this is what we had worked for, this was that old-fashioned gut check, this was why we had sweated on the practice field in those 100-play scrimmages, this is what it is all about.

We learned that it takes hard work and discipline in everything. It's how you raise your kids, it's how you do your job. You can push, or you can be average. You can be complacent, or you can be great. It's up to you.

I've been licensed and ordained as a pastor. I'm the assistant pastor at a small ministry called International Prayer Village. I've worked in the school system with a mentoring program for four years as an administrator, and I was an executive director for a year with the Overtime Youth Center, which is Alonzo Mourning's youth program. I have been assigned to coach with the Rhein Fire in NFL Europe and could return to coaching in the NFL.

E. J. Junior III was an All-American in 1980, SEC Defensive Player of the Year, and a finalist for the Lombardi Trophy in 1980. The three-time All-SEC selection was the fifth player drafted in the first round and played for the St. Louis and Phoenix Cardinals, Miami Dolphins, Tampa Bay Buccaneers, and Seattle Seahawks.

MAJOR OGILVIE

HALFBACK

1977–1980

WHEN I HAD THE OPPORTUNITY TO GO TO The University of Alabama and play football for coach Bryant, it was not a time of rebuilding. My first year, 1977, was his 20th year at Alabama, so things were in place. The tradition was established, the routines were set, and everyone knew coach Bryant's system of hard work, discipline, teamwork, and all the rest that went into success. I've always considered myself lucky to be able to go to Alabama at that time.

It was not a complicated situation. Coach Bryant explained things in basic terms. We learned about hard work and never quitting and telling the truth and being honest with yourself. Do those things and you had a chance—and I emphasize *chance*—to be successful. Because as he told us, sometimes you can believe in something and work for it and you may still come up short. And in that case, you circle the wagons and try a little harder. I have thought of these lessons in business and in raising a family.

After you have been out of it for a while, it's fun to talk about how you just survived. I know that it wasn't fun at the time. But we learned that we could do more than we thought, that when we were fatigued, we could go on, could take another step, and then another one and another. And that is a lesson that stays with you, one of many that I am so grateful for. But you don't realize that lesson until later, and you are not truly grateful to coach Bryant until it is too late to thank him.

Major Ogilvie (No. 42) raced for a 22-yard touchdown to start Alabama to a 24–9 victory over Arkansas in the 1980 Sugar Bowl and secure the 1979 national championship. Ogilvie was the first man in college football history to score touchdowns in four consecutive bowl games.

I don't know if any of us could be fully prepared for Alabama football when we arrived as freshmen. I knew something about winning, because my high school teams were very successful. In six years of playing high school and college football, my teams had a record of 71–4. Our Mountain Brook teams won two state championships; at Alabama we won two national championships. And that was a lot of fun. But getting started at Alabama was starting over no matter how successful you had been in high school. We all had to adapt to the new situation.

The four losing games I played in were at Alabama. But that was over a four-year period, and we were playing tough schedules. Our non-conference games in those days were against Nebraska, Southern Cal, Notre Dame, Washington, and Missouri, which were very good, and teams like Miami, Georgia Tech, Virginia Tech, and Louisville, which weren't as good then as they are now.

Like most players, I remember the losses. But we won 44 games, which was one of the best records of any four-year group in Alabama football and college football history. I don't remember all the wins, but I remember the significant ones, the championship games.

We played to win, and we wanted to win national championships. We played in a lot of big games, and I enjoyed those. I think our teams had an attitude of going out, playing the best we could, and seeing where the chips fell. Most of the time we were on the right side of the scoreboard.

The 1979 Sugar Bowl game against Penn State was one of those games you are proud to say you were a part of and that you made whatever contribution you could. That was the toughest and best football game I ever played in. Penn State had a great team and they were well-coached. It was the hardest-hitting game I ever played in. It seemed as if the game was meant to go our way.

Another tough game that year was the Nebraska game to open the season. They were a really good team. They had beaten us the year before and then we had lost a lot of people from that 1977 team, Ozzie Newsome and Johnny Davis, for instance. Our 1977 team had done well and actually had a chance to win the national championship. Then we came back and started the season with a win over Nebraska. That was a real confidence-booster for us.

Even though we were ranked No. 1, we needed something for our confidence. In our first three games, we were playing top 10 teams, and then we were going to Washington. Typically, Alabama teams got stronger as the year went on. In 1978 we had to be pretty good from the get-go.

People seem to think we just coasted through the 1979 season, maybe because we beat Arkansas pretty decisively in the Sugar Bowl for the national championship. We did win a lot of games handily, but we had tough games that year against Tennessee and LSU.

One of the things about being lucky to be in the right place at the right time was something I was never aware of until after it happened. They've started keeping records on just about everything. The only thing that matters in football is the team, but they keep individual things that don't really matter, and one of them was my scoring touchdowns in four consecutive bowl games. That really says more about the team than one person. It doesn't mean anything to me compared to those national championship trophies.

I was probably destined to go to Alabama. My uncle, Hayden Riley, was on the staff at Alabama, a football recruiter and basketball and baseball coach. So I knew about the caliber of programs, that Alabama was a place where it was important to win. And that was of interest to me. From an educational standpoint, I was interested in accounting, and Alabama had a good accounting school. I was recruited by two really great guys in coach Mal Moore and coach Bill Oliver.

All of those things made Alabama the right place for me. But even if somewhere else had those things, Alabama had coach Bryant. And who would want to pass up the opportunity to play for him? It was something for a young person to be excited about, and it's still exciting for me today.

After my Alabama playing career, I was drafted by San Francisco. I was one of the last ones cut, and that was it for me. I came back to Birmingham where I have worked ever since. I'm now with Block USA.

Major Ogilvie was a four-year letterman, All-SEC performer, and captain of the 1980 Crimson Tide. Ogilvie was the first man in college football history to score touchdowns in four different bowl games—three Sugar Bowl games (two national championship games) and one Cotton Bowl, all 'Bama wins.

JEREMIAH CASTILLE

CORNERBACK

1979–1982

PLAYING IN COACH BRYANT'S FINAL GAME WAS SPECIAL to all of us on the 1982 team. It was a very emotional game for me because I took it upon myself to express to him what he had meant to us. I think it caught coach Bryant off guard, because I was such a quiet person in college. We were in the dressing room in Memphis before going out to play Illinois in the Liberty Bowl, his last game. I stood up and said, "Men, I want to say something." I think it surprised me as much as anyone else.

I'm a religious person, and I believe the Lord put it in my heart to express what coach Bryant had done for me in four years. I had come to him as an 18-year-old boy, and I was leaving a 22-year-old man because of him. That is what he did—changed boys into men.

I think it charged our team emotionally. I told coach Bryant what he had meant to all of us and how we felt about him. And then I said, "Men, there is no way we are going to lose this game."

Coach Bryant didn't react too much. He just nodded his appreciation.

Playing for Alabama was important to me. How many schools have the tradition of Alabama? Not many. When you have played for the Crimson Tide, you have been a part of the elite of college football.

Every time I pulled on that jersey, I thought about the importance of continuing the tradition of winning. I thought about people who had worn the

Jeremiah Castille (No. 19) was an All-American cornerback for Alabama whose sons followed him to Alabama as Crimson Tide players.

jersey before I did, because they had told me about the man who wore it before I got it. And I wanted to be a champion, too.

When Alabama played football, I wanted to be the best I could be because I was representing the school, the alumni, and the fans. I was representing my coach. And I was representing my family.

Everyone talks about football teaching life lessons. It's true. What you learn on the football field can be applied to how you live your life off the football field. If you work in corporate America, you learn to be a team player. If you have your own business, you learn to be a self-starter. If you are raising a family, you apply the lessons of discipline. If you want to be successful in anything you do, you have an advantage if you have played football for The University of Alabama, because you know those things and have experienced those things.

I have been fortunate to have played at Alabama.

I was easy to recruit. I am from Phenix City and Alabama had signed Woodrow Lowe and Billy Jackson in football, and a couple of guys in basketball from there. So I naturally kept up with Alabama. And like everyone else, I watched coach Bryant's Sunday television show. I particularly remember being excited when he talked about Woodrow Lowe. So it was part of my dream to one day play at Alabama. The first recruiting letter I ever received was from Alabama, when I was a junior, and that meant something to me.

I was lucky to stay close to sports following my Alabama playing career. I played professional football for six years, then coached in college and high school. I'm now executive director of Jeremiah Castille Ministries and serve as chaplain for the football team.

I'm very fortunate to have two sons who have followed me to the university to play football: Tim, a fullback and halfback; and Simeon, who is really following in my footsteps as a cornerback. I didn't have advice for them specific to playing football at Alabama or even attending the university. We believe they have been brought up to live their lives along certain principles that will serve them in every situation. I consider it a blessing.

Jeremiah Castille was MVP as he had a record-tying three interceptions in coach Bryant's final game, the 1982 Liberty Bowl victory over Illinois. He had a then-record 16 career interceptions. He was an All-American in 1982 and member of the Team of the Century.

TOMMY WILCOX
STRONG SAFETY
1979–1982

I SIGNED WITH ALABAMA PRIOR TO THE 1978 SEASON, but didn't play that year. That was the first year freshmen could be redshirted, and coach Bryant held out all but about two of us. So in 1978 I was the quarterback on the scout team against the first team defense, and I don't have to tell any Alabama fans what kind of defense I was going up against every day. At the end of the year, I was beat up and homesick. I had been a big fish in a little bowl, and now I was a little fish in a lake. And I wasn't mature enough to handle it. I wasn't going back to Alabama in 1979.

I lived in Harahan, Louisiana, and coach Bryant flew down to talk to me. He got a room in a hotel and had me over to explain things. He told me what he thought of me and why he wanted me to come back, and why it would be better for me.

I was a quarterback, but Steadman Shealy was coming back as the starter. Coach Bryant gave me an option. He said I could come back as Steadman's back-up, or, if I came back and did what he said, he thought I could start on defense.

I told him I didn't want to sit on the bench anymore. I wanted to play.

I didn't report on time. In fact, I was about a week and a half late, which is a lot when you only have three weeks to get ready for the opening game. So, of course, I didn't come back as a starter on defense. I was back on the scout team. I ran the offense scout team and was on the scout defensive team.

218

Tommy Wilcox (No. 15) turned in four interceptions as a freshman defensive back, including this one against Virginia Tech, and was SEC Freshman Defensive Player of the Year for the Crimson Tide's undefeated national championship season.

I took some punishment. I never came out of scrimmages. I had to stay after practice. And I was thinking, "This isn't what we talked about in that hotel room."

I was probably thinking about going home again, but the coaches kept talking to me, telling me what I had to do and that I would pass the test. Everything would be all right. And eventually coach Bryant saw I could handle it, and I moved up to first team defense.

It's hard for people to understand this now, but when we stepped on the field back then, everyone expected Alabama to win. And we did, too. When I pulled on that crimson jersey and that helmet, I never thought of anything except winning. It was a given. Of course, we worked awfully hard to make sure we won.

We didn't always win. Probably the toughest loss for me was in 1980. We had a 28-game winning streak and went to Jackson and lost to Mississippi State 6–3. We played well defensively and almost scored as time ran out, but we didn't. I think we might have gone on to a third straight national championship if we had won that game.

Because I was from Louisiana, the LSU game was big for me—not that I had been recruited by LSU. My father had played for Tulane, so we were not LSU fans. Alabama and Notre Dame were the schools I considered. About 75 percent of the players on our team were from Alabama, and so the Auburn game had always been the big one for them. I always told the guys before the LSU game that they had to play hard because that was my Auburn game. We'd go down there, and there would be signs about Wilcox being a traitor. I was 3–1 against them.

The national championship season of 1979 was truly special to me because I was a starter and I contributed. In a period of eight months, I had gone from not being in school and not expecting to play football to being on a national championship team.

When coach Bryant had recruited me, he told my parents that he wouldn't promise anything except that we would be on television a lot so my family could see me and that we would compete for championships and the chance to have a diamond ring. He kept those promises.

There was something about Alabama and coach Bryant. Back when I was coming out of high school in 1977, they were winning 10 or 11 football games a year. I came to Alabama as a quarterback. In high school we ran the wishbone offense, so it was kind of a perfect match for me. I wanted to play for the best, and at that time the best was Alabama. I knew it was going to be hard because of all other great players that were there. I felt like if I could go and play at Alabama with the best players in the country, I could do anything. It was a challenge to myself to compete with the best.

Alabama was the best, and coach Bryant was bigger than life. That was like icing on the cake. Alabama came to play Ohio State in the Sugar Bowl my senior year in high school and invited me out to practice one day. Coach Bryant carried himself in a unique way. He walked real slow, and he was a big, big man. I had heard about things he'd done at Texas A&M and at Alabama when he first got there, so I was in awe of him. He was just bigger than life. He was the most celebrated man I ever met. I had never met anybody bigger than him. Everyone knew who the Bear was. When you meet someone like that, you're in awe of them.

I look back and think how my life would have been different if I hadn't come to Alabama—and if I hadn't come back. He could have said to heck with me, and who knows where I'd be now? Fortunately, he didn't give up on me, and I was able to get a college degree and be known as an Alabama football player.

It was an honor to play for him, and I wish more young people could have had that opportunity. He was a great teacher, and not just about football. His emphasis on getting a degree was the reason I came back to Alabama after pro ball to finish up. And when I worked for a company that was bought out by another company, leaving me without a job, I thought back to coach Bryant and could hear him say, "What are you going to do now, Wilcox? You gonna quit or you gonna suck it up?" It's been a long time since he passed away, but I know all of us who played for him think about him and his lessons.

I've been in pharmaceutical sales for 18 years, but I also have a little fun thing, a hunting and fishing show that I do on weekends. I have a lot of celebrity guests, and the ones who are most popular are the former Alabama players who come on and tell stories about playing for coach Bryant. And that keeps me in touch with the Alabama family, too.

I've always liked to hunt and fish, and so did coach Bryant. He didn't have a lot of social interaction with his players, but he did like to talk to me about hunting and fishing.

After I finished, I was projected as a third-round NFL draft choice. My agent told me I could go into the USFL and make twice as much money.

A lot of players chose the USFL. I played for Marv Levy in Chicago. He would later take all those Buffalo teams to the Super Bowl.

Pro football was like vacation for me. They didn't hit anything like what we did in practice at Alabama. Practices were hard for some of the players, but not for any from Alabama. After my second year, I hurt my neck and the league folded. I was bought by Denver, but couldn't pass the physical because of my neck and gave up football to return to Tuscaloosa.

Tommy Wilcox was a two-time All-American and named to Alabama's Team of the Century. He was SEC Freshman of the Year in 1979. The four-year starter had 243 tackles and 10 interceptions and helped Alabama to a 39–8–1 record.

JOEY JONES
SPLIT END
1980–1983

NOT LONG AFTER THE 1982 FOOTBALL SEASON HAD ENDED, I was walking down the hall near the locker room. I heard coach Bryant yell at me and went jogging back where he was about to get on the elevator. He told me to ride upstairs with him. He said he knew I liked to fish and that when it warmed up in the spring, he wanted me to go down to his son's lake in Greene County and do some bass fishing with him.

You can imagine how excited I was. The coach-player relationship coach Bryant had with us was great, but he had just retired, and I thought how it would be to know him at a different level, to sit down and talk to him on a personal basis. And I was flattered that he had wanted that, too.

And then he died just a couple of weeks later.

Like almost everyone who played for Alabama, I came to Alabama in great part because of what coach Bryant had accomplished. But it was the entire Alabama tradition, how Alabama football had represented the state so well. Alabama players always seemed to exhibit so much more class, and you knew that came from the leadership.

In those days, a team could give out 30 scholarships, and I guess I got the 30th one. During the recruiting process, I didn't meet with coach Bryant a lot, and I'm not sure he knew who I was. After I signed, I heard he looked at me and then had a few choice words for the coach who signed me—Bobby Marks; that I was too small, that I wouldn't be able to play here.

Joey Jones (No. 4) was considered too small to be an effective wide receiver, but he led Alabama in receiving for three consecutive years.

My freshman year was rough. I was about sixth string. And coach Bryant made some remarks in the newspaper that I was too small a target for the quarterback.

But my sophomore year, a bunch of receivers got hurt, and he pretty much had to start me. As luck would have it, I scored a touchdown and had a pretty good game. The next week we played Kentucky, and I had another good game and also started returning punts. The following Monday, coach Bryant told me not to dress out. He said I had been in a couple of physical games and was beaten up. I wasn't hurt, but it was his way of telling me I had finally made it. He winked at me and told me to sit out practice. My confidence meter was sky high after that.

I had a pretty good year. In the wishbone, we didn't catch a lot of passes, but I kind of made the 12 I caught that year pay off. I averaged over 30 yards per catch and had one against Vanderbilt for an 81-yard touchdown.

Anyone who played football for Alabama is honored to have been a small part in the tradition created by hundreds of coaches and players through the years. When you are playing, it means a lot to pull on that crimson jersey; 20 years later it still means something. I have great respect for those who played before me, those I played with, and those who have played since. I also sense respect from others for those who played for the Crimson Tide.

It means a lot to me to have a tie to the university, to be an alumnus. Alabama alumni and fans are everywhere, and it's always a treat to meet with them.

I was fortunate after my Alabama playing career to have an opportunity to play with the Birmingham Stallions and then with the Atlanta Falcons. I wanted to be a high school coach and got into the business as an assistant coach at Briarwood Christian, then got a head coaching opportunity at Dora.

There was a time when I thought I needed to do something to make more money than I could in coaching and got out for a while. But I found myself going to watch practices in the afternoons and going to games on Friday nights. I was fortunate enough to get back into coaching in 1996 at Mountain Brook.

224

Joey Jones was invited to play in both the Senior Bowl and the East-West Shrine Game following his Crimson Tide career. He was Alabama's leading receiver in 1981, 1982, and 1983. Since 1996 he has been a very successful high school head coach at Mountain Brook.

PETER KIM

PLACE-KICKER

1980–1982

IN HONOLULU THERE IS A LARGE KOREAN POPULATION that was quite isolated as I grew up there. As a result, I did not speak English well, even when I went to the University of Hawaii in 1978. When I transferred to Alabama, there was a joke that I had told my coaches at Hawaii that one of the reasons I was going to Alabama was to improve my English. "You couldn't pick a worse place for that," was the reported reply of my coach.

When I started playing football at Hawaii, I had a curiosity about playing at a higher level, playing big-time football. I watched teams like Alabama and Nebraska. In my freshman year, we played at Nebraska. We went into the stadium where everyone was dressed in red. I had no idea what that represented. Was it some kind of red day? It didn't occur to me it was the school color. At Hawaii our school color was green, but we only had a few thousand fans at the games, and no one wore green.

I watched the 1979 Sugar Bowl game, Alabama vs. Penn State, on television. The most memorable thing I had ever seen was the Alabama goal-line stand. I can't overstate how much that impressed me, and I had a burning desire to be in a program like that. I believed I had the talent to do that. I thought how wonderful it would be to play for one of the best teams in the country. And I kept going back to that goal-line stand.

I considered several schools. I had had a good game against Nebraska, kicking a 51-yard field goal, and they seemed to want me. Oklahoma did,

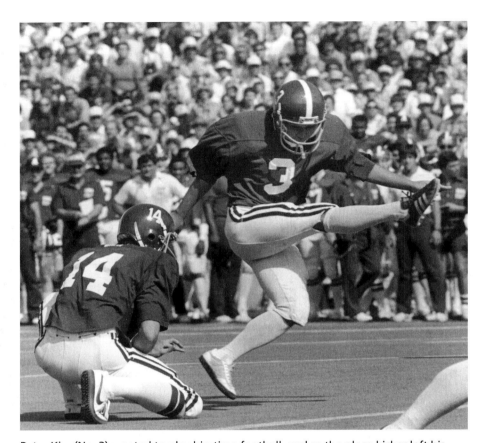

Peter Kim (No. 3) wanted to play big-time football, and so the place-kicker left his scholarship at Hawaii and walked on at Alabama. He kicked the final point of the Paul Bryant era.

too. Alabama didn't seem to care. But I looked at the weather belt and decided Alabama had better weather than Nebraska or Oklahoma.

Almost no one at Alabama knew—or seemed to care—that I was coming. I spoke to Dr. Gary White, the academic counselor, and to coach Jeff Rouzie. They told me if I wanted to come, to come ahead, but I was on my own. So I bought my plane ticket and headed to Tuscaloosa.

I have never regretted it. At least I don't regret it now, although I remember there were some bad days. I didn't get to play my first year as a transfer, but I did practice every day. And I got hurt.

I also have to admit there was some culture shock. I got homesick and couldn't sleep at night. I would think about leaving, but what would I go back to? I'd be a bum! I really had no place to go. I had to make it.

I even had a hard time adjusting to the food. I had never seen black-eyed peas, fried okra, or grits. The first two weeks were really bad. But I got hungry, and so I began to eat. I wasn't from a wealthy family. I didn't have a car. So when everyone went home for Thanksgiving, I was home alone in the dorm. I went to the Campus Party Store and bought a carton of milk and a sandwich and sat on the quad. The campus was deserted. I saw perhaps one car every other hour. I was very lonely.

It was a little bit of a joke, but also true, that when I first began eating in Bryant Hall, Alabama had only about 20 black players. All the black players sat together at lunch to eat. And all the white players sat together. I really didn't know where to sit. I didn't want to offend either group. So I sat by myself. And no one sat with me. Finally, my roommate, Woody Umphrey, who was our punter, started sitting with me, and then some other kickers, and eventually other players, black and white.

That seemed to me to be a culture thing. The black players sat together in meetings, and always in the same seats. But there was no resentment. And I didn't think it was bad then and I don't think now that it was bad. It was just a cultural thing. As we got more black players, it began to change. I had to think about Korea with a history of more than five thousand years. Cultural changes do not occur overnight.

I had many friends. I was not singled out as Asian. I made lifetime friends in Alabama and got along with everyone. I have nothing but good memories of my time in Tuscaloosa. Even in the fraternity houses, I was well-received. And I didn't even know what those fraternities meant until I was a junior or a senior. Now I appreciate the hospitality even more.

In those early, lonely days, what really kept me at Alabama was the desire to succeed. I saw the type of program and what coach Bryant had to offer. I didn't really realize how big coach Bryant was until I got there, but it didn't take long. And I had no idea that football was so important to the people of Alabama and how important coach Bryant was to the players and to everyone else.

It was quite a spectacle and eye-opener for the people of Hawaii when some ten thousand Alabama fans showed up for Alabama's game against Hawaii in Honolulu in 2003. I get a chill just thinking about it.

I went to Alabama to become a better football player. But what I became was a better person. And I wouldn't be where I am today if I had not gone to Alabama. Every bit of what little success I have had, I attribute to coach Bryant.

I learned hard work. Although I was a place-kicker, I didn't go in early after practice with the rest of the kickers. All four years, I stayed out and ran with coach Donahue and the defensive linemen—my being maybe 5'8" and 165 pounds with the biggest guys on the team.

I have been gone for more than 20 years, but there is not a day that something doesn't take me back to my days at Alabama. Not just football, but all the teaching I had from coach Bryant. We learned pride. We learned confidence. We learned to persevere.

There have been many days running my business that I have wanted to take a knee, just quit. But then I think about coach Bryant, who told us there would be days like that in life and that you have to get it done. And those thoughts get me going.

There may have been those who would have been uncomfortable walking into an executive office and trying to make a deal. But I had the confidence and poise to do that because of coach Bryant. I never took "no" for an answer without an explanation. And often I was able to turn a "no" into a "yes." And maybe not as much now, but when I have had to make a deal, I go back to it being "crunch time."

When I started my restaurants, I knew there were things that had to be done. That was what I had learned. Get it done. I had a few restaurants fail, but I had learned at Alabama that you learn from your mistakes, and so I think I may have learned more from those than the restaurants that have been successful.

I now own and operate five different ethnic restaurant chains throughout Hawaii, but also in shopping center food courts, on military bases, and now in university food courts around the nation. I look forward to one day having a Yummy Korean Barbecue in the food court at Alabama. I was quite honored to be 1998 Entrepreneur of the Year by Ernst and Young for the state of Hawaii, and that, too, is something I attribute to coach Bryant.

It was a great honor for me to play for him, to play in the game in which he became the winningest coach with 315 victories, and to play in his last game and kick the last point for him.

There is no way that I can ever repay what Alabama gave to me. I have been so happy that Mal Moore, who was offensive coordinator when I played, is now the athletics director, and I have been able to help a little through his Crimson Tradition campaign.

Peter Kim was a record-setting place-kicker for Alabama as he had records for field goals in a game with 4 (on two occasions), in a season with 15, and in a career with 37, all since broken, and also made 54 consecutive extra-point kicks.

WALTER LEWIS

QUARTERBACK

1980–1983

D ID YOU EVER THINK ABOUT WALTER LEWIS, HEAD FOOTBALL COACH, University of Alabama? I did. My coaching résumé is next to nothing—1989 as an assistant coach working with running backs at Alabama. But a few years ago, Kevin Scarbinsky of *The Birmingham News* wrote a column about Alabama having trouble getting a coach and maybe it was time for a black coach. I thought I had learned a lot from coach Bryant, and I felt like I had learned a lot from Homer Smith when I was on Bill Curry's staff. I thought I could bring some stability to the program. I went so far as to even talk to some guys about being coordinators. They told me I must be crazy. But later one of them called me back to see if I had heard anything, so that told me at least he was thinking about it. But of course I hadn't heard anything. Mal Moore would have had to have been athletics director from the moon to select me to be Alabama's head football coach.

I enjoyed coaching. If I had been mature enough, I might have stayed in it. I still think about it every day, Xs and Os going through my mind all the time.

I went to the Mississippi State game in 2004 and ran into Siran Stacy. He had been a tough customer when I was coaching him. And there he was with his beautiful wife and four beautiful children. And he was happy to see me. He said, "Coach Lewis, it's so good to see you." I never would have expected to hear that from Siran. He had been difficult.

Walter Lewis (No. 10) was a running quarterback in the wishbone offense of Paul Bryant's final season. He would become a passing quarterback as a senior under Ray Perkins.

But he told me that something I had told him in 1989 had registered with him. He said I told him I could either get a saddle and ride him or I could get a bridle and lead him, but however we did it, we had to get the job done. It was 15 years before I knew I had an impact on him.

But I'm not a coach. And I didn't really prepare to be one. I earned my degree from the university in engineering, and now I'm a partner and run an office in Birmingham for Gardnyr Michael Capital. It's an investment banking firm working with cities, counties, and universities throughout the state structuring bonds.

In a way, I prepared early to be Alabama's quarterback. But when coach Bryant first approached me about signing with the Crimson Tide, I turned him down. When it came time for recruiting, I thought Alabama was "slow playing" me, kind of keeping me as a prospect in case something better didn't work out. They were recruiting John Bonds, too. But when Bonds committed to Mississippi State, Alabama came after me. Auburn had been recruiting me hard from the beginning.

Alabama sent four assistant coaches to see me—Bobby Marks, Sylvester Croom, Bryant Pool, and Perry Willis. When they were leaving, Perry Willis told me it cost $45 per minute to make a call from the airplane, but that he was going to call me on the way back. And that if I'd commit they'd turn the plane around and come back. But I didn't commit.

I was in school, and it was getting late in the recruiting season, and my father came to the school. He said coach Bryant had called from practice— they were getting ready for the Sugar Bowl in December 1979—and they had only three scholarships left. They wanted me, but they had to know something. I called coach Bryant and committed.

I was at the funeral of my sister about 20 years later, and I heard a story I had never heard before, that a friend of coach Bryant, a Dr. Hays from Brewton, had written him and said Alabama had to sign me, that even if I never played a down, I'd be an asset to Alabama.

I couldn't really say that I was an Alabama fan growing up. I liked pro football. And I liked a lot of college teams, including Ohio State, Southern Cal, and Grambling. But I watched coach Bryant's show on Sundays, and I was so impressed because everyone lined up just perfectly. I thought it was awesome that every man was exactly where he was supposed to be. Things like that were what made a difference. And I'd go out in the backyard and practice running the wishbone the way Richard Todd and Gary Rutledge did it. I was able to run the option in junior high school and then became the quarterback at T. R. Miller in the 10th grade.

I made a recruiting trip to Alabama that fall, and really that's when I knew it was the place for me. Johnny Elias, Robert Russell, and I talked about it later. You just felt so at peace. There was no high pressure. They showed you what they were doing and told you that's what they intended to do, which was to win.

All of my friends weren't happy about me selecting Alabama. A lot of them thought coach Bryant would never play a black quarterback. But I wasn't the first. Coach Bryant had played Michael Landrum at quarterback. I think there may have been some skepticism in my house, but when coach Bryant visited, he erased any doubt.

Coach Bryant said we bled the same blood and sweated the same sweat. There was a bond among the players. Coach Bryant wasn't concerned about your color. He was interested in producing and performing, and that's what the players wanted.

I never thought being black was an obstacle at Alabama. All anyone got was an opportunity, and that was all I wanted. I thought if I had the opportunity to compete, I could do the job. And that's the way it was. I got the opportunity and took advantage of it. Coach Bryant said he wanted his players to remember him as being fair. I remember a lot of things about him, and that is one of the most important.

It wasn't easy. Coach Moore was my coach, and he was hard on me. I thought he was picking on me. It was demeaning. He'd grab my face mask and hold it so I had to look him in the eye while he cussed me out. I'd take it, but at night I'd go back to my room and cry and pray. Before he left Alabama to go to Notre Dame, after coach Perkins came in, coach Moore told me he had been testing me. He said if I folded on the practice field, I'd fold in front of eighty-five thousand. And he was preparing me for the day when I'd have to step into an office, maybe the governor's office, which I sometimes do, and I can stand the pressure. Being the quarterback at Alabama is about having courage.

233

But I also wanted to be out of the limelight. I enjoyed playing football, but I always felt my primary reason for being at Alabama was to get an education. Coach Bryant, and later coach Perkins, really helped me in that they stood in the gap for me. When things went wrong, they took the blame.

I was OK with coach Bryant retiring because he had prepared us for that. I thought coach Moore would replace him. Instead they brought in coach Perkins, and I resisted the change, having to go from wishbone quarterback to something else as a senior. But coach Perkins sold me on the fact that I'd be able to do it, and all the players bought into it, which really helped.

One thing I was not prepared for was coach Bryant's death. In his last game, the Liberty Bowl, I had thrown an interception and was down. And then coach Bryant wanted to change some personnel. I questioned him about it, and he jumped me, told me he was running the team. There was about a two-minute timeout, and I spent the whole time telling him how sorry I was. And after we got back to campus, I went to his office again and apologized. He said, "Walt, that's part of the game." It was four days before he died.

A few years ago, Major Ogilvie, Tommy Wilcox, and I were speaking at a Boys Club event for Paul Bryant Jr. I was telling that story, and Paul Jr. overheard it. He told me that was a story coach Bryant had told him in one of the last conversations they had.

I was coming out of an electromagnetics class about 1:00 P.M., and a cheerleader told me. I was in shock. I went back to the dorm, and it was full of reporters, TV trucks outside. I never realized how sick he was.

Mrs. Bryant and I had always had a nice relationship. It was an honor when she asked me to be a pallbearer. During that time, I thought how much he had done for us all. He had opened our hearts. He had built men of character.

My wife, Rena, who is also an engineering graduate from the university, and I have six children. One other thing coach Bryant did was to establish the Bryant Scholarships for children of the men who played and coached for him, and that certainly means something to me.

Walter Lewis quarterbacked Paul Bryant's final football game in 1982 and was unanimous All-SEC, MVP of the Sun Bowl, and team captain in 1983.

VAN TIFFIN

PLACE-KICKER

1983–1986

Every kicker would say that the situation that came to me was a dream come true, because a kicker always dreams of making the winning field goal in the last second of a big game. But when you're standing on the side-line and see the possibility of it coming down to you, you have second thoughts about it. And that was the situation in 1985 against Auburn.

As our final drive started with us trailing 23–22 and almost no time remaining, I didn't see us getting into field-goal range, at least not after Mike Shula got sacked on first down. But two plays later, we were up toward mid-field. I was still a little in denial that we would get into field-goal range, but the guys on the sideline with me were yelling encouragement, that it was going to come down to me. And when Greg Richardson got out of bounds at the 35-yard line, the opportunity was there.

Auburn didn't call a timeout, so everything was just rush, rush, rush. And that's the way I wanted it. I didn't want time to think about it. I never enjoyed having to wait through a timeout, even though by then I had gotten used to that and handled it better. But I'm glad Auburn didn't call a timeout, because I don't know how I would have handled it in that pressure situation.

Kicking is a lot like hitting a golf ball or a baseball. When you don't feel anything, you know you've hit it good. And that's the way it was. I can just remember getting back and kicking it, not feeling it, and looking up and there it was going right down the middle. I thought, "This can't be true. This

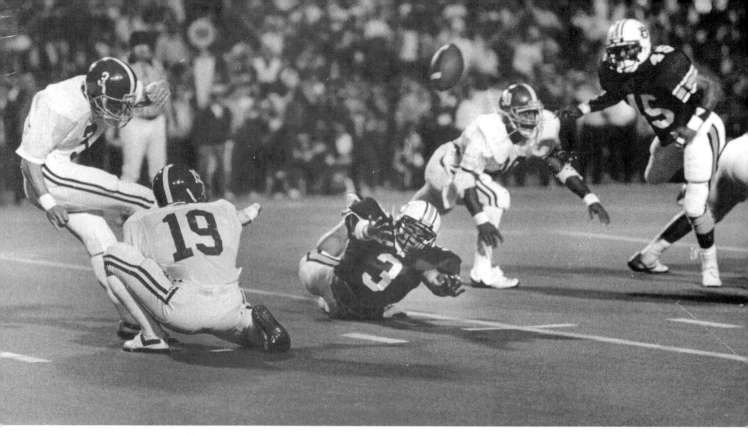

Van Tiffin kicked one of the most famous field goals in Alabama history, a 52-yarder as time ran out to beat Auburn in 1985. He never missed an extra point.

can't be real." Also, I could just feel Kevin Porter, the Auburn end, coming from the left side, and I knew it was going to be close. When I got out there on the field it was, "Line set. Snap." I was expecting more of a delay in snap-ping the ball, so I was just a little bit late getting to the ball. Kevin Porter was offside, so he was actually a little early. Had he not been offside, he might have blocked it.

It was like it happened yesterday. That's all people remember me for, and that's OK. At least they don't remember me for missing that field goal. That would really be bad.

It was particularly meaningful for me since I had grown up an Alabama fan. I was about nine or ten when I went to my first Alabama-Auburn game, and in the seventies my parents started buying season tickets. After the high school game on Friday night, we'd leave and go to the Alabama game. I was at the 1979 Sugar Bowl game against Penn State. So I was a fan.

But I almost didn't go to Alabama. Alabama wasn't going to give a kicker a scholarship, and I was close to going to Southern Miss. But about two weeks before signing day, coach Perkins called and said, "We want you to come to Alabama." That was all I needed to hear. And he said if I won the starting job, he'd put me on scholarship.

I won the kicking job as a freshman. My birthday was late compared to everyone else in my recruiting class. I think Cornelius Bennett and I were the youngest players on the team. Coach Perkins called me in on September 6, my 18th birthday, and told me I would be the kicker when we opened the season against Georgia Tech. Of course, he didn't know it was my birthday. The next January, coach Perkins called me in and gave me a scholarship. That was an exciting day for me and my family.

Perkins was intimidating to me. I would cringe every time he walked by, hoping he wouldn't say anything to me. He'd come up and stare right through you. He was a good man and always had good intentions with players. We all had such respect for him. I would do anything for him. I have talked to him some the past few years. If I talk to him even now, I start getting butterflies and on edge.

He was a high-class individual and expected high class out of players. He wouldn't tolerate anything the way it shouldn't be. I respected him and didn't realize that's what I had for him. I believe if he'd stayed at Alabama, he'd have won a national championship. In his and my last year, he was 10–3 and really strong, but you couldn't blame him for leaving for a better offer. I think he was a great coach.

I know kickers are sometimes considered strange, but I didn't think of myself that way. I got along well with my teammates. Coach Perkins always made kickers do everything everyone else did, except for the full contact. We did all the running and the off-season program everyone else did.

I really never got a big kick that had a bearing on the game until 1984 against Penn State. We won that game 6–0. In fourth quarter, the score was 0–0, and I tried a 53-yarder and made it.

I don't know if Alabama still has the record for consecutive extra point kicks, but I know we set the record. We reached 199 before we had a miss. It started with Peter Kim, who made his last 50 or so. Paul Trodd kicked one when Peter got hurt. I had 135 in a row when I was at Alabama. And then Philip Doyle finished it out. We went five or six seasons without missing one. I missed the first extra point I ever tried in high school, then never missed another one. But when we were breaking the NCAA record, I just barely made it. The pressure nearly got to me. It takes good holding, good snapping, good blocking, and good luck for a streak like that.

The longest field goal I had was 57 yards against Texas A&M. I made two or three that day. The 57-yarder was just before halftime, and we had a nice wind helping. You always wanted to be really positive with coach Perkins. In the third quarter, we had that same wind against us and were facing a 51-yard field-goal situation. He looked at me and said, "Can you make it?" Well, I wasn't going to tell him no, but as I was walking out there I was thinking, "No way." So I was a little surprised when I made it.

During my freshman year, Malcolm Simmons and Paul Fields held for me. Larry Abney held for me my sophomore, junior, and senior years. Darren Whitlock was the snapper, and he didn't do anything else but snap. He was a good one. When he snapped, eight of ten times the laces were turned up perfectly. All Larry did was hold. Anytime I wanted to snap and hold, they were ready. That's so important for a kicker. When I walked out there, I knew the snap and hold were going to be there. It was almost an unfair advantage.

I got to play a little professional football with Miami, but when I got cut the next year, I went back to Alabama to finish my degree work. I'm in the family business, Tiffin Motor Homes, in Red Bay, and we go to games as part of the big RV community. It's a good way to stay familiar with our products and our customers. Dr. Gary White, who was assistant athletics director under coach Perkins, helped me get a summer kicking camp started in 1987, and it's still going. That's a nice change of pace for a few days.

Playing at Alabama was a dream come true. I really enjoy seeing my old teammates at games. And I can see how football helps you all your life. You have to be able to focus, and you have to give full effort. That's every day in football.

238

Van Tiffin was an All-American in 1986 and was selected to the Team of the Century. He holds the NCAA record for best extra-point percentage for a career (135 of 135, 100 percent). He hit one of the most famous field goals in Crimson Tide history, a 52-yarder as time expired to beat Auburn 25–23 in 1985, and also kicked the winning field goal against Auburn in 1984. He had a school record 14 points by kicking (three field goals, five extra points) against Mississippi State (since broken).

MIKE SHULA

QUARTERBACK
1984–1986

THE FIRST TIME I STEPPED ON THE CAMPUS of The University of Alabama as a high school senior, I was very much aware of the rich tradition of Crimson Tide football. I knew it was a place you could win the national championship. But there were many things I didn't know. I was surprised at the atmosphere, exactly what a college town should be. It was a beautiful campus. I was surprised that it was a relatively small school, about fifteen thousand at the time. I loved it.

It may be that the reason I was so comfortable here was that the people were themselves. No one was trying to put on a face for you. It was, "This is Alabama. This is what we are about." It was so natural and made you feel real, real comfortable. You'd go to other places, and people were going out of their way to impress you. Think about it in terms of people you meet. Would you rather be with someone who was trying so hard to impress you or someone who was just himself, natural?

I had visited a few schools and had a few more scheduled. My father couldn't be really active in my recruiting because he was very busy with his team. They played in the Super Bowl that year. But when I returned from Tuscaloosa and told him I had decided on Alabama, he suggested I take at least one more visit to be sure. I made one more visit, and I was sure it was Alabama. I canceled the rest of my visits.

I had not been recruited by coach Bryant's staff. I was not a wishbone quarterback. When coach Perkins got the job, I knew a little about him, but I did not know him. My father did, of course. Coach Perkins hired George Henshaw from Florida State, who had been recruiting me, which is how I came to get a visit.

When I got here in 1983, I thought I knew a lot about SEC football. But I found out I didn't know the depth of feeling people in this state have for Alabama football. But I found out in a hurry, thanks to guys like Curt Jarvis who had grown up with it. Just about everyone who came in was from Alabama or near Alabama except me and Craig Epps, who was also from South Florida. And the more I learned, the more excited I got about being here.

I was fortunate to play in two of the most exciting games imaginable. I've always bragged about being the first one to reach Van Tiffin after his 52-yard field goal on the last play of the game to beat Auburn in 1985. I really wasn't the first, but I was close. I remember coming off the field after Greg Richardson had gotten out of bounds to stop the clock and thinking we had done our job. There was never any doubt in my mind that Van would make the kick. You never thought about a miss when Van was kicking. Later I saw an end zone shot of the kick. If there had been a pole going up 90 degrees from the exact middle of the crossbar, I think the ball would have hit it. But it would have to have been a long pole, because I think that kick would have been good from 60 or 65 yards.

And of course the Georgia game that year is one that is most fond in my memory. We needed a touchdown in the final moments to win that game, and as a quarterback, I knew I had to get the ball into the end zone. It was a two-minute drill situation, which is something a quarterback dreams about. I hear more stories about how people reacted when Georgia blocked a punt with a couple of minutes to go, and then how they reacted when we came back and Al Bell took the ball in for the winning touchdown.

My four years here just flew by. And I mean flew.

I always pictured myself as being in football as long as I could. I had been around football all my life, seeing almost all of my father's home games and some road games. I wanted to play as long as possible and then to stay in it. There's just something different about football.

It was a challenge to take the next step, whether playing in the NFL or getting into coaching. And I was fortunate enough to coach for 15 years in the

Mike Shula was an exceptional quarterback as an Alabama player. In 2003 he was selected as Alabama's head coach, one of a handful of former Tide players who have ascended to that position.

NFL, and I enjoyed it very much. I have said many times I would not have left that for any college job except one—this one.

I truly never allowed myself to think about becoming head coach at Alabama. I was asked about it, including by some close friends. Coach Perkins had asked me if I'd be interested. I never really answered anyone, just sort of blew the question off.

And I had never been approached about the Alabama job. I remember when coach Franchione left. One of the coaches at Miami put a list on my desk. He had gotten it off the Internet. It showed me 28th on a list of possible successors.

I heard about the incident involving coach Price. And then he was fired on a Saturday. We were in minicamp. That night coach Moore called me. I couldn't sleep after that call. We had practice again Sunday, and I don't think I could tell you what the quarterbacks did. I knew that coach Moore and Dr. Witt were coming in that night.

I knew I had to be one of the first people he called. I knew coach Moore a little, and we had mutual friends. I didn't know who else he might have called.

242

And after he talked to me, for the first time in my life, I felt something was tugging me toward this job. I had never had a feeling like that.

On Monday the Dolphins had an alumni golf tournament. The word was starting to get out. There was a cameraman there, but I just gave him a "no comment." But the neat thing was that all those former Alabama players who were Dolphins alumni were there—Don McNeal, Tony Nathan, Dwight Stephenson. Even Bob Baumhower came for the first time ever. He had his "Wings" cart on the back of his truck and provided wings for everyone. They were all fired up. They were "Roll Tide"-ing me.

On Wednesday there was another Dolphins function, an annual coaches-media get-together, and of course those guys were all over me. But I wasn't going to announce anything there. I left that function early, went home, and had about a two-hour conversation with coach Moore.

I had never had a representative, but after that conversation, I thought I needed one. I didn't have the job, but I was feeling good about it. I called a high school friend of mine, Mike Rodgers, who represents pro baseball players. He left his son's baseball game in West Palm, drove to Fort Lauderdale, and was with me Thursday to help me as we worked out the details. And Thursday night the Alabama plane came and picked us up.

From the first call Saturday to the final agreement on Thursday, my mind was flooded with all the great memories of being in Tuscaloosa. And yet I had to do some serious work in finding out where the program was so I could make an intelligent decision. I knew where my heart wanted me to be, though.

My wife, Shari, was not from South Florida. She was from Tampa, which is more like Tuscaloosa than it is South Florida. So in one respect it wasn't a big adjustment for her, but in another it was. People from outside the state of Alabama don't understand how the people of this state feel about Alabama football. And the people in Alabama think this is the norm.

As nice as I thought it would be, it has been 10 times better than I could have imagined or expected. Maybe 50 times better. We timed out right for these facilities. The people here are as good or better than I remembered. There's even more attention to Alabama football than when I was here as a player.

And I think there is a sense of pride that is even greater now in the players. Or maybe it's because I didn't see it as a player in myself, but I can see it in these players. I can see it in their eyes, what it means to them. They are proud to be a part of this football team.

Our assistant coaches all say that by far it is the best job they ever had.

People ask about dealing with the attention and pressure. To me, that's why you come here. The expectations are so high. They have always done things in a first-class manner. People here have lofty goals, and not in a pompous way. You can't say that about other places.

I came here as a player to win a national championship. We didn't get that done. So one reason I was happy to get this opportunity is I felt I had left some business on the table.

243

Mike Shula was an All-SEC quarterback at Alabama in 1985 as he became only the second quarterback in Alabama history to pass for more than 2,000 yards. He started three years and passed for 35 touchdowns. He became Alabama's head football coach May 8, 2003.

BOBBY HUMPHREY

TAILBACK

1985–1988

I KNOW THAT A LOT OF PLAYERS WHO WENT TO ALABAMA grew up fans of the Crimson Tide and were well aware of the great Alabama football tradition. That didn't have anything to do with me selecting The University of Alabama. The great Alabama tradition was not a factor in my decision because I was not aware of it. I didn't grow up an Alabama fan. Now, I did like it when Alabama played its games in Birmingham and I could sell Cokes and get into the games to watch. But I was a city boy, from the projects. No one in my family had gone to Alabama or knew anything about Alabama and its tradition.

That said, it was one of the greatest decisions I ever made and something I am very, very proud of. While I didn't know anything about the tradition before I got to Alabama, when I did get there, I began to find out about it. And the more I learned, the more I wanted to know, and so I found out even more. That made me even more proud of the decision I had made.

I think I decided on Alabama because I thought it was the place I would have the best chance for early playing time. At the time, I think, Auburn had several good running backs returning. Alabama had Kerry Goode, a premier back to be sure, but Kerry had been injured.

I wanted to stay close to home and had decided I was going to stay in the state. I knew it was going to be either Alabama or Auburn. So I decided to go to Alabama because the chance to compete for playing time seemed better.

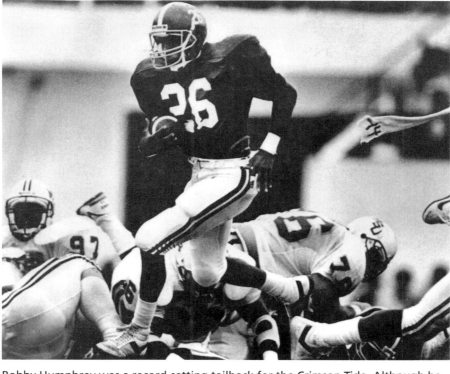

Bobby Humphrey was a record-setting tailback for the Crimson Tide. Although he grew up in Birmingham and sold Cokes to attend Alabama games at Legion Field, he had little knowledge of 'Bama tradition until playing for the Tide.

Once you have done it, you realize it means a lot to play for the Crimson Tide. There is something special about wearing the crimson and white and knowing you are a part of the best in college football. I look back and see that it was almost lucky that I ended up at Alabama and consider myself very fortunate.

Over the years, I have talked with a lot of football players from many, many colleges and universities, and I am convinced that no one has better fans than The University of Alabama. I have been amazed at the number of fans I have met and the places I have met them around the country. When I was playing in the NFL, I would see Alabama fans in the stadiums supporting me. I'm now coach of the Birmingham Steeldogs, and Alabama fans make up a great part of our fan base because I am part of the Alabama family.

Players from other schools are envious of the support that Alabama players get from Crimson Tide fans, who in my opinion also are a part of the Alabama family.

Alabama fans have great respect for the men who played football for the Crimson Tide. Most amazing, though, is the memories of the fans. The games sort of run together for me, but I have met many, many people who can tell me in detail about things that happened in games in 1985 and 1986 when I was a freshman and sophomore. They remember extraordinary details, and you know that you have given them something to be proud of.

After my playing career at Alabama, I played five years of professional football, three at Denver and two at Miami. I signed with Buffalo in 1995, but never played.

In 1997 I returned to the university to get my degree. And when I graduated in 1998, there were Alabama fans there to show their support for me as a student.

I worked for a semester in the Tuscaloosa County school system, then got the opportunity to coach the Birmingham Steeldogs in their first season in 2000.

Bobby Humphrey was an All-American in 1986 and 1987 and named Alabama's Offensive Player of the Decade. In 1986 he rushed for a school record 1,471 yards. He was SEC Offensive Player of the Year in 1987. He was MVP of the Sun Bowl. He played in the NFL for Denver and Miami and is coach of the Birmingham Steeldogs arena team.

DAVID SMITH

QUARTERBACK
1986–1988

I HAVE A RECURRING DREAM THAT I AM DOWN ON THE SIDELINES of an Alabama game and I am being told I have to go in and play. I'm the age I am now. It's explained that it's been discovered I have a year of eligibility left. But, of course, I don't know any plays and haven't played football in 16 years. But I've got to do it because it's Alabama. Fortunately, I wake up before anything bad can happen. I guess that's my version of the "not ready for the history test" nightmare.

I've loved Alabama football as long as I can remember. When we were kids we'd take T-shirts and put holes all in them so they'd be like Alabama's tearaway jerseys and put numbers on them, like 22 for Johnny Musso. We still love going to the games. My wife, Ali Blumberg, was an Alabama gymnast, and our children love sports, too. I do watch games a little differently than most people do. I'm not critical because I know what is going on and that it's a lot more difficult between those sidelines than it is from row 50.

Like most athletes, I don't think I appreciated the experience of being an Alabama football player as much then as I do now. But I do know it was different. I had played football all my life, every fall and practice every spring. I didn't think it was particularly special. But in my senior year at Alabama I could go out to eat or go to the mall and I would be amazed at the number of people who would recognize me and want an autograph or want a picture taken with them. And not just kids—adults, too. I guess I can understand how star pro athletes might get frustrated by it, but it was always special to me.

And just as amazing is that even after all these years it still happens, though not as often.

I'm also surprised that I don't remember the games as much as I remember the friendships I made at Alabama, players sitting around the dorm or running or lifting weights. I look back and can take some satisfaction in what we were able to accomplish.

Being elected captain was an honor following the 1988 season, but it is certainly more special now, particularly since the other captain was Derrick Thomas.

It is amazing that I ever played at Alabama. Following my junior year at Gadsden, I heard from Alabama and most of the SEC schools and several others around the country. Not a ton, but quite a few, and probably a lot of them were just standard letters they were sending out to a lot of players. But in my senior year, I got hurt in the second game, and the letters stopped. It was a torn cartilage, which isn't a big deal now, but was then. I had always played basketball, but couldn't play my senior year. I did get back to play baseball and some people thought I should try to play college baseball. I had a good year, pitching and playing first base. I struck out only twice and made the East-West All-Star Game. But I wanted to play college football.

Today you have guys who are delaying entry into college until midway through the next year. They call them grayshirts. I guess I was one of the original grayshirts, but without a scholarship. I decided to go to Tennessee Military Institute to get in another year of football. Unfortunately, after about five games, I broke my collarbone.

But I went ahead and enrolled at Alabama and was a walk-on in the spring of 1984. Mike Shula had a broken ankle, but there were quite a few guys in front of me—Hugh Smith, Jeff Webb, Larry Abney. And Gene Newberry had finished high school early and came in that spring. So I was just a helmet-holder. I did a little work in individual skills, but never got to participate in team drills or seven-on-seven. But Dave Rader was the quarterbacks coach, and he did include me in all the meetings and things like that. Then in the A-Day Game they sent me in, even though I had had no team work. I only got to play one series, and I threw only one pass, which was a completion, and I remember it as if it were yesterday. After that series, coach Perkins

David Smith was a walk-on quarterback for Alabama who became not only a starter but an all-star and Crimson Tide record-holder.

walked across the field and told me he hoped I would stick around. That was the first time I knew anyone was watching me.

I was still about seventh on the depth chart the next fall and didn't dress out for any games. I went to all the home games and sat in the stands. And during the week I was one of the scout team quarterbacks, which was good for me. I got to practice against some really good players on defense and got used to the speed and intensity of the game. You got beat up a lot, but it was a learning experience going against guys like Cornelius Bennett, Emanuel King, and Jon Hand.

I dressed out for the first time against Georgia in Athens in 1985. I had gone from about fifth on the depth chart the previous spring to number two. In fact, Mike Shula and I were splitting time at number one until a week or so before the opener when coach Perkins announced Mike as the starter. I about wore myself out in warm-ups before that game. Coach Rader had to settle me down, telling me the game didn't start for another hour. It was a great first game, although I didn't play. But I knew I was one play from being the quarterback, so I stayed in the game, really paying attention.

250

The first game I played in was against Vanderbilt, and I played in three or four more games, then got to play in the Aloha Bowl when we beat Southern Cal, which was a lot of fun.

I didn't letter in 1985, and I was still behind Mike in 1986, but I played more and lettered. They also made me the back-up punter late in 1985 when Chris Mohr had a little stress fracture, and I was listed as the back-up in 1986. Fortunately, I never had to punt.

Coach Perkins left after that year, and coach Curry came in. In February he called me into his office and told me coach Perkins had planned to put me on scholarship and so he was putting me on.

With a new coach, everyone was starting over in the spring of 1987. Mike was gone, but we didn't have a starter named after spring practice. Then about a week or two before the opener in 1987, I was named the starter. I'll never forget my first start, against Southern Miss, and my first touchdown pass, although I didn't see it. I threw about a 20-yard pass to Clay Whitehurst. I made the throw before his break and then someone hit me and knocked me on my back. But I heard the crowd cheer and I knew we had scored. We went up and beat Penn State, the defending national champions, when Bobby Humphrey had a great day, then lost to Emmitt Smith and Florida when I played about the worst game I ever played. Then I broke my collarbone against Vanderbilt and was out the rest of the year until the fourth quarter of the Auburn game.

We had another offensive coordinator in 1988, my senior year. Coach Homer Smith came in, and it was tough. Once again we didn't have a starter coming out of spring. It was me, Vince Sutton, Billy Ray, Jeff Dunn, and Gary Hollingsworth. And again, about a week before the first game, I was announced as the starter. Coach Smith expected nothing less than perfection. He was the best quarterback coach a man could have. He knew all our strengths and weaknesses and how to use us to Alabama's best advantage.

He gave me a lot of confidence. I always liked the idea of making decisions when I was at quarterback. I always thought I had a knack for being able to stay a step ahead. Before our opener at Temple that year, coach Smith told me he was going to sit in the press box, eat a hot dog, watch the game, and let me call the plays. And we did that. We ran a no-huddle offense and beat Temple pretty good. I probably called 90 percent of the plays. It was even set up for me to call the blocking checks, so I could go to the line and communicate the blocking we needed, as well as the play.

Then I tore my ACL and missed three games. It would have been four games, but we had the controversial Hurricane Bowl against Texas A&M, when we decided not to go when the game was scheduled. That worked great for me, because I got to play against Texas A&M and wouldn't have when it was originally scheduled. I was very glad we won that game—because of the controversy and also because we had lost the week before to a very good Auburn team. Against Auburn, we had closed to within five points late, and I thought if we could get the ball back, our two-minute offense could get us a touchdown. But we didn't get the ball back. So the A&M game was good mainly because we could get over the Auburn game.

251

One of the games I missed was homecoming against Ole Miss—the game where we didn't complete a pass and got beat. I remember being on the phone with Phil Savage, who was a graduate assistant and is now general manager of the Cleveland Browns, and his saying, "We're one play away from losing this game." And just then Ole Miss broke a long run and beat us.

I was able to start the next week. We went to Knoxville and beat Tennessee, which is always good.

I was sorry I couldn't play another year for coach Smith. You could see how the offense really grew, and Gary Hollingsworth got to run it the next year.

I was fortunate enough to receive a few awards, and I'm particularly proud of two of them. In fact, the only things I have that aren't boxed up are the Monday Morning Quarterback Club SEC Back of the Year and the Pat Trammell Award.

I have a State Farm agency in Birmingham now, and I'm involved with the university on the Planned Giving Advisory Committee. And I want to be even more involved in the future.

David Smith was Most Valuable Player as he set Alabama bowl records by completing 33 of 52 passes for 412 yards in Alabama's 29–28 come-from-behind victory over Army in the 1988 Sun Bowl.

The NINETIES

ROGER SHULTZ
CENTER
1987–1990

No one expected us to beat Tennessee in 1990. We had started that season with three straight losses, and Tennessee had not lost since we had beaten them the year before. I can remember Lee Corso on ESPN saying we would be like a high school team going into Knoxville. But we won the game, and I finished my career having never lost to Tennessee. In the locker room after the game, I said, "We ought to have to pay property taxes on Neyland Stadium, because we own it."

After that came out in the newspapers, coach Stallings said, "Man, why did you say that? We've got to go back and play them there in two years."

I said, "I don't." And added, "It was pretty good, though, wasn't it?" And coach Stallings said, "Yeah."

It must have stung them pretty good, because I still hear from Tennessee fans.

I came to Alabama from Peachtree High School in Atlanta, Georgia, but I had lived in Alabama from 1974 to 1980, in the Center Point area and in Homewood. I played little league football, and our uniform jerseys were red with white numbers. In fact, I think every team in the league had red jerseys with white numbers. Everyone was an Alabama fan.

At the end of the season, everyone on the team got a copy of a letter from Bear Bryant about "What are you going to do to make your mark?" The letter had been photocopied about a million times and you could barely read his signature, but to us it was like a personal letter from coach Bryant.

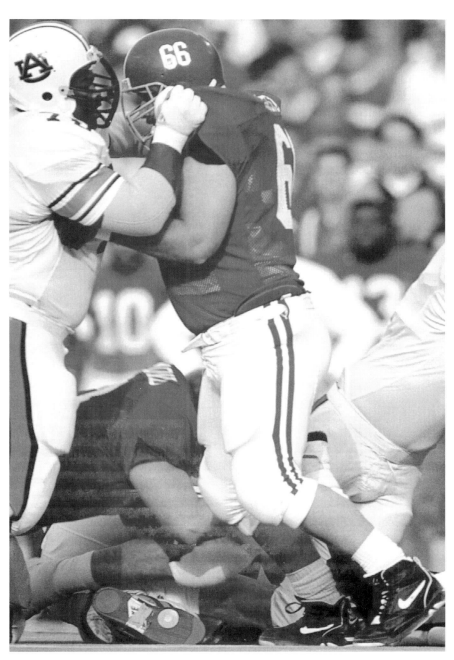

Roger Shultz (No. 66) was a two-time All-SEC center for Alabama, but is as well-known for his humor as he was for his excellent football play.

They put out this poster with coach Bryant pointing and saying, "The Bear Wants You," like the old Army recruiting posters, "Uncle Sam Wants You." I had it over my bed, and now my son has it over his bed. They didn't have nearly as much memorabilia as they do now, but I had everything "Alabama" I could get. Almost every day I wore something with Alabama on it. I still have an Alabama pillow my mother got for me in Tuscaloosa.

In 1980 I was in the sixth grade, but some of us were going to get to go with the high school team to Legion Field and sell Cokes for the Alabama-Auburn game. That would mean we could get into the game. But there was a mix-up and my name wasn't on the list. Three or four of us managed to scrounge up one ticket. Then we went to the gate and told the guy our mother had sent us out to get our coats. He let us all in on that one ticket.

We didn't have seats, so we stood around the fence. And they kept running us off. But I can remember how big Byron Braggs was. And we got to see coach Bryant in person. That's also when I learned that college students can get drunk. I had bought one of those big Alabama "Number One" hands with the finger sticking up, and an Auburn student took it away from me and tore the finger off.

256

Because of my father's job in hospital administration, we moved around a lot, finally ending up in Atlanta. My coach there told me if I worked really hard I might earn a scholarship to Furman. I thought, "Furman! I want to play for Alabama!" One of the doctors there, Dr. Milton Frank, had played for coach Bryant, and he got Alabama to write me a letter when I was in the 10th grade—the first recruiting letter I ever got.

I was recruited by coach Perkins, then played for coach Curry and coach Stallings. I had about three different coordinators and a handful of different offensive line coaches, although coach Fuller was always there.

When I went on my recruiting visit and coach Perkins offered me a scholarship, I said, "I'll take it." He said I didn't have to decide right then, and I told him I wasn't letting him take the offer back. The first person I met on that visit was coach Gryska. What a great guy, then and now.

A lot of guys on that recruiting trip ended up signing with Alabama: Lee Ozmint, Chris Robinette, John Mangum, Charlie Abrams, Danny Cash, Robert Stewart, Gary Hollingsworth. We all felt like teammates from the first time we met.

I remember meeting Wes Neighbors and thinking, "I'm taller than he is, so I should be able to play here." Of course, he was about the only one I was taller than.

Ohio State was recruiting me, too, and when I got back from my recruiting trip there, I told my father I might want to go to Ohio State. Dad had always said it would be my decision, but when I said that, he said, "No."

In a way it's a waste to have the opportunity to play football at Alabama when you are only 18 to 22 years old. I wish now I had paid more attention to things around me. It was so regimented—meetings, practice, meals, study halls, classes. I wish I had just taken a moment to stand in the middle of the field and look around at the full stadium.

Now I realize so much more what it means to pull on that crimson jersey, what it means to be a part of the greatest tradition in college football.

It's funny that I don't remember many of the games I played in. In fact, I was redshirted in 1986 but made the trip to New York for the Kickoff Classic against Ohio State, and I remember that game. We beat Ohio State, but had to hang on when Derrick Thomas got two pass interference calls. Of course, he wasn't *the* Derrick Thomas then.

I was part of an SEC Championship team as a player, and then I stayed around for a couple of years as a graduate assistant and got a ring when we won the national championship in 1992. One of the most amazing things is to go to the "A" Club Room before a game and see all those national championship rings, some from back in the sixties and seventies.

They picked an All-Century Team at Alabama, and you could be an All-American and not even get mentioned for it. I knew a guy at another SEC school who didn't make All-America and made their Team of the Century.

Alabama is just different. If someone writes a book about college football, you can bet Alabama and coach Bryant are going to be in that book. I have been across the country and even out of the country and people comment on my size and ask if I played football. I say "Alabama," and you can just see it register.

Think about how big it is for Auburn that Alabama went there to play a game? We went to Lafayette, Louisiana, to play a game, and they had parades, let school out, and I think maybe rededicated the town.

Can you imagine if an Alabama player ever wins the Heisman Trophy? He'll be able to be elected governor.

I'd like to be recruiting for Alabama now. I'd tell all those prospects that I would guarantee if they go to Alabama and we go 13–0, we'll win the national championship.

I never had any goal other than to play college football for Alabama. I didn't have any goals beyond that. When I got to Alabama I didn't even know what I wanted to major in. Shula and Neighbors were in business and Hollingsworth was going into business, so I went into business. If they had been in painting, I guess I'd be a painter now.

People always said I was a hard worker on the football field, and I think that's the main thing I took from Alabama. The difference in real life is that you have to do it every day. And that's what I do. I go to work every day and do my job with a good attitude.

I'm associate athletics director for external affairs at Troy University. Before that I did some radio work, which I enjoyed, too. And I don't mind saying that I'd be thrilled if one day Mama Called. I worry that she's lost my number.

Roger Shultz was unanimous All-SEC center in 1989 and 1990, and selected for the 1991 Senior Bowl.

GARY HOLLINGSWORTH

QUARTERBACK

1989–1990

You know what it means to be Crimson Tide? It means trying to explain to your children why someone would want Daddy's autograph. They have no clue. It is pretty amazing. I was lucky to go to Alabama, and then it took some bad luck for Jeff Dunn for me to have an opportunity.

Although I wasn't a big Alabama fan growing up, Alabama was the first school to show any interest in me as a prospect, and that meant a lot to me. Rockey Felker was recruiting North Alabama and had seen several games in which I had played. He was actually recruiting players on the teams we were playing against, but when he reported back after his scouting trips, he mentioned the quarterback from Hamilton. After that happened a few times, coach Perkins said, "Well, Rockey, don't you think we ought to be recruiting him?"

I didn't really have that great of an appreciation for Alabama football when I first got to Tuscaloosa because I hadn't followed it that much. But once I got there, I quickly realized the tradition. I particularly realized what an honor it was to be a quarterback at The University of Alabama, where people like Joe Namath and Kenny Stabler had played. That's pretty big to me now, and it was huge when I was 18 years old.

Gary Hollingsworth (No. 14) was an unheralded quarterback who was elevated to first team in 1989 when Jeff Dunn was injured. Hollingsworth took advantage of the situation to lead 'Bama to the SEC championship and earn Player of the Year.

In 1989 it was pretty much acknowledged that we could be written off if anything happened to Jeff Dunn. He was our only experienced quarterback. I had been redshirted as a freshman in 1986, then didn't play in 1987 or 1988. I threw one pass in our opening game, and then against Kentucky in our second game, Jeff hurt a knee.

The season was a satisfying one for me personally. I was able to come in and keep going what Jeff had started. We won a share of the SEC championship.

I like to think that I had the confidence I could do the job. That's part of football, that the back-ups are ready to step up and play. Everyone on the team has proven something to the coaches or he wouldn't be there. Sometimes guys aren't ready when the opportunity comes. But in football, and in a lot of other things, you never know when it's coming, and you have to be prepared as best you can. I think I've taken that from football to my business career.

It's possible that I wouldn't have been ready if the opportunity had come earlier. It worked out very well for me from the standpoint that I didn't play my first three years. A lot of guys, I think, are put in situations in which they're forced to play earlier, and sometimes they're not ready. I got to travel with the team a good bit. I got to go to Neyland Stadium and experience it without having to be the quarterback playing in Neyland Stadium. The same was true for Death Valley at LSU and some other places. You aren't under the gun, but at the same time you get to experience and feel what it's like. So then to play as a junior finally, I think I was better prepared for what I encountered than some of the guys who have to play the first time they ever go to Neyland Stadium. I think that can be hard sometimes.

I'm glad I got the opportunity and that it went the way it did. There's a satisfaction there because I could have had some opportunities probably to go play at some other schools and played earlier and maybe played more, but to look back and know that you're a part of one of the greatest traditions in college football is tremendous. It gives me great satisfaction to have been able to be a part of that and compete at that level.

I really enjoyed my time at Alabama. And I enjoyed living in Bryant Hall. We had a good group of friends. Once you finish, you stay in touch with a handful, but people begin to spread out and have families and careers, so you don't see or talk to one another. And this was a group of guys who were almost inseparable for four or five years.

There is one thing as a quarterback I know I am not remembered for, and that is running. But I remember one run. We played an unlikely game, playing at Southwestern Louisiana. I ran a naked bootleg and gained about 25 or 30 yards, which was easily the longest run I ever had in my career. I went out of bounds in front of their bench. And all of our linemen and the rest of the guys started laughing. I think it offended their team because they didn't really know how big the joke was. It wasn't that we were laughing at them; it was that I ran 30 yards.

In 1989 Bo Jackson won the Alabama Sports Writers Association professional athlete of the year award, and I was the amateur athlete of the year. Bo wasn't able to be there, so coach Dye was there and accepted the award for him. Coach Dye told a story about an Auburn spring game that Bo wasn't participating in. All the kids wanted to go see Bo play in the game, and they were disappointed when he didn't play, Dye said. So Bo came up with the idea to get a bunch of kids on the field and he would race them. To make it fair, Bo gave the kids a 50-yard head start, and Bo went on to win the race.

When I gave my acceptance speech, I said that coach Stallings had decided to hold me out of our spring game, too. And, I said, we had a similar event. Except in my case the kids gave me a 50-yard head start.

One of the most interesting games we played was the Mississippi game in Jackson in 1989. They got up 21–0 in the first quarter, but then we scored 62 straight points. We led 48–21 at halftime. We also outscored Tennessee 47–30. I threw a lot of passes to my fullback, Kevin Turner. And in 1990, after starting the season with three straight losses, it was satisfying to come back and beat Tennessee, LSU, and Auburn.

After finishing at Alabama, I went to the Houston Oilers as a free agent, but I had been in athletics long enough to know when I didn't belong. I came back to Alabama, and since 1991 I've been with Cavalier Home Builders in Addison where I'm sales manager.

Gary Hollingsworth was All-SEC and captain of the 1990 team. He holds Alabama records for completions in a game (32 against Tennessee) and season (205) in 1989. He also holds the Tide mark for all-purpose yards per game for a career (170.9). He was SEC Offensive Player of the Year in 1989.

ERIC CURRY

DEFENSIVE END

1990–1992

I KNOW COACH STALLINGS DIDN'T TALK ABOUT THE NATIONAL CHAMPIONSHIP until very, very late in the 1992 season. But we thought about it much earlier—the previous spring. During spring training, we hoped we wouldn't have to run after practice. Coach Stallings was a great believer in post-practice conditioning. One day before we ran, Derrick Oden, one of our captains, had the courage to say, "Coach, if you don't run us after practice today and just let us off every now and then, we promise you we'll win the national championship." He promised that everyone would give it his all in practice. I can't remember if coach Stallings ran us after that practice—I think he did—but from time to time he would reward a good spring practice by giving us a day off from running.

So that meant it was up to us to make good on Derrick's guarantee. And we made it through the regular season undefeated and had the opportunity to face Miami for the national championship in the Sugar Bowl.

Before every game, just before we went out on the field, coach Stallings would bring everyone together for a prayer, then the team would head for the field. For some reason, after the prayer before the Sugar Bowl, everyone seemed to be in a private little world. It was very quiet. A player or two would go out, then a few more, and so on. It was very different, very quiet, very focused. No one said anything.

Eric Curry was a unanimous All-American on Alabama's 1992 national championship team. He was leader of a defense that shut down Miami in the Sugar Bowl.

Eventually, we were all gathered in the tunnel, preparing to take the field. And when they announced us, it was showtime. We were insane. It was like a big-time fight, Tyson vs. Holyfield, or a barroom brawl. And it was like the roles were reversed. We were hyped up like you would expect Miami to be, although not in an in-your-face way like Miami.

Miami was intimidated before the kickoff. They lost the game before the first snap. They weren't ready.

We had worked so hard in practice that week we could have beaten the Cincinnati Bengals. I know when I was on that field that night, I didn't hear anything until there was only a minute or two left in the game and I knew it was over. It was the most focused game I ever played in. I look back on it now, and it's no wonder Miami didn't win, because I'm sure I wasn't the only

Alabama player in that type of zone. What Miami did was wake up a sleeping giant.

My favorite coach at Alabama was Mike DuBose. He was a difference-maker, my role model, my father figure. He put a fire under me and gave me that edge. His players gave 110 percent. He was a hands-on coach who molded each of us to be the best we could be. And he was always for the player, trying to make you better, whether coaching or talking or staying on you, or helping you off the field.

I also loved coach Stallings. He was a player's coach. As best I can tell, he was the next best thing to Paul "Bear" Bryant.

I remember coach DuBose's speeches before the Tennessee games. We would do sprints on the field before the game, and he would let us know that we were on our home turf. He would say, "Even though we're out of town, this is our field and this is our house." And that's the attitude we had. He would give some of the most memorable speeches I've ever heard. You'd have chill bumps. You'd be ready to play the game that very hour. He'd have you in the moment.

Being at Alabama was all about tradition. For a player to put his hands on the grass of the practice fields or at Bryant-Denny Stadium was an unbelievable thrill, a dream. You always felt the coaches and the students and the fans were all behind you, encouraging you to be your best. That's part of the tradition. As I got older, I'd tell the younger players to realize the importance of stepping onto that field, to remember they were representing The University of Alabama. That's prestige. That's honor. And every team that plays against Alabama knows they don't measure up to the Crimson Tide.

One thing I admire is our team fighting back now to get to that point where teams coming into Bryant-Denny are beaten before they step onto the turf.

After your years as a player at Alabama are over, you find there is a mystique about having played for the Crimson Tide. People know that if you could play for Alabama and earn a degree from the university that you will work hard, grind it out, and never give up.

I grew up in South Georgia in the Herschel Walker era, and everyone believed in the tradition of the Georgia Bulldogs. People lived Georgia football. I was also being recruited by Florida State, which was doing well.

When I came to Alabama for a recruiting trip, Steve Webb took me around and introduced me to Alabama players. And coach Larry New did an excellent job of showing me what Alabama football was all about. Although it was a fairly long trip, six or eight hours, I was taken by how people were so thoroughly involved in Alabama football tradition. You couldn't overlook the achievements of men like Cornelius Bennett and Derrick Thomas if you were an outside linebacker, which is what I played then.

And one other thing made a big impression on me. Alabama had those plain uniforms. Those guys might not wear a lot of colors, but they played hard. They kept the game as plain and no-nonsense as their uniforms. And I liked that.

After I finished at Alabama, I was drafted by Tampa Bay and played there from 1993 to 1997, then played in Jacksonville from 1998 through 2000. I still live in Jacksonville. But I also consider Alabama home.

Eric Curry was a unanimous All-American for Alabama's 1992 national championship team. He was Chevrolet Defensive Player of the Year and UPI and Washington Pigskin Club Lineman of the Year. He was a Lombardi Award finalist and finished 10th in Heisman Trophy balloting.

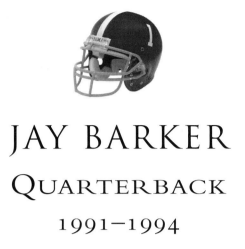

JAY BARKER

QUARTERBACK

1991–1994

IT WAS FUNNY THAT ALMOST NO ONE EXPECTED US TO WIN against Miami in the national championship game in the New Orleans Superdome at the end of the 1992 season. When we were preparing for the game, a reporter said to me, "Do you know what you're stepping into? This is like David going up against Goliath."

I said, "Well, I know who won that battle."

I believe the thing that defines Alabama football is the national championship. It is the great part of Alabama football tradition. And while the opportunity to play for the national championship is huge for the players and coaches, I believe it is most apparent in our fans.

I was fortunate enough to be a part of a lot of big moments as an Alabama football player, but probably nothing compares to running onto the field as a sophomore quarterback about to play against the No. 1 team in the nation with Gino Torretta, the Heisman Trophy winner, quarterbacking Miami. I can't even remember my feet hitting the turf, I was so nervous.

And then the most electrifying situation in my life was the Alabama crowd. Alabama fans filled the Superdome on January 1, 1993. I think Alabama fans turn into a new species when the national championship is on the line. That is when you see the true fans. They are home and in their comfort zone in that atmosphere.

Miami had the nation's longest winning streak, and almost all the talk was about Miami. But we thought we would win the game. Before the game, coach Stallings told me that he didn't think we would have to pass much to win, that we could run it just about every down. We saw a weakness that we could run right at them. They were very fast if you tried to go wide, but after looking at the films, we saw we could beat them. And it worked out just about like coach Stallings said it would.

To us it seemed like it was right winning against everything that was so wrong. And we did it the right way: with sportsmanship. I've always believed that the game was good for Miami, too, because they seemed to have a change in attitude that was for the better.

After that game, we were all so excited and, really, spent. But of course, everyone wanted to go out and celebrate. I went back to my room to get changed and decided to lay down on the bed and watch the highlights on television. I fell asleep. There was a banging on the door, and when I first woke up I thought maybe I had just dreamed the game. But then I realized how sore I was and knew that we had played.

It had seemed the city was covered with Miami fans before the game, although there were certainly more Alabama fans in the Superdome. But when we went to eat that night you could hardly find a Miami fan.

I can still remember the cry of an Alabama fan that night. "'Bama's back!" And that probably brought as much joy to me as it did to him.

I have never seen the videotape of the televised version of the game. I have gone through the coaching video. Between plays, the camera goes to the stands, and I have paused it to see how happy our fans are. I love to see people happy, and if I had a small part in that happiness, it means a lot to me. I've thought I might never look at the television version because I've got it in my mind how the game went, and I don't want that to change. But someday I'll probably watch the TV tape.

There are some games that would obviously be big ones, and that Miami game ranks at the top. Certainly our 29–28 comeback win over Georgia in a night game at Bryant-Denny Stadium in 1994 and the Citrus Bowl win over Ohio State at the end of that season were big.

But I also remember games like the comebacks against Mississippi State in 1992 and 1994.

The 1992 season was incredible. It is very, very difficult to go undefeated. Certainly we had some outstanding players, but we also had a lot of guys who

Jay Barker was quarterback of Alabama's 1992 national championship team as a sophomore and finished his career with a record of 34–2–1 as the starting quarterback.

were—for lack of a better term—role players. There were a lot of pressure moments, but I don't think we recognized them because it was the job that had to be done. How was I not nervous facing a must-make fourth-and-10 against Tennessee? I don't know, but I wasn't. In looking back, I have great respect for what my teammates and coaches did.

Other than the Miami game, it seems more people remember our comeback against Georgia than any other game. That was a humbling night for me. What most people don't remember is that I was benched, the only time in my career I was taken out of a game because I wasn't playing well. Coach Stallings took me aside and said, "Let's get over here and take a look." It was what I needed, and coach Stallings figured it out.

The 1995 Citrus Bowl in Orlando was the last game in my college career. I think Ohio State had about six first-round draft choices. They had an excellent team, and we were kind of the Cardiac Kids type of team. And we lived up to our name. I don't think any quarterback could have a greater thrill than the last play of his college career being to throw a pass to Sherman Williams that went for a 50-yard touchdown in the final minute to win the game. That gave us a four-year record of 45–4–1, the best of any class in Alabama history.

It's great to remember the wins, but there are so many things we got out of being Alabama football players. I tell my kids the same thing coach Stallings told us: "You'll never go wrong by doing right." That sticks with you. Our coaches cared about me as a person, how I was going to measure up as a husband and a father and a worker.

You hear Alabama players talk about "gut checks," that you are going to have them in life. And you learn that at Alabama. You learn about high expectations. You learn to be a team player.

I can never give back to Alabama football what it has given to me. Alabama football has impacted just about everything I have done, and there is not a day in my life that passes that someone doesn't say something to me about playing at Alabama. I think that's true for almost everyone who has pulled on that crimson jersey.

I've had a lot of men I have looked up to, and many of them are the products of athletics. And I always hoped that things I did off the field would live longer than what I did on the field. The greatest example of that is John Croyle, who has done so very much good in taking care of the children at his ranches.

John invited me up several years ago, and while I was there he asked if I would throw with his son, Brodie, to try to help him out. I threw a few with him, then said, "John, I don't want to mess him up."

I have the greatest admiration for Bart Starr, who played at Alabama, and Mike Kolen, who played at Auburn, as men of integrity.

I never wanted to appear "holier than thou," but I hoped that what was in my heart would shine through. It's a fine line. I believe that championship trophies are important, and I was competitive and wanted to win every game. But relationships last for eternity, and I like to think they made me a better person.

I was born to be an Alabama football player. My dad loved coach Bryant and Alabama, and we grew up cheering for the Tide and going to games when we could. At age five I was telling my friends that I was going to play for coach Bryant. I honestly think my class was about the last one that identified itself as the Bryant Generation. We didn't just wear the jersey. We represented it.

I almost wasn't an Alabama player. I only played one year of quarterback in high school, and coach Curry's staff was not recruiting me. But when coach Curry left and coach Stallings got the job, my prayer had been answered. Before that, I was afraid I was headed to Auburn. But coach Stallings called me the night he was hired.

271

I still see a number of my old teammates, but right now we're focused on the games our children are playing. Maybe soon we'll be sitting down and talking about our Alabama careers more. Meanwhile, it is wonderful to continue to be embraced by the fans for our accomplishments as Alabama football players.

I've been fortunate to stay close to sports and close to people as an on-air personality on WJOX radio in Birmingham and through speaking engagements and endorsements. And we have FaithWorks, a company involved in restaurants, real estate, and charitable foundations, and Nspira, a merchant services in the hospital field.

Jay Barker had the best record of any Alabama starting quarterback, 34–2–1, and was an All-American and winner of the Johnny Unitas Golden Arm Award as the nation's best quarterback in 1994.

KAREEM McNEAL

OFFENSIVE TACKLE

1992–1995

I NEVER DREAMED THE 1995 CITRUS BOWL GAME would be my last football game.

One of the most exciting games I ever played in was the Citrus Bowl at the end of the 1994 season. That was a really big win for our seniors because it gave Alabama a 45–4–1 record over four years, the best four-year record in Alabama history. That was my fourth season, too, but I had been redshirted as a freshman in 1991, so I had another season to play.

I was home in Tuskegee that next summer. In July of 1995 I was riding with my brother-in-law and a friend when our car left the road. We were all thrown out of the vehicle. My brother-in-law had a cut on his back. My friend had a concussion. I had the worst injury.

I don't remember the accident and don't remember the next week or so in the hospital. It was sometime after that I became aware of what was going on. My spinal cord had been crushed. I was paralyzed from the waist down.

I definitely felt I had been dealt a bad hand. It was a rough time for me and my wife and my family. And it was rough for my friends and for my team.

I had married my wife, Rene, the day after the SEC Championship Game in 1994, about seven months before the accident. Rene is from my hometown of Tuskegee. Seven years after the accident we had twin boys, Kevin and Carson.

Kareem McNeal (No. 74) was a starter on Alabama's 1994 Alabama football team, but prior to his senior year was paralyzed in an automobile accident. He is a junior college instructor in strength training.

Coach Stallings came to visit me on several occasions in the hospital. I know he was there when I came out of surgery to fix my back, but I really can't remember much about that meeting. I had the surgery to straighten my back and put rods in it to hold it in place. That was at Carraway Hospital in Birmingham. I was in Carraway for about a month, then I moved to Spain Rehabilitation. Coach Stallings came to see me regularly when I was there and was very encouraging.

I tried to stay positive, believing there would be a good outcome. And I have continued to stay positive. I can remember the May before my accident when Christopher Reeve had his accident that paralyzed him. I remember thinking, "Oh, man! Superman!" And I remember feeling sad for him. He became a great spokesman for people with spinal cord injuries and, I think, a lot of good has come from the attention he gave it. Naturally, I follow pretty closely the efforts being made. I think we're getting close to trying some promising work on people.

I was supposed to graduate in December 1995. That fall I went back to school, but I took it slow, taking some Internet classes and going at a slow pace. As it turned out, I took only one extra semester to earn my degree. I graduated with a degree in human performance in May 1996. Then I went to work on a master's degree and earned that in 1999 in health education. We have stayed in Tuscaloosa, where I am an instructor at Shelton State Community College, teaching weight training and health and serving as strength coach for a couple of teams.

Not long after I graduated, I had another surgery to remove the rods in my back. That was because I had become so active. I have stayed with a rehab program—swimming, stretching, and standing in a "stander" I have that keeps my legs accustomed to bearing my weight. The therapy is not as intense as it was the first three years after the accident, but I still do what I can.

I think having been a player helps when you face tough times. You can watch a football game and see the difficulties. A player puts in a lot of hard work, and I think I have continued to have a good work ethic and a good philosophy about life—things I learned on the football field.

I feel lucky to have been an Alabama football player. Alabama wasn't recruiting me very hard. Auburn and several other SEC schools were recruiting me, as were Wisconsin and Penn State. I knew I wasn't going to go play in the snow. I was seriously considering Auburn, because it was close to home. One day the coach recruiting me asked if I was an Auburn fan or an Alabama fan. I told him I had always been an Alabama fan. I think that killed the recruiting from Auburn, even though I had been in their football camp that summer. Fortunately, right after that, Mal Moore started recruiting me for Alabama. And after I made my visit and met coach Stallings, I knew this was the place for me.

I had to wait a long time to get to play. When Alabama was recruiting me, they told me they wanted me to gain weight. I overdid it, gaining 40 or 50 pounds before I got there. That made it awfully hard to practice. I was red-shirted in 1991, then just played a little on our national championship team in 1992 at left tackle and a little in 1993 as a tight end in goal-line situations. I hoped maybe I'd get a touchdown pass, but that never happened. I was a blocker.

In the spring before my junior season, coach Stallings sat a group of us linemen down in his office and asked us what weight we needed to be so that we would be able to play at a high level. And he wrote it down and said we'd better be at that weight when we reported in the fall. I had written down that I had to lose about 35 pounds. I really needed to lose more than that, and I did it. I lost 10 more pounds than I had pledged, and when I reported I was at 270. I told myself that if I could do that, I could accomplish anything.

275

That year I started my first game, the season-opener against Chattanooga. And I started every game that year. I was the right tackle. I think offensively we may have been a little better than the 1992 national championship team, although our defense might not have been quite as good. But it was definitely a good team.

I guess my first memory of really being an Alabama football player was the first game I dressed for in Bryant-Denny Stadium, coming out of that tunnel in 1992. It was breathtaking, the most exhilarating thing that had ever happened to me.

I remember big games that year I was a starter. We played Georgia in a night game and came from behind to beat them 29–28. Georgia had Eric Zeier, but we had Jay Barker. And we beat Tennessee in Knoxville and finished off an undefeated regular season by beating Auburn. Then we lost by one point to Florida in the SEC championship game.

That put us in the Citrus Bowl in Orlando against Ohio State, and I know we didn't play anyone with better athletes, except maybe Florida.

I was blocking on a guy, and I pass-blocked with my hands inside, but also inside his shoulder pads. It wasn't holding as long as I kept my hands in front of me. Their guy complained to the referee that I was holding him. I was relieved when the ref told him, "Just play ball." We got the winning touchdown with just a couple of minutes to play and finished the season 12–1.

As I look back, I am proud to have played a part in Alabama football tradition. It is so important. And it means a lot to me that people know who I am—a kid from a small town who was able to pull on that crimson jersey. It will always be special to me.

Kareem McNeal had been the state's 2A Player of the Year, performing for Alabama Christian Academy in Montgomery.

The
NEW
MILLENNIUM

ANDREW ZOW
QUARTERBACK
1998–2001

IT WAS AN UNLIKELY TRIP FROM LAKE BUTLER, FLORIDA, TO TUSCALOOSA. When I was first being recruited, it was the three Florida schools showing interest. Then, just before the start of my senior season, I tore the anterior cruciate ligament. That knee injury ended any interest the Florida schools had in me. Auburn and Alabama were recruiting me, and I committed to Auburn. Jeff Rouzie was recruiting me for Alabama and asked if I would reconsider because Alabama really needed a quarterback. Auburn had recruited me as a linebacker, but I wanted to be a quarterback.

I didn't take my commitment to Auburn lightly. I had given my word. But I had doubts. After talking with my family and my girlfriend—who is now my wife—and praying, I changed my mind. I told Auburn that I was going to Alabama because they had promised me a legitimate chance to play quarterback. Auburn then said they would give me a shot at quarterback, too, but I had made my decision.

It made me feel good when at the first practice at Alabama I threw a ball and Bruce Arians, who was the quarterbacks coach, said, "There's a quarterback." That's what I wanted to be.

Growing up in Florida, I didn't know too much about the Alabama tradition, or at least the specifics of it. But when you hear people say, "Alabama football," you know they are talking superior. Alabama was one of those teams that you expected to win the national championship every few years. And since we had won three straight state championships in high school, I had championship aspirations. I really thought we'd be in the hunt, and I wanted to be a part of that.

You also heard what a classy program Alabama has. That was a big part of my decision. Even the people in Florida who weren't Alabama fans knew that Alabama was a prestigious place, a great school to be associated with.

It meant a whole lot to me to put on that uniform. An Alabama football player can't help but think about coach Bryant and the great players who have gone before. A quarterback can't help but think about Joe Namath and Ken Stabler playing on the same field.

When you get to Alabama, you know you are in a family atmosphere. That's players, but it's also students and fans. You feel a lot of people are behind you.

When you finish playing at Alabama, the fans don't forget you. They continue to be supportive. Alabama fans make me feel that I did something that made them feel better about their school or that entertained them. It's a pleasure to give autographs to fans who are so much for you and for Alabama. I talk to friends who played at other schools, and they don't get that from their fans, particularly when their playing days are over.

279

After I finished playing at Alabama, I gave the Canadian Football League a short try at Montreal, then went home to Lake Butler, where I coached and taught school. But for the past two years I've been back in Alabama with my own business, Andrew Zow & Associates, in Birmingham. A main reason I came back to Alabama was the support I received as a Crimson Tide player.

And this is for a guy who quarterbacked that 2000 team that was so disappointing. A moment in the UCLA game was so typical of that season. My roommates were Jason McAddley and Shaun Bohanon. Shaun had a bad game against UCLA, fumbling a couple of times. And we were going into the huddle and Shaun said, "Give me the ball, Drew. I'm going to score this time." Real determined. Jason was a little skeptical, but I called Shaun's number. And he fumbled.

You can bet it wasn't funny then, but we think back to the look on Shaun's face and now we can laugh.

I prefer to remember better times. I certainly enjoyed my last trip to "the Swamp," Florida Field. One of my best friends, Gerard Warren, was at

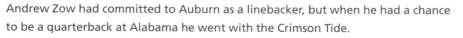

Andrew Zow had committed to Auburn as a linebacker, but when he had a chance to be a quarterback at Alabama he went with the Crimson Tide.

defensive end for Florida. He was taunting me that we couldn't run at him. I threw a few passes and completed them for long yardage. As I jogged downfield, I said to him, "We might not be able to run, but we're sure passing it." And a little later we had a nice run with Shaun Alexander running and Chris Samuels blocking to win the game in overtime.

Andrew Zow is the Alabama record-holder for career yards passing (5,983), and total offense (5,958 yards, including minus 25 rushing), and career plays (1,020 on 852 passes and 168 rushes). He also threw a school record 12 consecutive completions against Ole Miss in 2000. He was a 2001 captain.

SHAUD WILLIAMS
TAILBACK
2002–2003

YOU MIGHT THINK A KID IN ANDREWS, TEXAS, which is in West Texas, might never have heard about Alabama. But I had heard stories about the Crimson Tide when I was a small child. I can remember growing up and asking my dad, "Is the team with just numbers on the helmet playing?" I didn't know them as Alabama, just as the team that didn't have anything on its helmets but the numbers.

Later I heard more about the Alabama tradition, about Joe Namath. And I watched Shaun Alexander. But it took an unusual series of events for me to play at Alabama. I am grateful every day for those events that gave me an opportunity to put on that same jersey worn by so many greats. It was an honor to play for Alabama.

I signed with Texas Tech out of high school. Spike Dykes was the head coach, and I was a running back. After my freshman year coach Dykes retired, and they brought in Mike Leach, who brought a new passing style of offense. I didn't feel I fit that offense. Tech released me from my scholarship, but said I couldn't go anywhere in Texas or to any other Big 12 school. Then coach Fran got the job at Alabama. I knew him from when he had recruited me for TCU. And so I was able to go to Alabama.

I can honestly say that playing for Alabama is an honor, but I may not have seen it that way my first year. I had to sit out a year, which was the first time I had ever missed playing. And that was when Alabama had Saleem Rasheed,

Kindal Moorehead, Kenny King, and Jarret Johnson. I had to go out there every day and get beat up, knowing there was no chance I was going to get to play. It was tough. But that helped me, not only as a football player, but as a person. It helped me realize that there's going to be a time when I'm not playing football and not in the limelight. It was very much a humbling experience.

I was determined in spring training that year because I wanted to show I could play in the Southeastern Conference. I didn't get to touch the ball until the North Texas game in 2002, my junior year. In that game I got a few touches that boosted my confidence.

The Arkansas game was big for me. It was a night game on ESPN—always a good atmosphere. We were in Fayetteville before a full house of about eighty thousand. Our quarterback, Tyler Watts, was hurt, and it was going to be Brodie Croyle's first start. We were going to run the ball to keep the pressure off him and keep him relaxed. On the first play I went 80 yards for a touchdown.

All-in-all I had a decent year and we had a pretty good year, finishing up 10–3. And I never sensed the change that was coming. Of course, we heard the rumors that coach Fran was leaving. A lot of guys thought something was wrong when we were preparing for Auburn, but I never thought about Fran leaving.

283

I was home in Texas for a funeral when the news came that coach Fran was going to Texas A&M. I called back, and one of my roommates said they had just gotten out of a meeting and that coach Torbush had confirmed it. I could hardly believe it.

What upset me was that he had told us the rumors were not true, that he wasn't going anywhere. He had all the seniors convinced to stick it out through the tough times and he would stick it out with us. We were going to get through the tough times together. He hurt a lot of guys when he left like he did.

Coach Price came in and immediately put life into our football program. He made football fun again. I really thought we had a new energy with him.

We were at the football complex when they told us he was going to be fired. I put my head in my hands and wondered, "What is going to happen to us next? We bought into what coach Fran told us, and he left. Just when we bought into what coach Price told us, he gets fired. We're four months away from our senior year and we don't have a head coach." And I started crying.

Shaud Williams decided to leave Texas Tech when the Red Raiders changed from a running team to a passing team, and the tailback ended up as a thousand-yard rusher and team captain at Alabama.

Then someone asked me if I wanted to go make a statement to media. I didn't think I was going to cry then, but I looked over at coach Price. He had come over to us and said, "If you players ever need me, you can call me. I love each and every one of you."

My senior year was so close to being good. We had the great game with Oklahoma, which was No. 1 in the nation. Then we had the five-overtime game against Tennessee. We had near misses. We were close to being 9–4 instead of 4–9.

In the Tennessee game, I lost my temper with our offensive line. We had lost Wesley Britt early with a broken leg, but we needed people to step up. We had third and short, and a defensive tackle came through untouched and hit me. I was a little frustrated. Later I apologized to each guy individually for losing my temper. Most of them told me I didn't owe them an apology, but I felt I did. They were trying to do their job, just like I was.

Despite a few bumps, my whole career at Alabama was very much a positive experience. I don't regret one day I spent at The University of Alabama. Some of my best friends, who will be my best friends forever, I met at Alabama.

I was not surprised I wasn't drafted by an NFL team. A lot of teams don't want to take a chance on a small back. I just looked at it as another challenge. I knew if they would give me a chance, I would make the team.

285

Atlanta, Baltimore, Arizona, Dallas, and Buffalo wanted me to come in as free agent, and Buffalo seemed like the best fit. I had talked with the running backs coach [Eric Studesville] at an NFL combine, and we hit it off pretty well. He said they weren't going to draft a running back, but he was almost hoping I wouldn't get drafted because he felt like I could come in and make the team. And that's what happened.

You don't realize how special a place Alabama is until you're gone. In the NFL you may play in front sixty thousand fans, as opposed to Bryant-Denny where you have more than eighty thousand. I am very grateful I was able to be a part of the tradition and be a part of something that was so great.

Shaud Williams played at Alabama just two years, but along with another two-year player, Derrick Pope, was captain of the 2003 Crimson Tide. He signed as a free agent with Buffalo and made the team. He was 'Bama's leading rusher in 2002 and 2003.

WESLEY BRITT

OFFENSIVE TACKLE

2001–2004

How close did I come to not having a final year of football at Alabama in 2004? Not what you might think. Some people might have thought I was going to turn pro after the 2003 season, but that wasn't an option. The reason I played in 2004 is because I was redshirted in 2000. And the reason for that was a timeout by Ole Miss during my first year at Alabama. I wasn't happy about being redshirted. I came in with big expectations. I was the second-team tackle on both the left and right. I was traveling to every game. They were preparing me to play. And I was about to go in the game against Ole Miss.

Neil Callaway was my offensive line coach. He had me put the headset on so he could talk to me from the press box. He told me the play and what he wanted me to do, because of the way Ole Miss was playing. He was giving me the steps.

Then Ole Miss called a timeout, and coach DuBose and coach Callaway decided to not send me in. They knew I was having good practices, and I think they wanted to play me because they thought I was good enough. But once we started losing, I think they decided not to waste the year.

I wanted to play. I've been playing organized football since I was in the second grade. But I knew that God had a plan and I would have the faith to realize that plan.

Wesley Britt missed half of his junior season with a broken leg, suffered against Tennessee, but came back with an All-American season. He was joined on the 2004 Crimson Tide by brothers Taylor and Justin.

I've had an unusual career, with four head coaches and three position coaches. And I enjoyed it very much.

There was a time when it would have been unlikely that I would have been at Alabama. Growing up, we were Auburn fans. And then I went to a lot of Florida games, including the game in "the Swamp" when Alabama ended Florida's long home winning streak in 1999.

What really made Alabama different was the people. I'd go to Florida on a recruiting visit, and they'd look at the tag on my shirt and say, "We'd love to have you here." When I went to Alabama, the people didn't have to look at a nametag. They looked at my face and said, "Hey, Wesley. We can't wait to have you here. We can't wait to get you. You're an Alabama boy and we have to have you." That made me feel at home.

I think the reason we were Auburn fans growing up—everyone except my brother Taylor—is because we didn't go to Alabama games. Then we got some tickets for Alabama games, and comparing Alabama to Auburn changed my mind. I began to fall in love with Alabama. By the time I was a high school senior, Alabama and Florida were the only choices.

I liked playing for coach Fran and his offensive line coach, Jim Bob Helduser. He was a great motivator. We didn't really have a lot of technique in pass blocking or run blocking. He just wanted to see us get them on the ground. We learned a lot about becoming a physical football team.

They didn't care if the other team knew what was coming. We had a player transfer to Mississippi State, so when we played them, they knew all our audibles. We called a lot of plays at the line, and we'd hear their defense talking—"option right" or "belly left" or whatever. It didn't matter. We just ran over them because that's the kind of football we played.

We thought things were in pretty good shape. We had just had a ten-win season and had a lot of players back. And then Fran left. It was a hard process. We had just learned the system and were excited about having another year with it. The way he left kind of stripped away the foundation of what we were building.

I suppose that's the nature of the profession and that he did the best thing for himself and his family, but we were understandably let down.

Mike Price came in and he loved the opportunity he had. He was living a dream. And then he had that rude awakening. The way we practiced was great. I don't know how he did it, but he had us practicing so hard without being forced. He had us practicing and competing and wanting to work and get better. And I'm talking about the whole team, everyone. We had a great spring, and all of a sudden he was gone and we didn't have a head coach.

Coach Bob Connelly came in with coach Price. He is a real technician. I learned a lot of technique in the final two years of my career. I know it is going to be beneficial to take the technique I learned for pass blocking and run blocking to a chance in the NFL. I think I have a great base.

When coach Shula came in, we didn't have a playbook the whole summer. It was up to us to do it ourselves. We couldn't pick up a playbook or take one with us. We had to get together and learn how to play with a new system. We didn't have the season that we felt we should or could, but we kept fighting. We never gave up. We never made excuses. We played hard for The University of Alabama.

To play at Alabama will prepare me for the next level. My five years at Alabama, I went against six defensive linemen in practice who are in the NFL right now. You don't find that at many other schools. The level of competition we play at in the SEC, the media and fan attention, and the atmosphere you play in week-in and week-out is something you can almost directly compare to the NFL.

One other thing that I think will help me get to the next level is Justin Smiley, who left after his junior year to go to the NFL. We are really good friends, on and off the field. And we pushed each other to be better. We competed in the weight room and in drills. I'd break a record in the weight room, and then he'd come behind me and break it, and so on. That competition made us both a lot better.

The one game I hear the most about is one I didn't finish. The 2003 Tennessee game, which we would eventually lose in five overtimes, was the game in which I suffered a broken leg in the first half. I was blocking on the end, and a linebacker dived for Shaud Williams and landed on my leg. When I was carted off the field, I wanted everyone to keep supporting the team and not worrying about me, so I tried to give encouragement to my teammates and the fans. I was really pumping my fist for coach Shula and the players, telling them to keep going, to beat Tennessee, but I heard the crowd roar and felt they were fired up, too.

I hope it showed the faith I have in the Lord and that that is the way I'll be remembered.

The two games I remember the most are beating Tennessee in Knoxville and beating Auburn in Jordan-Hare my freshman year. Nobody thought we could win that Auburn game, and we beat them 31–7. We were playing so physically and having a great time out there.

Against Tennessee, we knew what we did best, and that wasn't throwing the ball. We just wore away the Tennessee defense and plowed the linemen and linebackers. We just kept pounding the ball. They knew what was going on, and there was nothing they could do about it. That's the best feeling—being an offensive lineman and knowing before the snap that you're about to dominate.

I am very fortunate that I was able to play the 2004 season with my brothers, Taylor and Justin. That was amazing. I'm really thankful to have my name and theirs in the books at this tradition-rich school.

Wesley Britt was captain of the 2004 team. He was winner of the Jacobs Award, voted by SEC coaches for the best blocker in the league. He was All-SEC and selected to play in the Senior Bowl.

...WARD CHAPPELL · BEN MCLEOD JR. · JOE DOMNANOVICH · DO

· TOMMY LEWIS · CECIL "HOOTIE" INGRAM · BART STARR · FRED

ARWIN HOLT · LEE ROY JORDAN · MAL MOORE · JOE NAMATH

NCAN · KEN STABLER · JOHNNY MUSSO · TERRY ROWELL · JOHN

EELER · WOODROW LOWE · MIKE WASHINGTON · RICHARD TOL

ARTY LYONS · DON MCNEAL · STEADMAN SHEALY · DWIGHT S

MMY WILCOX · JOEY JONES · PETER KIM · WALTER LEWIS · VAN TI

ARY HOLLINGSWORTH · ERIC CURRY · JAY BARKER · KAREEM M

APPELL · BEN MCLEOD JR. · JOE DOMNANOVICH · DON SALLS · H

VIS · CECIL "HOOTIE" INGRAM · BART STARR · FRED SINGTON J

LT · LEE ROY JORDAN · MAL MOORE · JOE NAMATH · PAUL CRAN

ABLER · JOHNNY MUSSO · TERRY ROWELL · JOHN HANNAH · JO

OODROW LOWE · MIKE WASHINGTON · RICHARD TODD · BOB B

ONS · DON MCNEAL · STEADMAN SHEALY · DWIGHT STEPHENS

LCOX · JOEY JONES · PETER KIM · WALTER LEWIS · VAN TIFFIN · M

LLINGSWORTH · ERIC CURRY · JAY BARKER · KAREEM MCNEAL ·

EN MCLEOD JR. · JOE DOMNANOVICH · DON SALLS · HARRY GIL

CIL "HOOTIE" INGRAM · BART STARR · FRED SINGTON JR. · TOMM

Y JORDAN · MAL MOORE · JOE NAMATH · PAUL CRANE · STEVE S